Industry Analysis
The Automotive Industry

January 25-26, 1994
Chicago, Illinois

Martin L. Anderson
Owen Bieber
Robert A. Brizzolara, CFA
Richard B. England, CFA
Philip K. Fricke
Stephen J. Girsky
David Healy, CFA

Michele Heid
Maryann N. Keller
Joseph G. Paul
James C. Rucker
Theodore Shasta, CFA, *Moderator*
Michael P. Ward, CFA

Edited by Theodore Shasta, CFA

To obtain an AIMR Publications Catalog or to order additional copies of this publication, turn to page 117 or contact:

AIMR
P.O. Box 3668
Charlottesville, VA 22903
U.S.A.
Telephone: 804/980-9712
Fax: 804/980-9710

The Association for Investment Management and Research comprises the Institute of Chartered Financial Analysts and the Financial Analysts Federation.

ISBN 1-879087-39-1

Printed in the United States of America

June 1994

Table of Contents

(continued on next page)

Foreword

Faced with saturated markets, rising costs, and increased competition, the automotive industry is testing new ways to stimulate demand and capture market share. Developments in the industry range from creative financing techniques being used by the automakers to the adoption of a consumer orientation and the establishment of market franchises by auto parts companies. As a result of these and other industry dynamics, the industry's power structure is shifting: Labor–management relations are changing, as are the relationships between manufacturers and dealers, dealers and customers. This proceedings offers readers the opportunity to understand and analyze both the cyclical nature of the automotive industry and the changes occurring within it.

The Automotive Industry is the seventh in AIMR's Industry Analysis series of seminars and proceedings. The series was conceived by Charles D. Ellis, CFA, to provide educational material on the nuances of individual industries that are relevant to securities analysis. This approach rests on the belief that the specific technical information that must be the backbone of any sound industry analysis is available only through personal experience with a particular industry. This series of seminars makes the fruits of that experience available to all.

The speakers at the seminar, whose presentations this volume reproduces, are among the leading industry participants and specialists in the analysis of the automotive industry. AIMR wishes to thank them for sharing their research and practical experience and for assisting in the preparation of this proceedings. Special thanks are extended to Theodore Shasta, CFA, who moderated the seminar and contributed the overview that expertly sets the stage for the presentations that follow.

The speakers contributing to the seminar were: Martin L. Anderson, Massachusetts Institute of Technology; Owen Bieber, the UAW; Robert A. Brizzolara, CFA, Harris Investment Management; Richard B. England, CFA, Putnam Investments; Philip K. Fricke, Prudential Securities; Stephen J. Girsky, PaineWebber; David Healy, CFA, S.G. Warburg & Company; Michele Heid, Cummins Engine Company; Maryann N. Keller, Furman Selz; Joseph G. Paul, Sanford C. Bernstein & Company; James C. Rucker, General Motors Corporation; Theodore Shasta, CFA, Loomis, Sayles & Company; and Michael P. Ward, CFA, Kidder, Peabody & Company.

Dorothy C. Kelly
Assistant Vice President
Publications and Research
AIMR

Biographies of Speakers

Martin L. Anderson is associate director of the International Motor Vehicle Program at the Massachusetts Institute of Technology (MIT). Prior to joining MIT, he was vice president of Gemini Consulting. He is co-author of *The Future of the Automobile* (Cambridge, Mass.: MIT Press, 1984). Mr. Anderson holds a bachelor's degree from Brown University and an M.B.A. from Harvard Business School.

Owen Bieber is president of the United Automobile, Aerospace and Agricultural Implement Workers of America's (UAW) International Union. Previously, he headed the UAW's General Motors Department and was also vice president of UAW International. Mr. Bieber is a vice president and executive council member of the American Federation of Labor and Congress of Industrial Organizations and president of the Auto Council of the International Metalworkers Federation.

Robert A. Brizzolara, CFA, is principal and research analyst at Harris Investment Management. He is a member of the Transportation Securities Club of Chicago. Mr. Brizzolara holds a bachelor's degree in business from Coe College and an M.B.A. in transportation from Indiana University.

Richard B. England, CFA, is vice president and analyst in the Equity Research Department of Putnam Investments. Prior to joining Putnam, he was at Aetna Life & Casualty. Mr. England holds degrees from the University of Florida and the University of Pennsylvania.

Philip K. Fricke is a first vice president and senior auto analyst at Prudential Securities. He was previously a vice president at Goldman, Sachs & Company and a senior auto analyst at L.F. Rothschild. He is a former president of the New York Automotive Analysts Group. Mr. Fricke earned B.A. and M.A. degrees in psychology and an M.B.A. from Fairleigh Dickinson University.

Stephen J. Girsky is first vice president and senior analyst of the Automotive, Tire, and Rubber Industry Research Group at PaineWebber. Previously, he was an analyst on the overseas financial staff of General Motors Corporation and was an assistant automotive analyst for PaineWebber. Mr. Girsky received a B.S. in mathematics from the University of California at Los Angeles and an M.B.A. from Harvard Business School.

David Healy, CFA, is vice president and U.S. auto industry analyst for S.G. Warburg & Company. Prior to joining S.G. Warburg, he was at Burnham & Company. Mr. Healy holds a B.A. from the University of Santa Clara and an M.B.A. from the University of California at Los Angeles.

Michele Heid is vice president of investor relations and planning for Cummins Engine Company. She is a member of the Financial Executives Institute and the American Institute of Certified Public Accountants. Ms. Heid earned a B.S. in accounting and an M.B.A. in finance and investments from Indiana University.

Maryann N. Keller is a managing director and automotive analyst at Furman Selz. She writes monthly on various automotive topics for *Automotive Industries* and the *Japan Economic Journal* and was awarded the Eccles Prize from Columbia University in 1990 for her book *Rude Awakening* (New York: William Morrow, 1989). She is also author of *Collision: General Motors, Toyota and Volkswagen and the Race to Own the 21st Century* (New York: Doubleday, 1993). Ms. Keller is president of the Society of Automotive Analysts.

Joseph G. Paul is a senior research analyst and principal at Sanford C. Bernstein & Company. Previously, he worked at General Motors Corporation in the marketing and product planning departments. Mr. Paul holds a B.S. from the University of Arizona and an M.S. from the Massachusetts Institute of Technology.

James C. Rucker is executive director of Industrial and General Assembly Engineering with the North American Operations Technical Center of General Motors Corporation. Mr. Rucker has held a variety of positions with General Motors, including computer systems analyst, plant controller, and corporate director of Capital Spending Analysis. He received his bachelor's and master's degrees in industrial engineering from Ohio State University.

Theodore Shasta, CFA, is vice president of equity research at Loomis, Sayles & Company specializing in the areas of the auto and insurance industries. Prior to joining Loomis, Sayles, he was an analyst with Dewey Square Investors. Mr. Shasta received a B.A. from Harvard University.

Michael P. Ward, CFA, is senior vice president and automotive research analyst with Kidder, Peabody & Company. Before joining Kidder, Peabody, he was an auto analyst at Ward Transportation Research. Mr. Ward holds a B.S. in accounting from St. Joseph's University and an M.B.A. in finance from Iona College.

The Automotive Industry: An Overview

Theodore Shasta, CFA
Vice President
Loomis, Sayles & Company

The automotive industry in the developed world is both mature and cyclical, and these characteristics create a challenge and potential rewards for investors. A special factor with respect to the domestic industry has been a steady loss of market share to Japanese manufacturers, many of which established new standards for development time, investment, product features, and quality. Although slow to respond, the domestic industry is beginning to close the gap, and the combination of a strong yen and a booming light-truck market (a traditional domestic stronghold) offers perhaps a unique opportunity for the Big Three (GM, Ford, and Chrysler) to recapture market share.

The proceedings from AIMR's seminar on the automotive industry is particularly timely because, with the recovery in demand now well under way, the investment perspective with respect to the automotive industry has shifted from earnings momentum to valuation. The presentations in the proceedings fall into four broad categories. The first five presentations cover the basics of security analysis in the automotive industry. Then, for those readers interested in deepening their understanding of the industry, the proceedings includes presentations on two important issues facing automotive managers—manufacturing practices and labor relations. Three additional presentations analyze the industry's suppliers—particularly their relationships with both manufacturers and consumers. The proceedings concludes with a discussion of the future of the automotive industry and the potential changes investors must consider in their analyses.

The Basics

Maryann Keller begins the process by providing an overview of the postwar industry, in which she notes that the U.S. market, with an average of two vehicles per household and nearly one vehicle per licensed driver, is approaching saturation. She includes an extensive discussion of long-term demand that covers foreign competition and offers insights as to the Japanese competitive advantage. With regard to the latter, Keller notes that the domestic industry was slow to realize that the Japanese advantage was a function not of culture, but of management and organization.

Keller observes that most industry participants are converging with respect to such standard measures of performance as design, cost, and quality. In the future, therefore, competitive advantage may be created by developments in the structure of supply and distribution. Keller believes that large swings in market share, a characteristic of the 1980s, are unlikely to occur in the future.

Robert Brizzolara addresses factors affecting industry dynamics, and he notes aspects of people's relationship with the automobile that might be more appropriately studied by a psychologist than an economist. Brizzolara discusses such factors affecting demand as the size of the driving-age population, total employment, consumer sentiment, lifestyle, and affordability. He cites Ford's recovery in the early 1980s and Chrysler's resurgence a decade later as powerful examples of styling and product design having more significance for investors than companies' immediate financial prospects.

In a detailed and highly informative presentation, Joseph Paul guides readers through the interpretation of U.S. automobile companies' financial statements. He recommends disaggregating an income statement by lines of business and by geographical units, examining the key components of revenue and cost, considering international operations, understanding operating leverage, and factoring in the companies' financial services operations.

An examination of the most recent labor agreement reinforces the fixed nature of labor costs and the subtleties of cash versus accrual accounting for contractual unemployment benefits. The discussion also notes the important role played by the demographics of a company's retired labor force. In this regard, Paul discusses the implications of charges arising from FAS No. 106 on accounting for retiree health care liabilities. He notes that the aggressiveness with which pension funding is undertaken affects cash flow: Aggressive funding reduces free cash flow but improves the quality of what cash flow remains. One of the special issues with respect to the balance sheet that Paul discusses is the funded status of pension plans and liabilities for retiree health care. He notes that, no matter how the U.S. automobile companies deal with the costs of current and future production, the cost of these liabilities is likely to remain as a drag to varying degrees on future earnings.

Paul's discussion of the cost and revenue footprints among different currencies represents a valuable analytical insight into important factors for analyzing international operations. He also offers valuable insights into analyzing cash flows and the significance of volume-driven swings in working capital.

Part of the information-gathering task analysts must carry out is to identify the competitive edge that will set a company apart from its peers. David Healy and Michele Heid demonstrate one aspect of this task in relation to the automotive industry—the company interview, specifically an interview with the investor relations (IR) contact. Healy, the analyst, points out that such interviews are not limited to company-specific matters; they also provide a good window on the industry. Matters appropriate for discussion include sales, production, pricing, trends in costs, taxes, accounting issues, capital expenditures, capital structure, and dividend policy. Whatever is learned, he recommends, analysts should always consider how it squares with consensus expectations. Complete and thorough preparation is essential to get the most out of a first visit, and analysts must always be wary of material nonpublic information.

Heid presents the point of view of the IR staff person. She notes that her primary objectives are to provide investors with the facts and to respond to inquiries on a timely basis. Consistency, fairness, and the avoidance of surprises are important guidelines. Key requirements for a successful IR effort include knowledge of the company, including its products and finances, and credibility. The mock interview included in this joint presentation is highly instructive and well worth the reader's time.

With a solid grasp of the industry, investors can turn to the stocks of the individual sectors and companies. Richard England tackles the difficult subject of valuing the U.S. automakers' securities, a process he considers as much art as science. He provides a historical perspective, analysis of the current cycle, and some thoughts on an appropriate entry point for the next cycle. The presentation covers many analytical tools, but England advises that investors be skeptical of any hard-and-fast rules. He also cautions that, once the peak in demand has passed, making money in this group is very difficult.

Management Issues

James Rucker provides insights on how the investor can assess competitive factors on the production side of automotive, or any, manufacturing companies. He begins by warning that, although manufacturing

is far from glamorous and may not attract investor attention, it is, nevertheless, central to a nation's ability to create wealth. Manufacturing's importance creates the importance of the automotive industry to the nation: The automotive industry, as the largest manufacturing segment in the United States, is vital.

In turning to the analysis of manufacturing operations, Rucker notes that technology alone does not ensure competitiveness. Today, virtually any entity can purchase technology. The key is the knowledge of how to apply technology successfully—that is, the current manufacturing paradigm. Rucker discusses the evolution in manufacturing paradigms—from mass production to lean production to the next step, agile production. He defines agile manufacturing as technology and techniques that promise the manufacture of unique products without the cost or delay normally associated with custom manufacturing.

Rucker closes by pointing out three factors investors need to look for in assessing a manufacturer: how technology is being applied, the role of process requirements in product development, and where process knowledge resides. With respect to the latter factor, Rucker states that all workers must have a view of the total production system and how they fit in it. He notes that the know-how that resides in human capital is the one competitive advantage that cannot be quickly copied or acquired.

The UAW perspective on the U.S. automotive industry is dynamically presented by Owen Bieber. He acknowledges that financial analysts and the UAW represent different constituencies, and therefore, do not always view events and issues in the same way. He goes on to suggest that the attitude of "what is good for labor is bad for the company" may be short-sighted. In support, he discusses the UAW's contributions to improving productivity and quality. Bieber also points out the stability the UAW has provided the industry; nine CEOs have come and gone at the Big Three during his tenure as president of the UAW. Bieber reminds readers that the UAW has an industrywide perspective and provides a structure for problem solving and dispute resolution. In closing, he states that the emphasis of the UAW will remain as it has been—people and the development of human capital.

Automotive Parts

The analysis of the industry cannot stop with the original-equipment manufacturers (OEMs). Investors and analysts may find some of the best opportunities in stocks of the automotive parts manufacturers and distributors. As discussed by Philip Fricke and Michael Ward, important structural changes are taking place in the parts industry—new customers in addition to the Big Three, a shrinking supplier base, increased outsourcing by all manufacturers, trade issues with Japan, and a demand for systems capabilities by OEMs. All these factors are working in favor of consolidation in the industry to fewer suppliers with greater capabilities and more financial strength. The approach to forecasting the fortunes of the industry promises to become less top down and more company specific. Analysts and investors will need to consider which companies are supplying what components to what models. Successful suppliers will have proprietary technology supporting a meaningful percentage of their revenues, and they will have the design, engineering, and manufacturing expertise to provide complete systems rather than merely individual parts. A low cost structure is essential, and rapid turnover in the specific components will serve as a buffer to OEM pricing pressure.

Stephen Girsky provides valuable insights into the hard-pressed participants in the tire industry. He notes that the industry takes on characteristics of the auto industry (sales to automotive OEMs are an important end market), the consumer products industry (sales to consumers are another important end market), and the chemical industry, which drives the cost structure. The tire industry's characteristics have resulted in poor returns, but solutions to these structural problems, at least partial solutions, do exist. Girsky describes two companies' solutions. The approach of Goodyear Tire & Rubber, as implemented by Stanley Gault in 1991, is to emphasize marketing and product development for the replacement market and expanded distribution. Cooper Tire & Rubber's approach has always focused on the replacement market but emphasizes low cost (Cooper does little in the way of advertising or research and development) and distribution through independent dealers.

In tracking the industry, Girsky notes, pricing is the most critical variable but is also the most difficult to pin down. While investors must always be sensitive to earnings risk, valuation risk also exists, as evidenced by the decline in Cooper's stock price in 1993. Conversely, Goodyear represented valuation opportunity at the height of its financial troubles.

The Future

Investor and analyst tasks do not stop with the past and present, of course; the future is the important arena. Martin Anderson provides a discussion of the future automotive industry from a global perspective. The global viewpoint is important, he notes, when one remembers that the North American market is but one-third of the 50-million-unit global market and is growing at the slowest rate of any geographical area.

In discussing the North American market, Anderson contends that the U.S. industry has an opportunity today to pull even with the Japanese. He views most European manufacturers as being where the U.S. industry was in the 1970s in terms of development times, cost, and quality.

Anderson sets forth five strategic factors that will determine the successful automotive companies of the future—the skillful use of scarce resources, a focus on knowledge, a close relationship with customers, vision, and strong supplier relationships. He cites Chrysler and BMW as examples of companies developing competitive advantages through supplier relationships, and he tells a wonderful anecdote about an escalator at Toyota's headquarters to illustrate operating with scarce resources.

In closing, Anderson suggests that the focus on manufacturing strengths and weaknesses, particularly final assembly, as a criterion for predicting success has gone to extremes. In the future, supplier networks, efficient distribution, and good service may well become the discriminating factors. He notes that a vehicle is sold between three and seven times before being scrapped and that each of these transactions creates the potential to add value and generate wealth.

The Basics of the U.S. Automobile Industry

Maryann N. Keller
Managing Director
Furman Selz, Inc.

Once considered a growth industry, the U.S. automobile industry has matured and is now heavily influenced by macroeconomics, demographics, and global competitiveness. Companies are seeking competitive advantages through product, production, financing, and service and distribution changes.

This presentation provides a historical perspective on the automobile industry focused on trends and issues that have shaped the industry. It details the substance behind the numbers that ultimately shape stock prices—specifically, macroeconomics, demographic trends, and shifts in competitive advantage among automakers, all of which collectively create the ebb and flow in the auto industry.

Overview

During the postwar era of the 1940s and 1950s, tremendous economic expansion in the United States opened the door for the auto industry to become a growth industry. In the mid-1960s, in addition to an increase in first-time buyers, the number of cars per household began to climb.

During the past two decades, however, the auto industry has become mature and cyclical. As the data in **Table 1** show, U.S. households today tend to own more than one vehicle. For cars alone, the average was 1.5 per household in 1992; add lightweight trucks, and the number would be 2 vehicles per household. Thus, the U.S. market, with nearly 1 passenger vehicle for every licensed driver, can be considered saturated.

Since the 1980s, the industry has experienced little real growth; demand has been rising and falling with the state of the economy. The recessions in U.S. economic history are easy to spot in the vehicle sales time series shown in **Figure 1**. Recessions have become deeper and peaks steeper since the end of the 1960s, and vehicle demand, especially for automobiles, has swung by millions of units from peak to trough. Light-truck demand has been more stable. Until the late 1970s, the truck business was essentially commercial. It ebbed and flowed with the

economy but had less dramatic swings than the auto sector.

In the late 1970s, American Motors Corporation, then a publicly owned company, enjoyed a flurry of investor activity because, for the first time, consumers developed a fascination with sport/utility vehicles such as the Jeep CJ-7 and CJ-5. These vehicles were not very safe and certainly did not qualify as family transportation, but they appealed to young male buyers.

Light-truck sales were approximately 4 million units in 1978. By the middle of the 1980–81 recession, however, truck demand was halved as personal usage dried up in the face of renewed fears of an energy shortage. Since then, the truck market has recovered to set sales records. With consumers shifting to trucks for personal transportation, lightweight trucks have outperformed cars.

The economy shapes auto company profitability, and that profitability, in turn, influences the long-term strategies of the companies. The volatility of the earnings of the Big Three (GM, Ford, and Chrysler) has been significant. As can be seen in **Figure 2**, the 1980–82 period was the most calamitous in recent history for the U.S. manufacturers. Chrysler required a government bailout; Ford was in desperate financial shape. GM lost only a modest amount of money in 1980, which set the stage for its spending spree in the first half of the decade. GM believed that a strategy of modernizing assembly plants and introducing new products would create a competitive advantage, but it did not. Ironically, Ford and Chrysler, because of their poverty, were spared GM's fascination with automation and wasteful spending.

The auto stocks vary with vehicle demand, as **Figure 3** illustrates, but the stocks perform best when the U.S. vehicle market is at the bottom of a trough.

Table 1. Cars per U.S. Household

Year	Cars	Households	Cars per Household
1960	61,419,948	52,799,000	1.16
1965	74,909,365	57,436,000	1.30
1970	88,775,294	63,401,000	1.40
1975	106,064,579	71,120,000	1.49
1980	120,743,495	80,776,000	1.49
1985	130,823,587	86,789,000	1.51
1990	142,391,229	93,347,000	1.53
1992	142,649,000	95,660,000	1.49

Sources: U.S. Department of Commerce, Bureau of the Census, and the U.S. Automobile Manufacturers Association.

The cliché is: Buy auto stocks when everything is bad. Most investors did just that during the 1991–92 period, when vehicle sales were at a low. With auto stocks so high today, the question is how much farther they will run now that the economy has turned up and the financial outlook is so positive.

As Figure 3 shows, GM, Ford, and Chrysler stocks essentially follow the same pattern, although the amplitudes vary. In Chrysler's case, the lows have been lower because of repeated fears about the company's viability in the mid-1970s, in 1980, and in 1990. In all three periods, Chrysler stock dipped briefly into the single digits. During the 1980s, Ford was one of the better performers of the group, which reflected its inherently greater profitability, rising market share, and strong financial condition.

Long-Term Demand

To forecast long-term demand, analysts usually consider the potential incremental growth in vehicle sales stemming from population growth. Typically, analysts use the number of people over age 16, the usual age at which a driver's license may first be obtained, as an indicator of new-demand growth.

The second contributor to long-term vehicle demand is scrappage, which represents so-called replacement demand. Scrappage has proved to be difficult to predict. During the 1960s and early 1970s, each model year had a shorter life expectancy than the one before it. Scrappage predictions typically assumed a four-month shorter life for every new model. This assumption was based on the rapid increase in the number of miles driven per year per vehicle. In addition, the increasing complexity of cars made them more difficult and expensive to repair. Scrappage occurred when a very expensive repair was required and the owner determined that buying a new car would be cheaper than fixing the old one. During this period, car prices were stable and personal income grew, which enabled people to replace their old vehicles.

Since about 1972, however, scrappage rates have fallen. In addition, during the 1980s, the age of the vehicle population began to rise. The average car on the road today is more than eight years old. Cars today are lasting longer than in the past; people today expect a car to last more than 100,000 miles. And quality has improved, so cars do not require as much repair. Problems with body corrosion, for example, have significantly declined as galvanized steel and double-coated steel have come into use as protection from rust. In fact, auto companies now offer warranties of 50,000–100,000 miles on body corrosion.

While the number of vehicles per household has risen, the number of miles driven per vehicle has stabilized. Total mileage continues to rise, but the limit per vehicle per year appears to be about 10,000 miles.

Another factor that has reduced scrappage is the price of vehicles. As car and truck prices have risen,

Figure 1. U.S. Car and Truck Sales
(units)

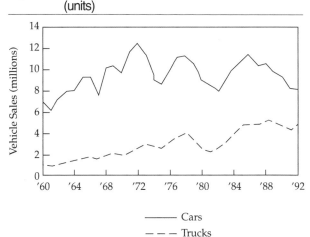

Source: Furman Selz.

Figure 2. The Big Three's Earnings per Share

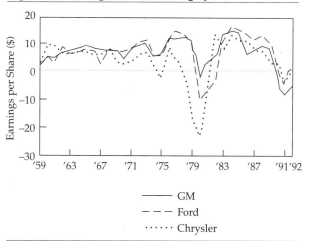

Source: Furman Selz.

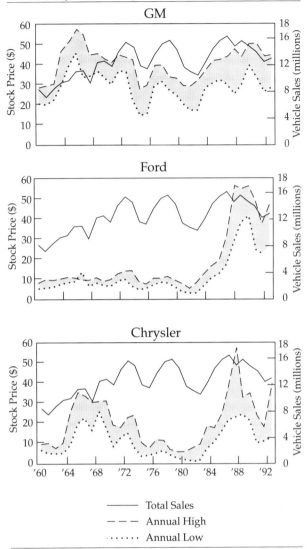

Figure 3. The Big Three's Stock Performance versus Total U.S. Market Vehicle Sales
(sales in units)

GM

Ford

Chrysler

——— Total Sales
– – – Annual High
········· Annual Low

Source: Furman Selz.

repairs have become more worthwhile. An owner who might have scrapped a car 20 years ago because it needed a new engine would probably replace the engine today rather than replace the car.

The first energy crisis produced high inflation and escalation of car prices in 1974. By the late 1970s, trendline demand held the unit growth rate at 2–3 percent, but slowing scrappage shifted the trendline lower.

Because of slower scrappage, the vehicle population will remain older than it was in the 1970s. Vehicle population age is often mentioned as an indicator of future replacement sales. The below-normal scrappage that occurs in a recession is seen as creating pent-up demand, which is seen as an indicator of future sales. An aging vehicle popula-

tion does indicate the potential for future sales, but ability to afford a newer car determines replacement as much as the age of a person's car. People who have eight-year-old cars in their garages may have pent-up demand for new ones, but the new ones may be unaffordable.

Demographic change also shapes the industry over long-term periods; it has had a tremendous impact on total demand, market shares, and the types of vehicles sold. In the late 1950s and early 1960s, the country underwent tremendous social changes that set the stage for the need for a second car. Women were entering the work force in large numbers. People were migrating to the suburbs. Acquiring a driver's license at age 16 became a rite of passage. Simultaneously with the social changes, public transportation deteriorated. U.S. cars of that era were monsters, however; they had fins, weighed about 2.5 tons, and averaged about 8 miles a gallon of gasoline. All these factors created a perfect environment for the inexpensive second car.

The aging of the Baby Boomer generation has had significant repercussions for the auto industry. As the Baby Boomers settled down, married, and had children, the 1980s became the decade of family transportation—the Ford Taurus, Honda Accord, Toyota Camry, and four-door sport/utility vehicle. The percentage of four-door vehicles soared while the percentage of two-door vehicles fell. One significant mistake Japanese carmakers made was their continued emphasis on sporty coupes as the model mix shifted away from such models.

Baby Boomers have been unpredictable consumers. As the 1990s began, some automakers believed that as the Baby Boomers aged, and achieved their peak earning power and discretionary income, they would spend more of their money on automobiles. Luxury-car makers anticipated that the 1990s would produce record volume for them. The weakest segment of the vehicle market since 1990 has been luxury cars, however, despite high manufacturer incentives. Older Baby Boomers are not buying Cadillacs, Mercedes, BMWs, or Lincolns; instead, they are buying sport/utility vehicles and upgraded minivans. These consumers are paying $30,000 for a Jeep Grand Cherokee. This "lifestyle" vehicle fulfills their driving needs at a price well below the amount they would have spent on a Mercedes.

Vehicle technology has also contributed to less interest in high-end, high-priced models. Twenty years ago, a luxury car contained unique features and sophisticated technology not available in a standard car. Luxury cars were notable for engineering excellence as well as size, weight, and such comfort and style items as leather seats and unique audio systems. Today, ordinary cars contain luxury-car features.

The Neon, for example, has dual air bags and will be available with a leather interior. Small cars are available with traction control, antilock brakes, and compact-disc players. It is hard to rationalize paying a stiff premium for a model that offers few obvious distinctions from ordinary models.

The luxury tax on cars priced above $30,000 has also deterred purchases. Consumers question why they should pay extra taxes just to own an expensive car that will get them from point A to point B with no greater comfort or features than they could get in a car costing much less in basic price.

Short-Term Cyclical Demand

The two key economically sensitive factors that cause vehicle sales to rise and fall over the short term are income and vehicle affordability. The cyclical ebb and flow of sales of big-ticket durables such as vehicles reflects general economic trends—trends in real GNP, income growth, consumer confidence, employment levels, and so forth.

Affordability became a major factor in determining vehicle sales in the early 1980s. Car prices rose rapidly, as shown in **Table 2**'s figures on average transaction prices of new cars, because of inflation and government regulations covering emissions,

Table 2. Average Consumer Expenditures per New Car

Year	Domestic	Import	Average	Import Price/ Domestic Price
1967	$3,310	$2,272	$3,212	68.6%
1968	3,531	2,353	3,406	66.6
1969	3,697	2,496	3,557	67.5
1970	3,708	2,648	3,542	71.4
1971	3,919	2,769	3,742	70.7
1972	4,034	2,994	3,879	74.2
1973	4,181	3,344	4,052	80.0
1974	4,524	4,026	4,440	89.0
1975	5,084	4,348	4,950	85.5
1976	5,506	4,923	5,418	89.4
1977	5,985	5,072	5,814	84.7
1978	6,478	5,934	6,379	91.6
1979	6,889	6,704	6,847	97.3
1980	7,609	7,482	7,574	98.3
1981	8,912	8,896	8,910	99.8
1982	9,865	9,957	9,890	100.9
1983	10,559	10,873	10,640	103.0
1984	11,172	12,354	11,450	110.6
1985	11,733	12,875	12,022	109.7
1986	12,526	13,815	12,894	110.3
1987	13,239	14,602	13,657	110.3
1988	14,029	15,537	14,468	110.7
1989	14,947	16,126	15,272	107.9
1990	15,638	17,538	16,157	112.1
1991	16,487	17,795	16,838	107.9
1992	17,252	20,552	18,078	119.1

Source: U.S. Department of Commerce, Bureau of Economic Analysis.

safety, and fuel economy. In this period, auto financing was extended from three-year to five-year loans, which pushed up volumes, especially of more expensive cars. The industry's profitability also rose, reflecting the fact that consumers were buying well-equipped cars.

The year 1993 marked a solid recovery over depressed sales in 1991 and 1992. Trucks, including minivans, were at record demand levels. Although personal income growth was not spectacular in 1993, automobile affordability improved. Income growth improved as the unemployment rate fell and the workweek lengthened. In addition, mortgage refinancing was tremendous as people took advantage of low interest rates. This factor increased household cash flows and is believed to have contributed to the increase in consumer spending.

One predictor of the new-car market that is related to affordability is used-car values. Rising values mean more people are buying used cars. As used-car demand rises, trade-in values increase. The higher the trade-in value, the more equity the current owner has and the more affordable a new car becomes. Since 1993, the used-car market has been strong, and the value of four-year-old models has risen throughout the period.

During 1989 through 1991, the auto industry subsidized rental-car companies to encourage them to buy cars and turn them over every four months to relieve excess capacity. After limited use, the four-month-old models were auctioned off. This program-car phenomenon pushed sales to rental companies up to 1.6 million cars. By 1991, the auto industry was in the business of manufacturing used cars. The buying public became aware that they could buy one of these cars with 7,000–10,000 miles on it for about 30 percent less than they would pay for that same car new. Thus, the program-car phenomenon killed used-car values through 1992. One of the first steps Jack Smith took as GM's new president in 1992 was to reduce program-car sales at GM by changing the terms under which the cars were sold. Dealers had been making more money per unit on the program cars than they did on new cars, but by 1993, that distortion was eliminated and used-car prices began to rise.

Weak demand created a battle for market share and necessitated various incentives in 1991 and 1992. Since early 1993, however, per-unit promotions have fallen. By the fourth quarter of 1993, incentives were costing the industry only half as much as they had been—about $650 versus about $1,100. Nevertheless, they still played a role in boosting affordability while other factors—income, used-car values, consumer confidence, and so on—were turning positive.

Two other elements have been affecting the industry since 1992: special-value pricing and leasing. GM emphasized special-value pricing on 1993 and 1994 models. Ford invented the idea a few years ago with special-priced Escorts and Thunderbirds, but GM uses the concept more than Ford or Chrysler today. In special pricing, the dealer's margin is cut and a model is advertised at a set price that is much lower than the price would have been with such features in the previous model year. Special-value prices helped stabilize GM's share even as the company was slashing program-car deliveries.

Personal vehicle leasing is a fairly new phenomenon that has made vehicles more affordable. Corporations have always leased vehicles, but personal leases were generally confined to luxury models. Seventy percent of all Porsches, BMWs, and Mercedes were leased in the past. Today, however, all models can be leased, often on attractive terms. For the industry as a whole, personal leases now account for about 20 percent of transactions, but the percentage is rising. Leasing a car is not strange to consumers, who already think in terms of monthly payments for mortgages, utility bills, and so on.

Leased vehicles are a rising portion of vehicle deliveries. Ford has been the strongest proponent of leasing; Chrysler the weakest. Chrysler and GM are being propelled into leasing because of Ford's success and because of customer demand.

Leasing will have an eventual impact on the cycle of vehicle demand because today's lessors will be forced into a second transaction in two or three years irrespective of underlying economic conditions. This could moderate cyclical demand at the bottom and top of the economy, thus flattening out the cycle. Leasing also offers the possibility of improved customer loyalty; satisfied lessors have shown a tendency to re-lease the same brand. In Ford's experience, 50 percent of its lessors subsequently lease a second Ford.

Foreign Competition

In the late 1950s and early 1960s, the Big Three thought Detroit was the epicenter of the auto universe and that its dominance would never be challenged. Moreover, the first wave of imports in the 1950s justified the Big Three's disdain for these automobiles. The Peugeots, Fiats, and Renaults of that era were not great cars, and service on them was inadequate. Consumers realized that the vehicles were unreliable under U.S. driving conditions and almost impossible to repair.

Volkswagen was the only European manufacturer to hold its own in the U.S. marketplace. By the late 1960s, Volkswagen was selling more than half a million Beetles a year. Volkswagen recognized the importance of service and a strong dealer organization. VW dealers had ample parts inventories and trained mechanics to repair VW cars. With a nationwide network of VW dealers, owners were confident that their VWs could be fixed anywhere. Volkswagen became the model for Japanese manufacturers when they focused on the United States.

The Big Three initially responded to European imports with compact cars, such as the Falcon, Dart, and Corvair. American consumers needed and wanted cheaper transportation, but the Big Three's costs of producing a small car were nearly identical to their costs of producing a big car. Because of foreign competition, prices of small cars were too low for the Big Three to make money. Thus, they only reluctantly developed another generation of small cars in the 1970s and early 1980s. Then, the Chevrolet Vega and Ford Pinto contributed to the image that the Big Three built inferior-quality cars. The Vega became notorious for engine problems, and the Pinto for exploding on impact in rear-end collisions. Moreover, although these Detroit-made vehicles sold in large numbers, they did not stop import demand.

In the late 1960s, Japanese automakers became a factor in the market, and in the early 1970s, their share climbed above 10 percent, which surpassed the earlier success of the Europeans. The Japanese followed the VW model. They set up good dealer networks and effective service systems.

The Japanese automakers believed they could claim 15 percent of the U.S. car market before incurring the wrath of Congress or having the U.S. automakers discover that they were around. They started on the West Coast and eventually dominated that market. Then, they gradually moved to the East. Not until the mid-1980s did the Japanese begin to build a significant dealer presence in the Midwest.

The Japanese were helped by U.S. companies' policies that prevented dealers of U.S. brands from acquiring multiple dealerships of the same brand. In other words, a Chevrolet dealer was not permitted to set up another Chevrolet dealership in or near the same town. The idea behind the policy was that dealers would best serve the customers and the company if their focus and concentration were limited to one store. Good businessmen were not to be denied, however, and as the Japanese became a factor in this market, dealers often "dualed" their stores (sold more than one brand of vehicle) with a foreign brand.

It was the better, profitable dealers who were looking to expand their organizations. Therefore, ironically, the U.S. automakers' policies enabled the Japanese to attract some of the most ambitious and effective dealers. The subsequent profitability of Japanese brand dealerships encouraged even greater dealer commitment to the foreign brands.

The development of suburbia and the entry of women into the work force had created a need for second or third cars, and the small Japanese cars became the vehicle of choice, especially among the Baby Boomer generation. After Boomers had rejected domestic cars and bought their small, cheap Japanese cars in the 1970s, they moved upmarket with them in the 1980s and eventually supported the Japanese entry into the luxury sector.

For a variety of reasons, the Japanese ignored the light-truck market; their share of this market is only 12–13 percent, half their share of the car market. Politics may have been a factor in their weakness in this segment; the Japanese may have reasoned that the light-truck market was the Big Three's last profitable stronghold. Another factor may have been a concern that these vehicles are unique to the North American market and not likely to generate satisfactory sales in Japan or other markets outside North America. The Japanese understand car buyers, but truck buyers are another matter. They may have difficulty relating to truck consumers and may never have anticipated that light-truck sales would account for more than 40 percent of passenger vehicles sold. Finally, few Japanese assembly plants can handle vehicles as large as lightweight trucks, and overcoming dimensional limitations would require huge capital investments.

The Japanese Competitive Advantage

The competitive advantage of the Japanese automakers can be measured in both relative and absolute terms. The Japanese were the beneficiaries of doing many things very well—things that happened to be the things Detroit did poorly. The cumulative impact elevated the status and reputation of all Japanese makes while diminishing the value of domestic models.

During the past 20 years, the Japanese have set the industry standards for cost, quality, and efficient vehicle development. In the 1970s, the Japanese developed a reputation as the world's most innovative producers of small, affordable vehicles. Quality was acceptable, although far from perfect, and prices were right.

The Japanese companies' low costs were thought to be the result of inexpensive labor. In the late 1970s and early 1980s, U.S. managers attributed the Japanese competitive advantage to a docile work force willing to work 60 hours a week for little compensation. They argued that the Japanese workers were much less costly than the unionized North American employees and blamed their high costs on this, presumably, insurmountable labor difference.

As a result, Roger Smith's commitment to automation in the early 1980s had a twofold purpose: to eliminate high costs (namely, hourly workers) and to improve quality through automated processes. He believed that GM could overcome the advantage the Japanese had attained through their automation by massive investment in production robots. The results were, of course, disastrous. GM spent heavily on untested technology, became the high-cost producer, and watched its quality worsen in some of its newest factories.

The American perception of the Japanese competitive advantage was naive. In the late 1970s and early 1980s, few American executives traveled to Japan, so few managers really understood the many facets of Japan's competitive advantage or, indeed, how many facets could be transferred to the United States.

U.S. managers underestimated the drawbacks of Japanese automakers establishing factories in the United States. Indeed, in the early 1980s, Henry Ford II complained that the Japanese *should* shift production to the United States and become employers and taxpayers in this country. When they did, the U.S. auto companies did not resist the first wave of Japanese transplant investment because they assumed that high costs, poor quality, and low productivity would characterize the Japanese experience here. Americans linked competitive advantage with culture rather than management and organization. After years of analysis, however, domestic manufacturers did recognize and adopt many Japanese processes, systems, and organizational structures, especially platform teams for new-product development.

The period in which the Japanese automakers were entering the U.S. market, the mid- to late 1970s, was a period of intense government regulation in the United States, which is often cited as benefiting the Japanese. The Big Three had to increase vehicle fuel efficiency, tail-pipe emissions were ratcheted down, and increasingly stringent safety standards added to vehicle weight and costs. The Japanese had no problem meeting some of these standards because their small cars were fuel efficient and pollution was somewhat easier to control. The Japanese were able to follow a natural process of moving their cars upscale in the 1980s with little concern about fuel-economy targets, whereas the Big Three had to spend billions to downsize and reduce weight. Honda, with its CVCC engine, actually avoided using the catalytic converter for several years. Honda cars could thus use leaded gasoline, which was cheaper than unleaded. This characteristic also gave the company a reputation for engineering superiority.

As the Japanese companies' share climbed in the

1980s, many U.S. automakers also blamed the exchange rate—an overvalued dollar—for their worsening problems. Even after the dollar's steep decline, however, Japanese cars continued to claim a growing share of the car market. (During the late 1970s and early 1980s, the dollar fell to about 140 yen and then rose to about 250 by the mid-1980s.) The Japanese cars were perceived as offering superior value despite higher prices because of their superior quality and high residual values.

In the 1980s, analysts increased their understanding of the Japanese automakers. Several significant studies were conducted, including one by the Massachusetts Institute of Technology's International Motor Vehicle Program that produced *The Machine That Changed the World*.[1] This book probes the means by which the Japanese achieved high quality and high productivity, and it identifies the many dimensions on which the Big Three have been coming up short against their Japanese competitors.

Experts in the United States who studied Japanese methods learned that automation contributed little to the Japanese car companies' productivity. They found, instead, that productivity was a by-product of design, complexity, training, and numerous other factors overlooked at the time—for example, how many parts the vehicle had and how much an automaker relied on suppliers. The famous *keiretsu* system enabled the Japanese to work confidently with suppliers, as opposed to the adversarial relationship with suppliers that had traditionally existed in the United States. Eventually, American appreciation of the true nature of the challenge grew.

The Japanese joint ventures with U.S. companies were also a learning experience. GM entered its joint venture with Toyota believing that it would learn the secrets of the production processes that made Toyota the low-cost assembler. And indeed, the joint venture, NUMMI (New United Motor Manufacturing, Inc.), was quite remarkable in what it taught. NUMMI took a work force notorious for high absenteeism and a factory noted for building low-quality vehicles and transformed the situation into a model of good labor relations while producing quality vehicles at reduced costs. NUMMI demonstrated that the workers were not at fault; they could be organized, motivated, and trained to be efficient and productive. In the process, NUMMI revealed that most of Toyota's systems were not culturally bound to Japan but, rather, were transferable to the United States and elsewhere.

When Toyota later built a wholly owned plant in Kentucky, it practiced what it had learned at NUMMI about approaches that worked and approaches that should be rejected. Unlike NUMMI,

[1]James Womack, Daniel Roos, and Daniel Jones (1990).

the Kentucky plant has no labor union. Toyota carefully screened job applicants and created a population of employees with mind-sets close to those of workers in a Japanese factory—that is, people dedicated to the company, willing to work overtime, and willing to work in teams. Both Honda and Toyota attract a large number of people with college educations in areas that do not offer a large number of good-paying jobs.

Competitive Advantage in the Future

Eventually, productivity will no longer define competitive advantage; the productivity gap will close because the automakers know how to assemble a car in 20 man-hours or less per car. General Motors is certainly not at 20 man-hours, but it knows how to get there. That potential is part of the optimism about GM's future. In addition, every automaker knows that it has to reduce vehicle development cycles to 36 months. So these numerical, quantifiable differences between U.S. and Japanese automakers are narrowing.

Quality no longer confers a competitive advantage; high quality is a necessity. Cost and the product will always, however, constitute competitive advantage. Some products will always be perceived to be great, while others will be perceived, for whatever reason, to be missing the target. Chrysler has been hitting home run after home run during the past couple of years and will likely continue because the new concept in vehicle design, "cab forward," is as significant as Ford Taurus's aerodynamic look of the mid-1980s.

During the 1980s, the Japanese were great proponents of multivalve engines—small, high-output, high-performance engines—while the U.S. automakers continued to make push-rod engines. Ford did not introduce a new engine anywhere in the world during the 1980s, despite its high profitability. Today, however, the rate of new-engine introduction in the U.S. auto industry is without precedent. Practically every new U.S. car comes out with a new engine that equals or exceeds those made in other countries. Any Japanese competitive advantage in engines today is difficult to identify.

In the 1980s, a restructuring occurred at the assembly level. The focus was on what assemblers did and how they did it. As a result, capacity was closed and employment levels fell. Competitive advantage in the 1990s could shift to suppliers and distributors.

Chrysler has already demonstrated the advantages of working cooperatively with a small group of suppliers. General Motors and Ford, to varying degrees, will reduce the number of their suppliers and use more long-term contracts. The supply industry is likely to experience a transformation during the 1990s as outsourcing, concentration, and the development of a tier structure continue.

Auto retailing is undergoing a revolution as automakers try to establish brand loyalties to gain competitive advantage. For several years, Ford has focused on developing brand loyalty by, among other things, altering its policies in such a way as to encourage dealers to upgrade service and facilities and by improving warranties.

During the next ten years, the number of dealers in the United States will shrink. In the past, dealerships were established on the theory that the more dealers competing with one another to provide customers with the best service and best price, the stronger the brand. But it does not work that way. Brands such as Saturn, Lexus, Acura, and Infiniti have demonstrated that a few carefully chosen dealers can provide that high level of customer service with much better results. Therefore, most auto companies have a "Project 2000" review under way to optimize the number and location of dealers in order to improve their organizations' customer service.

The model for this improvement is Saturn, which has a competitive advantage in its dealer body. About 300 Saturn dealers sell approximately 300,000 cars a year, which makes this network very profitable, indeed, formidable. Saturn is always at or near the top of the list in unit sales per outlet; Saturn dealers sell nearly 100 cars a month. They also provide very good customer service; they can afford it because their franchises are so profitable.

Oldsmobile's dealers present a contrast. In 1993, about 3,000 Oldsmobile dealers sold approximately 450,000 cars. Thus, Oldsmobile needs to take one of two steps: sell more cars or reduce the number of dealers so that those who remain can afford to support the brand.

Low costs will always constitute a competitive advantage. Therefore, the auto companies should be trying to reduce distribution costs. Auto companies struggle to save 5 cents per part on assembly and then spend billions of dollars on incentives. They also spend billions of dollars supporting a large field staff to serve their large dealer networks; a small dealer network, however, requires a smaller field staff, as Saturn has demonstrated.

Depending on how analysts calculate the numbers, distribution costs are 20–25 percent of total expenses if items such as warranties and dealers' margins are included. These costs are a high proportion of total costs, but they have been given little attention during the last decade because companies have concentrated on production and development. In the next decade, automakers will pay more attention to how and where consumers buy their cars and how they get them serviced. Those companies that do it right will gain tremendous competitive advantage.

Market-Share Trends

Changes in competitive advantage translate into market-share trends. The Japanese automakers have been gaining share for years, as shown in **Figure 4**. In 1993, however, the Japanese share of the U.S. car market declined 1 percentage point, although some anticipated even worse performance. That their performance was not worse is remarkable considering their price disadvantage, the improvement in U.S. products, and the fact that they have 50 percent of the California market, which has been besieged by natural disasters and recession.

Figure 4. Japanese Share of the U.S. Car Market
(units)

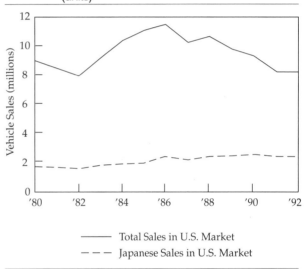

Total Sales in U.S. Market

– – – Japanese Sales in U.S. Market

Source: Furman Selz.

Analysts would be advised not to assume that the Japanese automakers will be down and out in the North American market; they always respond to crises effectively. As an example, in the second half of 1993, the Japanese caught on to leasing. Traditionally, Japanese cars have had a higher residual value than U.S. cars because they depreciate less quickly. The Japanese have used the lower depreciation rate to offer superior leasing terms, which in turn, have offset some of the price disadvantage.

Market shares among the Big Three have shifted during the past 30 years, as can be seen in **Figure 5**. Despite GM's launch of many new models in the 1980s, the company was the decade's biggest loser of market share. GM went from being the low-cost producer in 1980 to being the industry's high-cost producer in 1983. As the high-cost producer and

Figure 5. The Big Three's Share of the U.S. Car Market
(units)

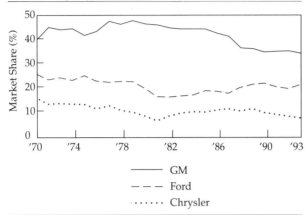

Source: Furman Selz.

simultaneously the largest carmaker in the country, GM set prices. Competitors then set their prices generally lower to maximize capacity utilization. This pattern is contrary to what is typical of the largest competitor in a marketplace. That competitor is supposed to have the economies of scale to make it the low-cost producer. In the auto industry during the 1980s, however, because GM always had to set prices against its own cost structure, which was significantly higher than that of its competition, it created a distortion that enabled Ford and Chrysler to decide whether to go after market share or profit per unit.

GM's costs are falling rapidly today, and it is making a concerted effort to prop up its market share so that it does not sag any farther. Even at the cost of somewhat lower margins, GM has gotten a lot more aggressive on price than it has been, especially through special-value pricing.

Collectively, the car market will probably not experience in this decade the huge swings in market shares it had during the 1980s. The Japanese share of the U.S. car market is likely to remain at about 25–27 percent for the foreseeable future. Some shifting among the brands will no doubt occur. Among the U.S. automakers, Chrysler should gain a little more market share this year as a result of its Neon and JA models. Ford and GM are launching new car models, however, so the gains and losses among domestic makes will probably be small. At the end of the decade, GM is likely to have a slightly higher market share than it has today. GM is probably at its low point because it has lacked significant new product, but that problem could well be rectified starting with the next model year.

Question and Answer Session

Maryann N. Keller

Question: With respect to vehicle demand, is buying a new car ever a fashion issue? What has been the impact of demand for air bags and antilock brakes? What is the effect of interest rates?

Keller: Fashion does not affect the total market, but it does affect market shares. The Ford Taurus, for example, was such a phenomenon that it pulled a significant amount of market share from both Chrysler and GM.

The issue of safety is very interesting because, until a few years ago when Lee Iacocca boldly installed air bags, talking about vehicle safety was unfashionable; it reminded people that they could die in a car. In 1956, Ford had marketed a car with special safety features and the model failed. That lesson stayed with the industry for years. Today, people are interested in safety, and features such as air bags and antilock brakes have had the ability to attract consumers. One of GM's problems during the past three years has been a low installation level of air bags. On the other hand, Chrysler air bags have contributed to an increasing share. Safety helped Chrysler sell models that were unattractive from the standpoints of performance and quality. Antilock brakes are gaining acceptance, but the air bag seems to be a much more visible manifestation of the desirability of safety equipment.

Interest rates have been an ingredient in affordability, not just in the rates charged on car loans but also in the cost of capital factored into lease terms. Lower interest rates on auto loans have a positive impact on demand.

Question: What was the auto companies' rationale for their rental-car business in the 1989–91 period? Was their motivation related to costs?

Keller: Auto rental companies were never owned for the rental business. They were owned by conglomerates for their tax benefits in the early 1980s. In 1987, however, the investment tax credit on cars was eliminated and the three-year depreciation of cars was lengthened. As a result, car-rental companies were sold off, often to the managements, with financial participation by the automakers. GM participated in the employee buyout of Avis Rent A Car, for example. Ford participated in the Budget Rental Car buyout and owns a majority stake in Hertz Rent A Car. GM also participated in and now owns National Car Rental. That acquisition necessitated a huge write-off in 1992.

In the late 1980s, a frenzy to capture rental-car businesses developed because U.S. companies wanted to keep them away from the Japanese. The Big Three justified their investments as insurance against excess capacity and as free marketing and advertising. That is, if the fleets kept cars clean and low on mileage, then drivers were likely to have good experiences with the cars, which might help sell more cars.

The automakers did not realize that, once these program cars came back into circulation—and in such large numbers—they would be viewed by consumers as "nearly new" and perfectly acceptable as substitutes for new cars. The auto company managers argued that new-car buyers would never consider purchasing used rental cars, but the dealers advertised and sold them as "nearly new" cars, and 70–80 percent of them were sold to new-car buyers, which destroyed the argument that they represented incremental production.

The current rental programs are reminiscent of the mid-1980s: Rental cars generally have 20,000 miles on them and are a little shabby and worn. They are definitely not substitutes for new cars when they come back into circulation.

Question: To what extent is the Big Three's success in the light-truck market attributable to the 25 percent tariff on imported lightweight trucks? Also, please elaborate on the history of the "chicken tax."

Keller: The tariff on lightweight trucks was imposed in retaliation for Germany's tariff on U.S. chickens. The United States retaliated by putting a 25 percent duty on the few VW Microbuses coming into the country at the time. Although the tax on light trucks was aimed at Germany, not Japan, it nevertheless had some adverse impact on the Japanese and their light-truck development.

The tariff had an effect ten years ago, but it has gradually been weakened and does not apply to many vehicles today. The definition of a truck, and thus what is subject to that duty, has changed. Today, all four-door vehicles, such as the four-door Isuzu Trooper, are treated as cars for the purposes of taxation although from the standpoint of emission, safety, and fuel-efficiency standards, they are trucks.

Question: With respect to leasing, have residual values been inflated in order to lower monthly payments? What is the risk to both the used-car and the new-car markets as these vehicles come off lease?

Keller: The cars now coming off lease are actually worth more than the residuals that were assumed two years ago. The reason is that the used-car market has been very good. The question is whether the used-car market will remain very good so that cars coming off lease in two years will have the same experience. The answer may depend on what the manufacturers do to protect residual values. Vehicle quality plays a role in residual values and attracting used-car customers. For many years, Mercedes carried high residual values because of the great market for used Mercedes; in fact, they depreciated only slightly in the early years of their lives.

As more cars come off lease, auto companies will encourage their dealers not to send those cars to auction but to sell them in their used-car lots. Ford had assumed 50 percent of the cars coming off lease would go to auction, but fewer than that actually go to auction because dealers have caught on to the fact that they not only have to sell new cars but they also have to have complementary used-car businesses.

Car dealers now look at their stores as multidivisional businesses, with service and parts operations, used-car businesses, financing, and insurance as well as new cars. The new-car operation is the least profitable part of the business today. Dealers recognize that used cars are a profitable source of income because they can play with price more than they can on new cars, especially with the auto companies cutting margins.

We can't predict the impact on used-car prices when leased cars come on the market, but it is safe to assume there will be no shortage of cars. The industry will have to work hard to sell so many used cars without depressing residual values.

Question: Can Volkswagen reduce costs in the next two years? Do you think it will follow Fiat and Peugeot and pull out of the U.S. market?

Keller: VW has enormous structural problems related to a production philosophy that does not apply in the modern automotive world. Heinz Nordhoff, the father of the contemporary VW, developed a production system that was efficient when it produced millions of the same model. The issue is whether there is a market for millions of Golfs a year. Every VW factory around the world—from Brazil to the new Spanish plant, the SEAT (Sociedad Española de Automóviles de Turismo) factory, to the VW factory in Mosel or the Mexican factory—is dedicated to high-volume production of the same vehicle. The market today, however, even in Europe, is demanding variety. VW's factories are not capable of the necessary flexibility, which is a fundamental problem for the company. Its production system, which is predicated on economies of scale, might limit VW's ability to reduce costs.

Also, VW is partially owned by the State of Lower Saxony, so politics could restrict the company's ability to lower costs. Gerhart Schroeder, a member of the VW supervisory board, is up for reelection, and VW has promised Lower Saxony that it will maintain employment at about 100,000 people.

I am not sure whether Fiat or Peugeot voluntarily made the decision to pull out of the U.S. market or whether the marketplace made the decision for them, but I speculate that, unless VW responds with better quality, lower prices, and more product variety, it will become less of a factor in this market. The customer will ultimately determine whether VW survives in the United States. If VW continues to produce and sell the kinds of cars it is selling at the prices it is charging, it is not a matter of whether VW wants to stay in the United States but a matter of whether the U.S. customer wants it to stay. Increasingly, the answer seems to be no.

Question: Can the Chrysler dealers carry the torch the manufacturer has given them in terms of better products and a better buyer profile?

Keller: Distribution is the most difficult area to change in this industry. Neon may in many ways be better than Saturn, but the average Chrysler dealer's store is older than other dealers' and many are not in the best location. Chrysler management wants to sell cars to people with college educations and high incomes who will bring down the average age of the Chrysler customer. The Chrysler dealer has been selling to older customers, is not quite in the right location, does not have quite the right store, and does not have quite the complete commitment to customer service and customer satisfaction. This disparity is probably the biggest problem facing Chrysler today in achieving its goal.

The willingness of the Chrysler dealer body to accept a new way of thinking varies. When the LH cars came out last winter, some Chrysler dealers bemoaned the fact that they could not put vinyl roofs on them. Dealers were concerned that they had nothing for the blue-collar, 65-year-old crowd.

The dealers will have to

change, however, and will in the long term. Gradually, the perception is developing that a Chrysler franchise is a superb profit maker, so a lot of Chrysler dealerships are turning over and going into stronger, better hands.

Question: How much of a cost advantage does Chrysler realize by virtue of its lower development costs ($1 billion for the JA versus $6 billion for the competing Ford Mondeo)? What does the difference in development costs mean in terms of per-unit costs?

Keller: I would guess production of the Neon is roughly 300,000–400,000 units a year. The fixed costs per unit are easy to figure out if a life expectancy of, say, five years is assumed. The volume for the Mondeo is 2.5 times the Neon figure, with the same sort of life expectancy. Thus, Chrysler seems to have a significant advantage.

It is not a make-or-break advantage in terms of costs per unit, but what Chrysler has demonstrated in that billion-dollar, 36-month product development is the ability to react quickly to the market. Rapid product development gives a manufacturer the ability to incorporate new features fairly quickly. A company that is wedded to a very long product-development program has a much harder time reacting to changes in the marketplace.

Question: Please comment on GM's ability, given the terms of the 1993 UAW contract, to make the productivity improvements required to be an effective competitor.

Keller: The 1993 labor contract was a disappointment. As soon as the UAW chose Ford to lead negotiations, it was a foregone conclusion that GM would not have the ability to bargain away some of its problems.

A cynical approach would be to look at the unfunded pension liability, the health care liability, and ask what the likely Financial Accounting Statement No. 112 charge will be for people on extended disability. GM has 17,000 people on extended disability. In this sense, GM is owned by its employees. Making productivity improvements is not difficult; getting the cost savings by eliminating those employees made redundant by productivity is a lot harder.

This problem affects both GM and VW. In the case of GM, successive contracts written during the 1980s tightened up job security and income protection. Chrysler and Ford have a significant advantage in that they eliminated a large number of jobs and closed many factories in the late 1970s and early 1980s before such job guarantees. In those days, they could simply shut a factory down and walk away from it. That cannot be done today. Reducing employment will be a long-term problem that GM can solve only gradually, not with the great speed that Chrysler and Ford enjoyed.

Question: What effect will the North American Free Trade Agreement have on automotive production and investment in North America?

Keller: NAFTA will probably have less effect in the short term than one would imagine because of all of the controversy about the agreement. Some people believe that every factory in the United States will close and companies will rush down to Mexico to open factories. The fact is that setting up factories in Mexico is not easy. Mexico does not have a tremendous infrastructure to accommodate massive shifts in capacity.

The Mexican market will grow gradually, and additional auto assembly capacity will be developed in Mexico during the next decade.

The U.S. automakers are going to change what they produce there; Ford has already indicated such a change. Today, they produce five or six different models in many of their factories, but they will shift to one or two models and then import from the United States the remaining vehicles that they sell in Mexico. Investors will also see more Japanese investments in Mexico; Toyota is looking now for a factory site there.

More auto parts vendors will certainly migrate gradually to Mexico over the next decade. Hundreds of parts factories, with a tremendous amount of automotive parts investment, are already located there.

Question: What is your assessment of the new senior management teams at the Big Three? What are the key differentiating factors among them?

Keller: I see similarity in these companies today—much more so than ever in the past. First, the new senior management teams are very different from the teams they replaced. The industry is past the era of imperial management. Lee Iacocca was an autocratic manager; he was replaced by Robert Eaton, a very low-key man for whom the word "democracy" has meaning. The fact that he could walk into Chrysler and work comfortably with Bob Lutz is a testament to the kind of person he is. The CEOs of Chrysler, Ford, and GM—Robert Eaton, Alex Trotman, and Jack Smith, respectively—are younger than and come from completely different backgrounds than their predecessors. Their experience with the auto industry has not been seeing their companies as great, arrogant overachievers but as companies being demolished by the Japanese. That experience will definitely reshape the way these companies are managed. Younger people are getting more responsibility. Terms such as "team," "group," and "president's council" apply to the kind of collegial management that will develop.

Second, the Big Three's new senior managers have had international work experience and understand the term "global industry." They will not ignore the presence of foreign manufacturers the way their predecessors did.

GM's biggest risk is that it became too profitable too fast; its success so far could actually stop the revolution it needs—the kind of revolution that Chrysler has had. Although the commitment to the revolution is strong at the top of GM, that "frozen" middle management is hard to move if movement affects the way the managers' lives are conducted. Profits have a way of causing people to sit back and think everything is fine so they don't have to worry. I hope that will not be the case at GM.

Question: If a peak in retail auto demand in North America comes in the 1996–97 time frame, when should investors sell these stocks?

Keller: When the combined car and light-truck selling rate gets close to 16 million units, I think a confluence of events may occur. Interest rates will probably rise as a by-product of a strong economy, and portfolio managers will consider late-cycle stocks as investors perceive that production capacity and earnings are nearing a peak.

Question: What is your opinion of the outcome of the California legislation pushing electric cars versus the Big Three protestations that major technical/cost hurdles block the meeting of the emission and electric-car requirements?

Keller: So many companies are working on electric cars that someone will make the breakthroughs required to produce an acceptable electric alternative. The innovator may not be an auto company.

Question: Do you anticipate that the trend in demand for sport/utility vehicles will continue in the future? How far will it go?

Keller: I believe the demand for sport/utility vehicles will top out sometime in the next few years. Their popularity is partly a fad. It also reflects the fact that automakers emphasized capital investment in such models at the expense of cars, and the industry is now in the throes of a wave of new-car launches that could shift demand back to cars.

Factors Affecting the U.S. Automotive Industry

Robert A. Brizzolara, CFA
Principal
Harris Investment Management, Inc.

The fortunes of the U.S. automakers depend heavily on demographic and economic developments. Also important to the fortunes of car companies are qualitative factors (styling, creativity, and marketing) and psychological factors (ego gratification, optimism versus fear, rising frugality, and perceptions of quality). Affordability, a major factor today, is being affected by psychological factors, rising prices, and tax changes. The response has been a significant rise in leasing, which has important implications for industry growth.

Humankind's relationship to the automobile should be studied by a psychologist rather than an economist. Analysts grapple with this aspect every day: When we talk about the auto industry, everybody has an opinion and everybody has a knowledge base.

Qualitative versus Quantitative Analysis

Two of my more notable recommendations—Ford Motor Company back in the early 1980s and Chrysler Corporation in 1991—were not based on the traditional analytical structure of earnings forecasts, price-to-earnings ratios, cash flows, spreadsheets, and so forth. Rather, they were based on styling. I visited the rotundas of Detroit and saw the Taurus/Sable in late 1981, and then in 1991, I saw the Chrysler LH cars. They really impressed me. The industry and these companies were in bad shape in those years, and therefore, anything that would be an improvement was welcome. These automobiles certainly represented a substantial improvement in styling, so I made favorable recommendations, and they worked out rather well.

This experience proves that looking at the numbers may not always be the key to answering all the questions and solving all the challenges analysts face, because the auto industry is more than just numbers. Entering into the early and mid-1990s, analysts have realized that creativity, styling, and marketing should be given weight. As Maryann Keller mentioned in reference to Volkswagen, what automakers produce is not as important as whether they produce what the customers want.[1]

[1]See Ms. Keller's presentation, pp. 4-12.

The automobile has redefined life. It has extended peoples' abilities to work and play, and it also has changed demographics, land values, and social mores. It represents a freedom experienced by only a few nomads before us; cars allow people to move around freely when and where they want to go. The automobile accounts for 95 percent of the miles traveled in the United States, and we have created a huge industry that caters to every facet of designing, building, and maintaining these vehicles.

Today, the industry is looking for buyers. The United States has about 200 million vehicles on the road, and every year, some of those vehicles are replaced. The trick is to convince an additional 2 or 3 million people to replace their vehicles, which can make the difference between a mediocre year and a very profitable year. Another 1 or 2 million sales can increase profits dramatically. Selling to an extra 3, 4, or 5 million people out of 200 million would not seem to be too large a task, but for many reasons, it has become a substantial one.

The growth rate of vehicles in use is thus slowing precipitously, as shown in **Figure 1**. The U.S. auto industry is mature: Everyone owns a car. Everyone also owns shoes, of course, another vehicle of transportation, but people have several pairs of shoes for various occasions—shoes are in demand for working, shopping, dancing, sporting, and so forth. Obviously, the cost, maintenance, and space requirements of a car make car demand different from demand for shoes, and most people have only one car. Like shoes, however, cars do more than merely transport people from point A to point B. They have an element of fashion in their appeal; they

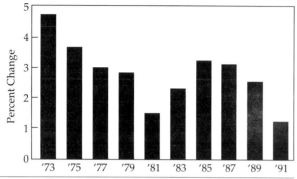

Figure 1. U.S. Growth of Total Vehicles in Use
(year-to-year percent change)

Source: PaineWebber.

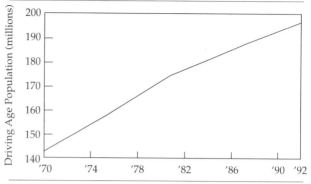

Figure 3. U.S. Driving Age Population

Source: PaineWebber.

provide ego gratification. This characteristic of demand should not be treated lightly.

Demand Factors

Secular and cyclical trends in the auto industry are affected mainly by, respectively, demographics and the economy. The total employment numbers in the United States, as shown in **Figure 2**, indicate that the U.S. economy has a basic underpinning, however, that supports vehicle purchasing. The figure reflects the effects of recessions and some secular flattening, but the overall upward trend in employment is quite discernible.

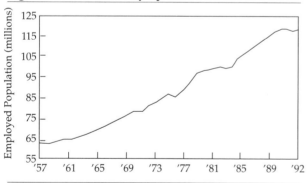

Figure 2. Total U.S. Employment

Source: PaineWebber.

The driving age population is also important to automobile sales. Because the Baby Boomer period has passed, the growth rate in this sector of the population has slowed, as shown in **Figure 3**. This trend should be considered a negative for auto sales.

The number of women who are employed has increased dramatically, as shown in **Figure 4**. More than half the married women in the country today are working, which means that many households need two cars. This upward trend in female employment has matured, however, so analysts cannot ex-

pect any increase in auto sales from this factor.

As shown in **Figure 5**, new vehicle sales closely track changes in real GDP. Real GDP dips slightly during a recession, but a –1 percent change in the great wave of economic value created in this country every year is really a very small amount. What happens is that a recession creates a fear factor that acts as a barrier to people's desires to be optimistic and spend money. Time is needed for the fear factor to pass. My and other analysts' forecasts expect the next peak in vehicle sales to occur in two-to-three years and to be near 17.5 million vehicles.

Each year, consumers spend differing amounts of disposable personal income (DPI) on autos and light trucks. As shown in **Table 1**, the range is 2.8–4.3 percent. Automakers could sell about 18 million vehicles this year if consumers were to increase their personal consumption expenditures to 3.7 percent of today's DPI.

Government economic statistics count all lease auto sales (including personal leases) as business expenditures. Because of the larger growth in lease sales than purchases, this cycle's peak will not have a personal consumption expenditures level of spending for motor vehicles equal to the 4.3 percent of DPI

Figure 4. Women in the Labor Force as a Percentage of Total U.S. Female Population

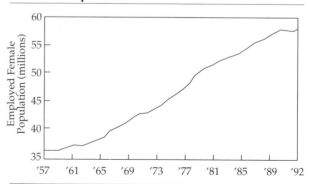

Source: PaineWebber.

Table 1. U.S. Personal Consumption Expenditures for New Light Vehicles

Year	Personal Consumption Expenditures on Autos/Trucks (percent of DPI)	Light-Vehicle Units (thousands)
1982	2.8	10,364
1983	3.4	12,130
1984	3.7	14,216
1985	4.1	15,450
1986	4.3	16,077
1987	4.0	14,926
1988	4.0	15,480
1989	3.8	14,425
1990	3.4	13,894
1991	2.8	12,332
1992	3.0	12,883

Source: Merrill Lynch.

during the last peak. A level of 3.7 percent is more appropriate, with an additional estimated 0.5 percent in the value of new vehicles being tied into leases (counted as business expenditures) and not reported as personal consumption expenditures.

Although the auto companies are trying to recapture people's hidden purchasing demands so consumers will step forward and buy, analysts do not expect a significant amount of secular growth in vehicle sales per se. Several million additional vehicles will be purchased and leased, however, when optimism grows and personal consumption expenditures for vehicles as a percentage of DPI increases by an incremental 0.7 percent.

Analysts study economic data, but the most important variable in car purchases is consumer sentiment. People interested in purchasing a new vehicle first ask themselves: How am I doing at my job? How secure am I? How much money am I making?

Figure 5. U.S. New-Vehicle Sales and Change in Real GDP

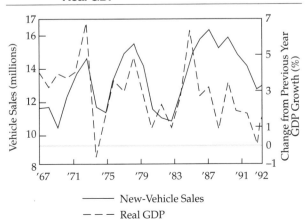

Source: PaineWebber, based on data from the U.S. Department of Commerce.

Am I going to make as much this month as last month? What other requirements do I have? What other problems are there? How people feel about life can be translated into an index such as that shown in **Figure 6**. This index has a close correlation with auto sales; if people feel good, they are likely to buy a new car.

The Affordability Issue

A continuation of the trends in cyclical peaks depends on the affordability of autos. Analysts' sales projections are predicated on the assumption that cars will be as affordable in the next cycle as they were during previous cycles. Thus, the prediction of 17 million in vehicle sales assumes that income levels and the rate of affordability will stay the same. That is a very big assumption and one that should not be taken for granted.

As shown in **Table 2,** from 1982 to 1992, the average transaction price of an auto doubled, but the average loan payment was up less than 50 percent. The major reason is that the average loan maturity increased from 46 months in 1982 to 56 months in the 1987–88 period. By the end of 1992, however, the average maturity had decreased to 54 months. One explanation for the decrease is the heightened experience of bad loans, which caused financial institutions to tighten the reins with respect to extending credit.

Table 2. U.S. Auto Price and Loan History

Year	Average Car Transaction Price	Average Loan Payment (monthly)	Average Loan Maturity (months)
1982	$ 9,890	$238	46.0
1983	10,640	242	45.9
1984	11,450	257	48.3
1985	12,022	248	51.1
1986	12,894	259	50.0
1987	13,657	264	56.2
1988	14,468	276	56.2
1989	15,272	292	54.8
1990	16,157	291	54.6
1991	16,838	298	56.1
1992	18,076	310	54.0

Source: Merrill Lynch.

Another interesting phenomenon is that, although the consumer price index (CPI) has not doubled since 1982, the price of cars has doubled. Industry people point out that the inflation-produced price of autos has gone up less than the CPI. What they mean is that the prices of traditional components have increased less than the CPI. But their attitude is analogous to "not seeing the forest for the trees." They are correct in a very precise economic sense, but they are not considering the costs of meeting CAFE (Corporate Average Fuel Efficiency), safety, or emissions standards or putting radial tires on a car that formerly had bias-belted tires, or price increases to make smaller cars ride nearly as smooth as larger ones. The price of cars has, in fact, increased considerably, and people are having trouble affording them.

Note, however, the role of the ego-gratification factor. Basic transportation does not cost much, and many cars on the market today are relatively inexpensive. The problem arises when consumers try to gratify their egos by demanding luxury or high-performance vehicles. A car that looks the same but is more powerful than the basic model can cost $1,000–$5,000 more than the basic model.

Many people cannot afford to buy the car that has been luxury priced, and all they have is basic transportation. If their cars run well, they wait to buy a newer, perhaps more luxurious car. When their cars stop running well, they take them to a dealer, trade them in for $500, and buy a new piece of basic transportation.

All kinds of costs are embedded in cars. The industry is facing a new round of CAFE and safety requirements to be met by the end of the decade. California is mandating that a small but definable percentage of its vehicles be nonpolluting. This requirement could mean consumers will be driving electric vehicles, which will need a new set of batteries every 20,000 miles or so at a cost of a few thousand dollars.

Despite the industry costs, the auto industry is potentially profitable, especially considering that automakers are charging consumers $500 for bags

that fill up with air. Selling bags that hold air and making a lot of money at it is not a bad business.

One way the manufacturers are attempting to keep their products *apparently* affordable is by squeezing dealer markups. The 1994 Cadillac Sedan deVille, for example, is a new model that replaces the 1989 design. It is essentially a brand-new car—new body, new interior, improved engine performance— for the same base list price, $32,990. The automaker raised the wholesale price by $1,500, however. A price increase of $1,500 is about 5 percent of the total price, and in relation to coming out with a new auto, that does not appear to be confiscatory. The price is still being increased, however, despite the lack of sticker-price increase.

Leasing

The industry cannot lengthen loan maturities on auto purchases to offset rising prices as it once did, so the average loan payment will increase at the same rate as the price of the car. One solution is the lease. For several years, retailers have been using the marketing tools of "90 days same as cash" and "buy now, pay later." Now, the auto industry has a new slogan: "Buy now, never pay." At a 6 percent interest rate, consumers can use $20,000 of vehicle value for $100 a month. If they were to buy that same $20,000 vehicle value, they would pay more than $600 a month for three years.

The leased cars are not fully sold, because the only part that has been sold is the depreciated value. Somebody has to pay for them, however, because General Motors, Ford, Chrysler, and Honda need the money. The stockholders are receiving dividends, yet those cars have not been sold even though the companies are recording the revenue as if the cars had been. The cars have been financed, but they have not been sold yet. The consumers do not own them.

The expansion of leasing will aid the new-car situation during the cycle because leasing reduces the average monthly cost of having an auto at a consumer's disposal. The industry will also see many leased used cars, and they will be relatively high-priced vehicles because they will be like-new autos.

Taxes

In 1986, the Tax Reform Act brought about considerable change. It eliminated the deductibility of interest payments. Prior to 1986, consumers bought cars and could deduct the sales tax and the interest; today, they cannot. The federal government also phased out sales taxes, but it later established luxury taxes. According to economists, no economic data directly correlates these taxes with declining auto sales. I refer to this response as the *Predator* movie

Figure 6. U.S. New-Vehicle Sales and the University of Michigan Confidence Index

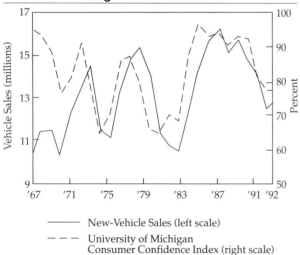

New-Vehicle Sales (left scale)

– – – University of Michigan Consumer Confidence Index (right scale)

Source: PaineWebber, based on data from the University of Michigan.

syndrome: Some factor is making things disappear, but economists do not see what it is, so they say it cannot be there. Something is out there, and it is affecting luxury car sales. My suspicion is that it has a lot to do with U.S. tax policy, particularly at the luxury end of the market.

Consumer Psychology

American automobile culture has undergone a change. Years ago, cars were the most predominant form of gratification for people. Today, however, people enjoy traveling in airplanes and on cruises. In the late 1930s, the great French passenger ship *Normandy* made a winter cruise from Europe to Rio de Janeiro with only the richest people on board; today, millions of people take cruises from various U.S. ports. Millions of people fly to Europe every year. Millions of people join health clubs and buy all sorts of electronics, such as stereo equipment and computers. Simply put, people are still gratifying their egos, but the auto is not necessarily the main part of such gratification. An obvious, but perhaps arguable, reason for this shift is that people see better value for their money in these trips or devices than they see in autos.

A change in the auto industry that has affected demand is quality. In the mid-1970s, people from another culture almost halfway around the world figured out that Americans wanted reliability in their autos. In 1977 and 1978, the Japanese began building quality into their cars. The styling and performance were no big deal, but Japanese cars did something that many U.S. cars were not doing: They started and they transported people reliably from point A to point B. Ford caught on to the idea somewhere in the early 1980s, during a time when it had lots of financial problems. It created the slogan, "Quality is Job One." Some other U.S. and European manufacturers picked up on this three or four years ago. Although most companies have made improvements, many are still trying to figure out how to get quality up to where it should be.

Another phenomenon occurring today is a return to a frugal lifestyle. Perhaps people think they pampered themselves too much in the 1980s. People today want to buy light trucks; they feel good driving around in their trucks. The truck segment of the market is predominantly domestic, with the Big Three (GM, Ford, and Chrysler) in control, and it is more profitable on a unit basis than the auto segment. **Figure 7** shows changes in demand for new trucks and new autos during the past 20 years. The trend favoring trucks is forecast to continue.

Another way to demonstrate the new psychology is that a decade ago, when people bought new

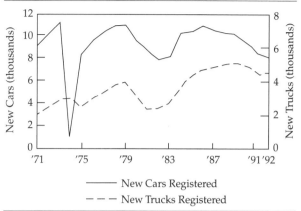

Figure 7. U.S. New-Car and -Truck Registrations

Source: PaineWebber.

autos, they showed them off, calling neighbors and relatives over to see them. Today, when people have to buy a new car, they feel apologetic about it, as though they got suckered. Such a change in attitude limits the ability of the auto industry to continue to grow.

From an economic perspective, people know they do not need to replace autos every three, six, or eight years. The average auto lasts 15 years before it is scrapped. People think about selling sooner because they believe they deserve a new vehicle and because they want to flaunt it. When consumers do not feel good about what is going on around them, however, they will not make trades to the degree they had been. This reaction can be discerned without looking at economic data. The economy is not as morose today as it was, but consumers are not rushing to invite everyone to see their new purchases either.

Labor–Management Issues

If the auto labor force can negotiate the pay and benefits that management gives them, I say they have earned it. The situation is really no different from the companies agreeing to give stockholders dividends. Sometimes, however, we find out that they have been giving too much in dividends. Perhaps labor's demands have also at times been too great.

The labor–management situation is very fluid. When a unionized company is closing plants and another, nonunionized company is replacing the unionized company, a problem exists. It may be an attitudinal problem rather than a structural problem. That is, I am not criticizing the union–management structure, but I question some of the attitudes among the unions and the managements in not recognizing the need for everybody to work together to take care of the most important person—the customer.

Today, a change is occurring in the attitude of

corporate managements; they are realizing that assets are not the sole answer to selling autos, that they need to get back to people again. On the cover of GM's 1992 annual report, for example, is the statement, "We will maximize value to our customers and restore GM's profitability." In 1991, the statement, "Customer satisfaction: Our master plan" appeared on the report's cover. As a result, the customer is now the focus, and we can look at some of the products and services offered and be optimistic about them.

Conclusion

In conclusion, I propose that analysts keep two ideas uppermost in their minds when considering the future of the automotive industry. First, the cyclical rebound that is forecast to continue to take place is being substantially accomplished by the implementation of consumer lease financing. Leasing can bring monthly vehicle payments close to the historical relationship between auto payments and income levels; it has made auto payments affordable. In turn, leasing allows a forecast that the secular trend's peak sales will be achieved. No doubt, something as dramatic as auto leasing—unknown to us at present—will have to be created in order to rekindle auto sales growth at the bottom of the next cyclical downturn.

Second, toward the top and the bottom of the auto industry cycles, analysis of the industry requires approaching it as a game of psychology, cultural changes, and style rather than as an economic numbers game. Looking at the psychological phenomena, should aid in your analytical endeavors.

Question and Answer Session

Robert A. Brizzolara, CFA

Question: Why are light trucks so much more profitable for the Big Three than cars?

Brizzolara: The major reason is less competition in light trucks. Only three manufacturers produce full-sized trucks. The Japanese do not compete in this market because it has been narrowly defined—about a million total units. The small-truck market has had tremendous growth, however, and the Japanese producers compete in that market. In the light-truck market, the competition has been more interested in making money than in using large price incentives.

Question: How will the recently completed General Agreement on Tariffs and Trade affect the Big Three?

Brizzolara: The agreement will help reduce costs by increasing flexibility through lowering import/export barriers—the flexibility of producing vehicles at given plants and taking advantage of economies of scale by producing one type of vehicle at one location. It may help the companies deal with the labor unions and, therefore, hold down costs and promote efficiency. It also increases the Big Three's marketing ability in Mexico.

Question: What percentage of cars does each of the Big Three sell through leasing arrangements?

Brizzolara: I think about 25 percent, but this share is growing substantially. Consumers cannot go wrong: Buy now and never pay. Welcome to Pleasure Island!

Question: Are leased vehicles serviced any differently from purchased vehicles, and does this factor have a bearing on the replacement-parts market?

Brizzolara: They are serviced the same way. Therefore, leasing should have no impact on the replacement-parts market.

Question: If you view leasing as a form of financial leverage, do you anticipate a period of financial dislocation in the auto industry similar to what happened in the real estate and jet aircraft industries?

Brizzolara: People who lease autos based on residual values will obviously run some risk. To say that no problem will manifest itself would be very naive on my part. Financial dislocation is not a big problem today, but it certainly could be in the future. What is going to happen when large numbers of these cars come back on the market from one- and two-year leases? Who is going to buy them? This point is critical, and I think the automakers will lease them again. After all, if consumers can lease something new, why can't they lease something used?

Question: If the financial tail wind of mortgage refinancing and lower interest rates has run its course, what do the next two or three years hold for leasing, sales, and affordability?

Brizzolara: This leasing trend is like a Catch-22 situation. For it to slow down, it must be overdone. The uptrend in penetration of leasing has just begun. We have had two years of modest recovery, and in the past several cycles, the rate of recovery of vehicle sales has been substantially more vertical than the present uptick. Although some analysts are bemoaning the uptrend and some did not even see it until January, analysts now have 12 months of information on economic recovery. They can now say all of 1993 was a year of economic recovery for the auto industry, which matches 1992's recovery performance. Now, analysts have two data points connecting an upward-slanting line, so they can forecast that 1994 will be another year of recovery.

The industry has a long way to go. The worst thing that could happen would be for car sales to go through the roof, because then, interest rates would rise. High interest rates hurt auto sales and auto stocks, and they hurt leasing perhaps the most. The components of a lease entail a lot more interest relative to the total cost than in a purchase. In leases, consumers have to pay interest, but they do not pay any principal on the residual value. In purchases, principal declines to zero. Thus, if interest rates rise, the cost of a lease increases more than that of a purchase. If the cost of financing rises to 12–14 percent, much of the monthly cost savings of a lease versus purchase will be lost.

Question: What does GM need from the UAW in the way of cooperation for GM to become competitive and recover its financial strength? Can GM get what it needs from the UAW?

Brizzolara: The biggest single

thing GM needs to do is to have the union rank and file come to work every day with the idea that they want to make the best cars in the world. That would mean more than any changes in labor rates and productivity. The problem is attitudinal, not structural. It is a question of getting everybody together.

Seniority is important to the rank and file in the unions. Making the best cars at the lowest possible costs and satisfying the customer does not seem to have quite the same priority as seniority. Somewhere along the line, however, workers must understand that if the company does not win, they will be gone. That is what happened in the railroad unions, and it is happening to the UAW. The sooner that point gets across, the better the auto industry will become.

Figuring out whether GM will be successful is why I go to work every day. As long as the auto industry is getting better, the profitability of the companies will improve. A rising tide lifts all the ships. I just hope the economy keeps rising while the auto companies work to improve costs and products.

Question: The next sales peak, 18 million vehicles, does not conform with the leveling off of the percentage rise in female workers and driving age population. Will sales be a disappointment, and is extending the trendline safe?

Brizzolara: The peak will near 18 million vehicles because of leasing. Many factors are negative, but don't forget the pent-up demand, or that about 200 million vehicles out there will eventually wear out. Today, we do not have the secular 3–4 percent growth in demand that we had in the past. The total rate of secular growth in the auto industry is down to about 1 percent, partly

because of the maturity in the trend of women entering the work force.

Question: Does the industry have the productive capacity to produce 18 million vehicles?

Brizzolara: The amount of additional capacity is substantial and quite elastic. If manufacturers want to sell cars at a constant price, they have ample capacity. A lot can be done within the constraints of union contracts, productivity, and line speeds. There could well be shortages, however, of the most popular models.

Question: Are the manufacturers making special efforts to sell to female buyers? I have read that females make more than 60 percent of car-buying decisions.

Brizzolara: Years ago, when women were not considered the decision makers, salespeople did not want to spend any time with them. Today, they find that women are the ones buying cars, and therefore, to survive, they cater to women as well as men.

Question: What are the prospects for the U.S. automakers?

Brizzolara: Barring the specter of higher interest rates, all the Big Three have attractive prospects, but for different reasons. According to the auto critics, Chrysler has the best products today, whether in full-sized trucks, vans, LH models, or the subcompact Neon. The company is also coming out with the new compact Stratus and Cirrus in the fall. The principal reason to buy the stocks of an auto company, provided that it is decently run, is that it has great products in a recovering market.

Ford has the best balance sheet. It is very profitable, has significant financial strength, and

has the highest dividend. It is experiencing a substantial restructuring in Europe, which should enhance the company's profitability even before Europe recovers.

GM is the quintessential turnaround. Some substantial changes are taking place at GM. The challenge is that the list of *needed* changes could fill a phone book; the company could make 20 or 30 changes and just begin on what needs to be done. But the direction is correct. GM is enhancing its profitability, and its products are improving substantially. It has product capability and pricing power it did not have before. In the late 1980s, GM recognized it had a problem; in the early 1990s, it admitted its problem; today, as we enter the mid-1990s, it is doing something about the problem. GM is a big boat and the rising tide of industry recovery could have trouble lifting it, but right now, it is rising, not sinking, which offers some good investment value.

Question: What are your major sources of information on the auto industry, and what are some of your sources that your competitors may not appreciate?

Brizzolara: Investors do not need an economist to tell them whether the auto industry is doing well. My sources are my relatives and friends. They *are* the auto industry. This industry is about them, their friends and neighbors, their ability and desire to buy, and their choices among the sellers.

Friends and relatives are my secret sources. They tell me the auto industry is doing much better. The industry managers sitting back with the pencils and looking at the trendline sometimes don't see a recovery or a downturn until it is two or three years old Then, it is too late to buy or sell the stocks.

Interpreting the U.S. Automaker Numbers

Joseph G. Paul
Senior Analyst and Principal
Sanford C. Bernstein & Company, Inc.

The financial statements of the U.S. automakers contain subtleties and possible surprises that might elude the unwary analyst. Important elements to examine carefully in the income statement are disaggregated business and geographical data, key components of revenue and costs, overseas operations, operating leverage, and financial services. Analysts will also find nontraditional sources and uses of cash, and balance sheets may contain ominous news about pension funding and liabilities for retiree health care.

The irony of the automotive business is that the companies' financial statements reduce a particularly complicated business to a deceptively few simple numbers. Some dimensions of the complexity of the auto business are as follows: On average, more than 14 million vehicles are sold in the United States each year. The average new car has 3,500 parts. The number of brands has risen to more than 40, and the number of models to more than 260. Keeping up has become much more difficult for the consumer than in the past—and even more difficult for the analyst because the standards of knowledge are higher for the analyst than for the consumer.

Understanding the Income Statement

Despite the increased complexity along many dimensions, the income statement of a typical assembler is simple—at least as far as the operating income line. As an illustration, General Motors' income statement for 1992 is given in **Table 1**. GM reported almost $119 billion in revenue for the year and lost about $4 billion on operations. The company had $105 billion in cost of sales, representing almost 90 percent of its total costs.

Changing the gross margin by 1/10 a point can add or subtract about $120 million in operating profitability. This factor is the principal problem facing a forecaster of automotive earnings. That is, the forecaster is dealing with very large numbers in which small changes in assumptions can cause large changes in outcome. When forecasters take a broad financial statement and combine it with the industry's inherent volatility—demand can fluctuate 40 percent from peak to trough—they encounter trouble trying to forecast how much these companies will earn.

When looking at income statements, forecasters should disaggregate the statements by business and by geography, examine the key components of revenue and cost, consider overseas operations and any financial services, and understand the operating leverage (distinguishing between fixed and variable costs). Such an approach will help forecasters determine whether times will get better or worse for the industry and for particular companies.

Disaggregating the Income Statement

Ford Motor Company has two primary businesses: manufacturing cars and trucks, and financing cars and trucks. In the second category, the company also has a consumer finance company handling home equity loans and heavyweight-truck financing, and a savings and loan operation.

Ford organizes operations primarily by the three geographical groupings that are the major profit centers in the international automotive industry—North America, Europe, and the rest of the world. As shown in **Table 2**, with respect to pretax profitability in 1992, about two-thirds of the money lost in the automotive business was lost in North America. Thus, forecasters trying to determine how much better Ford can be in 1993 relative to 1992 would be well advised to focus on what may happen in the North American automotive operation.

Key Components of Revenue

The first area forecasters should tackle when analyzing elements of an income statement is future revenues. Therefore, they need to determine the key

Table 1. GM 1992 Income Statement
(dollars in millions)

Item	Dollars	Percent of Revenue
Manufactured products	$113,489	95.7%
Computer systems services	5,083	4.3
Total revenue	$118,572	100.0%
Costs of sales	105,239	88.8
Selling, general, and administrative expense	9,955	8.4
Depreciation and amortization	6,174	5.2
Amortization of intangibles	189	0.2
Special provision for plant closing	1,237	1.0
Total costs	$122,794	103.6%
Operating profit (loss)	(4,222)	(3.6)

Source: GM annual report.

components of revenue in the auto industry. The approach to understanding and forecasting revenue components is essentially a reversion to basic economics: price times quantity equals revenue. Forecasters must try to determine the quantity of cars and trucks a company will sell and at what price.

Table 2. Business Disaggregation: Ford, 1992
(dollars in millions)

Item	North America	Europe	Rest of the World	Total
Revenues by business				
Automotive	$55,398	$22,777	$6,233	$ 84,408
Financial services	12,514	2,051	1,160	15,725
Total	$67,912	$24,828	$7,393	$100,133
Pretax profit by business				
Automotive	(1,069)	(370)	(145)	(1,584)
Financial services	1,452	266	107	1,825
Total	$ 383	$ (104)	$ (38)	$ 241

Source: Ford annual reports.

The Big Three's (GM, Ford, and Chrysler) total revenues, units manufactured, and revenues per unit for the North American sector in 1992 are given in **Table 3**. Note the disparity in revenue per unit among these three companies: Chrysler, earning about $16,100 per vehicle sold, is at the top end of the range, and GM, with slightly less than $15,400, is at the bottom.

Table 3. Revenue Determination, 1992

Item	GM	Ford	Chrysler
Total North American auto revenue (millions)	$74,726	$55,398	$30,973
Units manufactured (millions)	4,856	3,594	1,923
Revenue per unit	$15,388	$15,414	$16,107

Source: Company annual reports.

The production data used in Table 2 to determine revenues are available from several industry sources. The companies are relatively cooperative about revealing the expected levels of production, at least for the short term. Determining expected revenue per unit is more problematic. One factor is that determining automotive revenue involves some important accounting principles. First, revenues are booked when vehicles are manufactured, not necessarily when sold at retail. The car sales reported in government statistics every month are retail sales, but the auto companies book revenues when a unit is shipped from the factory to the dealer. In the United States, auto companies do not own dealerships; dealerships are separate legal entities, and dealers are independent businesses. Thus, revenue is booked when the title transfers from manufacturer to dealer.

The second accounting item forecasters should keep in mind is that incentives, such as cash-backs, discount financing, and leasing deals, are booked as reductions in revenue, not expenses. Tracking the incentives is particularly difficult because the financial statements show only the net results. They show some sort of preincentive revenue less incentives; the reported figure is the net of the two. Figuring out what the incentives are is important, however, because they can make or break a forecast's accuracy depending on whether the incentives turn out to be higher or lower than forecasters anticipated.

The third accounting subtlety forecasters should remember when predicting automotive revenue is that incentive costs are accrued at the time a unit is produced, not necessarily when the unit is sold at retail, which further complicates the determination of what will actually happen. This accrual practice stems from the principle of matching revenues with costs. Because incentives are a marketing cost, when auto companies manufacture a unit and book the revenue, they also book some forecast of the incentives. The companies predict how much money will be needed two months down the road to move a unit off the lot. Clearly, the timing can be difficult to predict, especially if the industry is either coming out of a recession or entering one. Forecasters can badly miss what is going to happen with revenues as the competitive nature of the business changes.

Many factors influence how much revenue a company receives on average for a vehicle. A principal one that forecasters often miss is the mix of products sold. Forecasters know, for example, that GM might manufacture 1 million vehicles in an upcoming quarter, but whether it is manufacturing 1 million Chevy Cavaliers with a wholesale price of $7,000 each or 1 million Cadillacs with a wholesale price of $28,000 each makes a difference. **Table 4**

Table 4. Production Mix, First Quarter 1993

| Vehicle Type | Share of Production | | Average Revenue per Unit |
	Ford	Chrysler	
Small car	12.9%	17.7%	$11,000
Midsize car	21.2	14.0	16,500
Large car	4.4	0.0	18,000
Luxury car	5.4	3.2	26,500
Sports car	5.9	2.0	17,000
Minivan	7.5	28.0	19,500
Sport/utility	11.3	19.9	22,000
Small pickup	8.0	8.2	12,000
Full-size pickup	15.7	3.2	15,500
Other truck	7.7	3.8	17,500
Total vehicles	100.0%	100.0%	
Weighted-average revenue	$16,835	$17,424	

Sources: Ward's Automotive Reports and Bernstein & Co. estimates.

shows the differences in production mix for Ford and Chrysler in the first quarter of 1993 and the average revenue-per-unit figures. Such figures clearly indicate the significance of changes in mix. Ford's average revenue before incentives is about $16,800, and Chrysler, which is selling a greater proportion of its product in higher priced minivans and sport/utility vehicles, is averaging about $17,400. These mixes can change significantly from one quarter to the next, depending on whether products are in production, out of production, ramping up, or phasing out.

Tracking rebates and promotions from quarter to quarter is also extremely significant in estimating revenues. Companies are fairly cooperative in talking to analysts about the level of marketing money they have in the market on a particular day, which is a good indication of what was accrued the previous 60 or 90 days. It also provides some direction about the per-unit spending occurring at retail.

These figures are only half the story of revenues, however. To avoid being fooled on the revenue side, the analyst needs to keep track of how much of production is being sold to fleets and rental car companies as opposed to retail buyers. The discounts given to fleets and rental companies are generally multiples of the discounts to be given to the retail buyer. By noting small changes in mix, analysts can determine significant changes in the weighted rebates. **Table 5** shows the influence of rebates and promotions on per-unit revenues for the Big Three during the first quarter of 1993. Ford spent more money than GM or Chrysler but not necessarily at retail, because a higher percentage of its total production went to fleets. The ratio of retail to fleet sales often indicates the competitiveness of a company's product line; companies would rather sell a product at retail because the marketing costs are lower than in selling to fleets. To do so, the company must have a product people want to buy.

Table 5. Influence of Rebates and Promotions on Per-Unit Revenues, First Quarter 1993

Item	GM	Ford	Chrysler
Retail rebate or incentive	$ 960	$ 900	$ 950
Fleet incentive	2,500	2,800	2,200
Retail sales mix	80%	69%	74%
Fleet sales mix	20	31	26
Weighted rebate	$1,268	$1,489	$1,275

Sources: Company reports and Bernstein & Co. estimates.

Key Components of Cost

Analysts should also dissect the huge number representing cost of sales, such as GM's 88.8 percent figure in Table 1. Information that is publicly available allows investors to estimate the cost structures of these companies. As seen in **Table 6**, of the Big Three's North American operations, only Chrysler was profitable in 1992. GM lost about $1,400 per vehicle manufactured.

Of the several costs listed in Table 6, some of the biggest are materials, labor, capital (depreciation and amortization), and benefits (retiree health care and pension).

Table 6. North American Automotive Cost Structures, 1992

Item	GM	Ford	Chrysler
Revenue	$15,388	$15,414	$16,107
Costs			
Materials/overhead	8,063	11,075	10,412
Labor	5,280	2,499	2,850
Depreciation	644	348	398
Amortization	337	364	295
Intangibles	39	0	0
Retiree health care	762	373	390
Pension	260	94	402
Selling, general, and administrative expense	1,292	781	1,200
Extraordinary warranty	124	167	0
Total costs	$16,801	$15,701	$15,947
Operating profit (loss)	(1,413)	(287)	160

Sources: Company annual reports and Bernstein & Co. estimates.

Note: Chrysler's 1992 earnings restated to put accounting for retiree health care on a comparable basis.

■ *Materials.* The cost of materials is the largest component of cost in the industry and the most difficult to grasp because the companies provide little information about materials costs. The average car has about 3,100 pounds of materials, with steel of varying grades being the largest on a weight basis. Breaking the elements down on a value basis, however, indicates that steel is not the largest cost component of the car. Other major raw materials used are as follows:

Raw Material	Pounds in Average Car
Steel	1,727
Iron	412
Aluminum	177
Rubber/plastic	377
Glass	89
Other	367
Total	3,149

Analysts can follow the costs of these primary commodities to obtain some idea of how they will influence the average cost structure. For example, analysts may not be able to determine exactly how much the steel in a car costs, but if the price of steel doubles, they will be able to determine that 1,700 pounds of it is going to be twice as expensive as it was.

The complexity of a vehicle also influences material costs. Stripped-down compact cars are cheaper to manufacture than luxury cars simply because luxury cars are built with much more material content.

Depending on the accounting used for cost of materials, the portion of total costs represented by materials costs will vary with the degree of the company's vertical integration. For example, conventional wisdom is that GM has a lower proportion of materials costs than Chrysler because GM manufactures about 70 percent of the value of a car in house whereas Chrysler manufactures only about 30 percent of the value of a car in house. Chrysler is buying more parts than GM. GM will have higher labor costs per unit than Chrysler, however, because it is adding more value internally than Chrysler.

Materials purchasing has become the focus of cost-reduction efforts in the automotive industry, perhaps because materials costs are the only element of costs that managers can truly control today. As discussed later, labor costs and capital costs are largely fixed, and benefit costs are determined by actuarial tables. What remains, in terms of a large area of costs, is purchased materials.

Auto manufacturers are making substantial, and varying, efforts to reduce the prices they pay for purchased parts and to improve the efficiency of the purchasing processes. According to conventional wisdom, Chrysler has taken the cooperative approach, whereas GM has taken the confrontational approach. In reality, the approaches are probably closer than those labels indicate; essentially, both approaches focus on gain sharing. In other words, the auto companies are increasingly listening to their suppliers' ideas for reducing costs and then sharing the savings. This approach will be a substantial source of future savings for the industry, but because all the companies are doing it, the savings will probably not confer an advantage on any one company. Moreover, gain sharing will not necessarily improve the profitability of the industry as a whole.

■ *Labor.* Perhaps the most important aspect to understand about labor costs in the auto industry is that the overwhelming majority of the hours in a vehicle and of the costs of labor in a vehicle are controlled by the UAW. The cost of labor is set by a pattern agreement, which means the union chooses a particular company with which to negotiate, sets a contract, and then drags those terms, adjusted only for the scale of the company, to the other manufacturers. So, each manufacturer in the industry has the same set of conditions. These contracts are negotiated every three years; the most recent was in the fall of 1993.

Also, the union contracts contain strong provisions for income security. Labor, therefore, is essentially a fixed cost. For example, union contracts are written so that people laid off for volume-related reasons (e.g., no work to do) or for productivity improvements continue to collect pay anyway. Specifically, laid-off workers receive about 95 percent of their after-tax pay through a combination of state unemployment benefits and supplemental unemployment benefits provided by the company for 36 weeks. The actual cost to the company during this period, because of the state contribution, is about 65 percent of a worker's normal pay. (The companies have to pay the states back eventually, but the auto industry tends not to worry about things that are far down the road.) After 36 weeks, laid-off workers then go into the Jobs Bank, where they receive full pretax pay and full pretax benefits until the money runs out. As a result of this labor control, what really matters is not how many units are being manufactured but how many employees a company has and at what rate of pay.

Another important subtlety about the contracts' income-security costs is that, since the 1990 contract, those costs are expensed rather than accrued. Prior to 1990, a portion of each hourly wage was put into a fund to create supplemental unemployment benefits, and when employees needed the benefits, they drew down the funds. These costs were accrued and, therefore, did not represent a current expense. Because of the peculiar nature of GM at the time of the 1990 negotiations, however (larger numbers of hourly workers were laid off even though industry demand was still robust), and because the fund was empty, the UAW decided that to protect its members, layoff costs should be expensed rather than accrued. This move showed tremendous foresight on the union's part, but it increased the burden of the recession on the automobile industry.

Actual labor costs for the Big Three vary significantly. As shown in **Table 7**, GM had about 316,000 hourly employees in North America and paid them slightly more than $42 an hour, fully loaded (i.e., including benefits). The numbers include both working and laid-off employees because everyone is receiving pay. The company manufactured almost 4.9 million vehicles, which (using a standard labor-hour) gives it about 125 fully integrated hours per vehicle, or a labor cost of nearly $5,300 per vehicle. Ford is at the other end of the spectrum with 120,000 employees and approximately $2,500 per vehicle in labor costs. Chrysler has about $2,850 per vehicle in labor costs.

Table 7. North American Labor-Cost Comparison, 1992

Item	GM	Ford	Chrysler
Hourly employees	316,000	120,000	70,000
Labor cost per hour	$ 42.12	$ 39.16	$ 40.40
Vehicles produced	4,856	3,594	1,923
Hours per vehicle	125	64	66
Labor cost per vehicle	$5,280.00	$2,499.00	$2,850.00

Sources: Company annual reports and Bernstein & Co. estimates.

Several reasons explain how labor costs can be so different in an industry as concentrated as the automotive industry. The principal one is the degree of vertical integration. GM simply adds a lot more value to the car internally than Ford or Chrysler. By buying parts outside, Ford and Chrysler are not dependent on the UAW and the generally high union wages; thus, overall, the lower cost strategy is to have less vertical integration. Of course, the problem with setting out to reduce vertical integration is that a company has to pay the workers anyway for awhile. As a result, it is easy to improve productivity but difficult to realize the gains from that improvement.

The second important influence on labor costs, because labor is essentially a fixed cost, is degree of capacity utilization. If a company will be paying 300,000 people $60,000 a year whether it is making 1 car or 5 million cars, the per-unit cost will be influenced by the total level of production.

The third influence is the demographics of the hourly labor force. In the auto industry, wage is generally a function of age. As seniority goes up, so does the hourly wage, and the auto companies' hourly labor forces have different demographics.

Particularly important are the demographics of the retired labor forces. That $42-an-hour labor cost for GM, for example, is fully loaded, so it includes the cost of supporting the retiree base in the industry. Retiree costs are determined by the age of the retirees, whether they are pre-Medicare or post-Medicare and pre-Social Security or post-Social Security. After a retiree reaches age 62 or 65, the government provides substantial Social Security and/or Medicare subsidies, which lower retirement costs to GM.

Another aspect of labor costs are those costs that drive write-offs. For example, almost every day, GM faces the question of what to do about too many employees. In the past four years, GM has taken about $9.6 billion in restructuring charges, most of which were for employee-related costs. These write-off costs cover employee buyouts and unaccrued pension costs to the standard retirement date. For example, if an employee is supposed to retire at age 62 but retires at, say, age 55, the company must accrue at that time of early retirement the pension costs it would have accrued during the next seven years. The same is true for health costs to the standard retirement date.

■ *Capital.* As with some other costs, capital costs vary with the degree of vertical integration. The more volume a company manufactures in house, the more tooling and equipment costs it will have. Many companies, however, account for tooling and equipment differently. The issue is how conservative management is. As shown in **Table 8**, Ford, writing off tools over about four years and plant and equipment over about eight years, has the most conservative capital expensing policies. Chrysler appears to be the least conservative. These differences in accounting for costs are important when comparing the profitability of one company with another.

Table 8. Average Lives for Tools and Equipment as of 1992
(years)

Item	GM	Ford	Chrysler
Tools	4.3	4.0	5.9
Plant and equipment	8.9	7.8	11.5

Sources: Company annual reports and Bernstein & Co. estimates.

Notes: Tooling amortization is based on estimated lifetime production. GM and Ford use accelerated depreciation; Chrysler uses the straight-line method. In 1993, Ford switched to straight-line depreciation.

■ *Benefits.* An American car contains more health care than steel. As shown in **Table 9**, GM spent about $1,350 per vehicle manufactured in health care expenses in 1992—about $760 for active employees and about $600 for retired employees. GM's expenditures were twice those of the other two automakers.

Relative to foreign competition, health care costs are a big problem for U.S. automakers. My company estimates that Toyota spends only about $250 a vehicle on health care. A prime reason for the difference is the Japanese government subsidies for health care that the United States does not have. In addition, Toyota has been more productive than the U.S. companies, so its number of retirees and its bills for retiree health care are lower.

Table 9. Expenses for Health Care: North American Automotive Operations, 1992

Item	GM Total	GM Per Unit	Ford Total	Ford Per Unit	Chrysler Total	Chrysler Per Unit
Active employees	$2,882	$ 762	$ 824	$229	$ 553	$288
Retirees	3,701	593	1,364	380	750	390
Total	$6,583	$1,355	$2,188	$609	$1,303	$678

Sources: Company annual reports and Bernstein & Co. estimates.

Overseas Operations: Cost-and-Revenue Footprints

Foreign operations and currencies can have an influence on automobile companies' income statements. The cost drivers in a company's overseas operations will be much like they are in its U.S. operations, but in Europe, the selling and manufacturing are occurring in different currencies. Significant changes in the exchange rates for currencies in Europe can thus lead to difficult problems.

From a company's sales and production data, analysts can construct a matrix such as that shown in **Table 10** indicating where the company sells units and where the company manufactures units—that is, the company's cost-and-revenue footprint. For example, 1.7 percent in the first cell means that about 1.7 percent of Ford of Europe's business is sold in France but manufactured in Belgium.

Understanding such relationships can help analysts determine a company's vulnerabilities to currency fluctuations. For example, Ford had substantial exposure between the German mark and the Italian lira; 8.1 percent of revenues came out of Italy, but the costs were in marks. This dichotomy is the principal problem that Ford had been experiencing. Ford estimates its profits are about $500 million lower in Europe as a result of the movement of the lira against the British pound and the Belgian franc. GM has a much more balanced cost-and-revenue footprint in Europe than Ford, and therefore, it will not suffer as much from the kinds of exchange rate changes that occurred in Europe in 1992.

Fixed versus Variable Costs: Understanding Operating Leverage

Because of the relationships of fixed costs to variable costs in the automotive industry, a small change in demand can have a significant impact on operating profits. **Table 11** shows the theoretical effect of a small change in production. Production in GM's North American automotive operations increased by 5 percent from about 4.8 million units in

Table 10. Ford of Europe's Cost-and-Revenue Footprint, 1992

Cost Sources	Revenue Sources France	Italy	Spain	United Kingdom	Germany	Other	Total
Belgium	1.7%	0.7%	0.8%	6.7%	4.7%	5.4%	20.0%
Spain	6.2	3.2	8.2	0.0	0.0	3.4	21.0
United Kingdom	1.7	0.0	0.0	19.3	0.0	0.0	21.0
Germany	1.4	8.1	0.0	7.0	15.3	6.2	38.0

Sources: Agency for International Development and Bernstein & Co. estimates.

Table 11. Operating Leverage Example: GM North American Operations (dollars in millions)

Item	1991 Total	1991 Per Unit	1992 Total	1992 Per Unit	Percent Change Total	Percent Change Per Unit
Production (thousands)	4,856	—	5,098	—	5.0%	—
Revenue	$74,726	$15,338	$78,448	$15,338	5.0	0.0%
Variable costs						
Materials	28,091	5,785	29,492	5,785	5.0	0.0
Fixed costs						
Labor	25,624	5,280	25,624	5,026	0.0	(4.8)
Capital	4,955	1,020	4,955	972	0.0	(4.7)
Selling, general, and administrative expense	6,274	1,292	6,274	1,231	0.0	(4.7)
Other	16,629	3,424	16,629	3,262	0.0	(4.7)
Operating profit (loss)	(6,847)	(1,413)	(4,526)	(888)	(33.9)	(37.2)

Sources: GM annual reports and Bernstein & Co. estimates.

1991 to nearly 5.1 million units in 1992. The increase in production caused a 5 percent increase in revenue and also a 5 percent increase in variable expenses; the fixed-cost component at GM is quite substantial. The company reduced operating losses by nearly 35 percent by effecting only a 5 percent change in production.

This demand–profitability relationship produces the most difficult forecasting problem with respect to the automotive industry. It may also be largely the reason the stocks respond strongly to economic cycles.

Understanding operating leverage provides only half of the equation, however; the other half is revenue. As demand strengthens or weakens, price per unit reacts accordingly. Prices rise when demand is strengthening and fall when demand is weakening. As shown in **Figure 1**, when industry capacity utilization increases, the balance between supply and demand tightens and the discounts or rebates given in the marketplace fall. Changes in rebates have a substantial impact on the profitability of this industry. Every $100 per vehicle GM saves in discounts generates $500 million in operating profitability.

Also note from Figure 1 that the industry's behavior has changed. In the early 1980s, discounts peaked at about 10 percent and capacity utilization was about 60 percent. In the early 1990s, discounts peaked at about 16 percent and the capacity utilization rate dipped only to 70 percent. Pricing has become more sensitive to operating rates than previously, perhaps because labor costs that used to be variable are now fixed, which means that the marginal cost of production is lower than it ever was in the past. Therefore, companies can afford to cut prices more than in the past. That is, companies have huge fixed-cost bases, and when demand starts to

fall, they cut prices drastically in an effort to try to stimulate that incremental sale to get an extra dollar to cover the fixed costs. Analysts have been surprised by how strong pricing has been at retail and how quickly profits have come back since the latest recession, which illustrates the tremendous implications this aspect has for the speed with which the industry's profitability can recover and will recover from the next downturn.

Automotive Financial Services

One final area of importance in the income statement is automotive finance operations. Auto analysts typically do not spend much time on finance companies because the volatility in earnings is generally concentrated in the auto business. If the finance operations were stand-alone companies, however, analysts would pay considerable attention to them. They are hundred-billion-dollar banks that the financial services community virtually ignores.

The growth of automotive financial services is influenced by marketing promotions. If the auto companies choose to subsidize sales by offering discount financing, the asset base of an operation such as General Motors Acceptance Corporation or Ford Motor Credit will grow much more rapidly than had discount financing not been offered.

The other factor influencing the rate of growth in the finance operations' asset bases are longer terms on loans, which have lengthened significantly since the early 1980s. Cars today tend to stay on the balance sheets as assets longer than in the past. The effect compounds over time and tends to balloon the size of the automotive finance operations.

Longer terms also raise loss rates, however. Thus, the industry has probably hit a ceiling in terms of extending loan terms; the cost of reserving for losses has simply grown too great.

Leasing has little effect on the way the industry functions; it is primarily a transfer of residual risk from the consumer to the credit company. Leasing should probably be considered more a deferral of earnings than a sacrifice of earnings.

Finance companies provide a way to defer earnings from the automotive side of the business. The auto companies sacrifice some money on the manufacturing side in order to earn money on the financing side. These operations have a tendency to smooth earnings over time.

Understanding Cash Flow

The auto manufacturers' cash flow statements contain some nontraditional sources and uses of cash. Particularly important are elements of working capital and long-term liabilities.

Figure 1. Capacity Utilization and Discounts

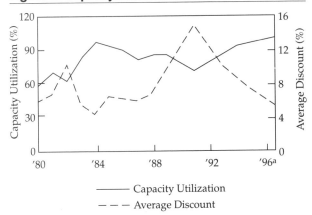

- —— Capacity Utilization
- --- Average Discount

Source: Bernstein & Co.

[a]Estimate.

Working Capital

Working capital is generally a source of cash for the automotive industry when business is improving and a use of cash when business is worsening. Manufacturers collect from dealers daily, so if sales increase, the cash comes in quickly. Manufacturers tend to pay suppliers on a 60-day basis, so as production increases, liabilities can swell but the asset base may not grow quickly. The companies expand the business by using somebody else's—generally, the suppliers'—nickel. When business turns in the other direction, they have to pay all the money back. This aspect often causes analysts to miss how bad downturns can be in this industry; analysts forget the substantial absorption of cash that will occur in a downturn by the reversal of this working capital phenomenon.

Long-Term Liabilities

Another source of cash that every company has since the adoption of Financial Accounting Statement (FAS) No. 106 is health care accruals. FAS No. 106 essentially changed the accounting for retiree health care from a cash basis to an accrual basis. Manufacturers are taking large charges for retiree health care, but the cash outlay does not necessarily match those charges. GM had a substantial mismatch in 1992, for example. The company accrued $3.7 billion in retiree health care costs, but it actually spent only $1.6 billion of cash at the doctor's office. The noncash differential is almost $2.1 billion, a substantial source of cash and something that traditional analysis might miss.

Depending on the rate of inflation in health care, this situation will probably reverse in 10–15 years because the inflation rate in cash outlays will exceed the rate in accruals. At some point, companies will be paying out more to the doctor than they will actually be accruing.

Pension funds have also been a source of cash in the past, but the companies will be spending cash on them in the future. GM's cash flow and pension fund numbers for the 1989–92 period, shown in **Table 12,** illustrate how analysts can be fooled by the quality of the balance sheet. When the contributions in a year are less than the expenses, the companies are actually running their automotive business off the

cash that is supposed to be in the pension funds. A particularly interesting example is 1989, when GM had $811 million in pension expense and put $1 million into the pension fund, so cash from operations was actually enhanced by about $800 million. During the last several years, the enhancement has totaled about $2.6 billion.

Clearly, this use of the pension fund leaves a company in bad shape; it has to pay this money back eventually. People often miss this source of funds, and it is not often discussed, especially by the automotive companies. Nonetheless, the information is in the cash flow statements and in the footnotes to the financial statements.

Special Issues on the Balance Sheet

Analysts should be wary of some of the bombs that can be hidden on the balance sheets of the auto manufacturers.

Pension Funds

The issue that has received the most press attention recently is the funding of pension funds in the industry. Chrysler has been in trouble, and GM's situation has substantially deteriorated recently. As shown in **Table 13,** in December 1992, GM owed pensioners almost $57 billion and had nearly $43 billion in assets, so it was underfunded by about $14 billion. During 1993, GM made the situation worse by signing a new labor contract that increased pension benefits. The present value of that contract was about $3.6 billion; the workers earned slightly more than $4.5 billion in benefits. Interest on the liability was almost $4.8 billion, and then, the biggest factor occurred—a fall in interest rates. Falling interest rates push up the present value of what companies owe because the benefit obligation is a stream of payments into the future that are discounted back to today's dollar. The discount rate controls how large the present value of that stream of payments will be. When interest rates fall, the discount rate falls. The interest rate fall in 1993 pushed up what GM owes by almost $9 billion. Then, the company paid out about $4 billion to existing retirees.

On the asset side, GM contributed $4.4 billion in cash to the pension fund and the fund earned about

Table 12. Cash Flow and the Pension Fund: GM
(millions)

	1989	1990	1991	1992	Cumulative
Pension expense	$811	$369	$1,520	$1,982	$4,682
Pension contribution	1	5	352	1,708	2,066
Net cash flow to operations	$810	$364	$1,168	$ 274	$2,616

Source: GM annual reports.

Table 13. Anatomy of the GM Pension Fund
(millions)

Item	Amount
1992 asset value	$42,831
Contributions	4,400
Return on assets	7,750
Payouts	(4,000)
1993 asset value	50,981
1992 projected benefit obligation	$56,841
New labor contract	3,600
Early retirements/benefits earned	4,560
Interest	4,750
Discount rate change	8,850
Payouts	(4,000)
1993 projected benefit obligation	$74,601

	December 1992	December 1993
Pension asset value	$42,831	$50,981
Projected benefit obligation	56,841	74,601
Funded status	(14,010)	(23,620)

Sources: GM annual reports and Bernstein & Co. estimates.

$7.8 billion. The company wrote checks to retirees for about $4 billion, however, leaving it with about $51 billion in assets for a net underfunding of nearly $24 billion.

Retiree-Health-Care Liabilities

The other big bomb on the balance sheet also has to do with retirees—the auto companies' liabilities for their health care. **Table 14** breaks down the Big Three's accounting for retiree health care and shows the assumptions used for inflation and discount rates so that the discussion can focus on the differences in terminal inflation rate and discount rate. The smaller the difference, the more conservative the accounting for retiree health care. Just as changes in inflation or the discount rate can influence the pension fund, they also substantially affect retiree-health-care liabilities. GM's liability is about $35.5 billion, and the difference between the terminal inflation rate and the discount rate is slightly more than 3 points. Chrysler's difference is about 3.2. On average, companies tend to have a difference of about 2 percent, so the Big Three are at the upper end of the range of non-conservative accounting for retiree health care.

One final point with respect to retirees is that, in this industry it is difficult for a company to escape its past. Even if a company has changed size recently—

Table 14. Retiree-Health-Care Accounting

	GM	Ford	Chrysler
Retiree-health-care liability (millions)	$35,551	$13,588	$7,645
Beginning inflation rate	10.10%	10.30%	9.10%
Terminal inflation rate	5.50	5.50	5.40
Discount rate	8.55	8.50	8.60
Difference	3.05	3.00	3.20
Effect of 1 percent change in inflation or discount rate			
Liability (millions)	$ 4,650	$ 1,700	$ 800
Annual expense (millions)	500	190	100

Source: Company annual reports.

through loss of market share, a reduced level of vertical integration, or both—that company will continue to have difficulties altering some aspects of its cost structure. As **Table 15** shows, GM has 358,000 retirees and produces about $75 billion of revenue in North America, which means retirees left behind a company that is producing about $200,000 in revenues per retiree. In contrast, Ford's retirees left behind a company that is producing more than $400,000 in revenues per retiree, a substantially more productive company than GM on that basis. Although GM focuses a great deal on costs today, the retiree burden is a function of what the company used to be. It is a function of the fact that GM once had 60 percent of the market in North America and that it has always been more vertically integrated than its competitors. GM retirees from a time when the company was substantially stronger are a drag on its revenue base. Thus, retiree burden is another subtlety of the balance sheet that will influence how well companies will compete in the next several years.

Table 15. The Relative Burden of Retirees

Company	Retirees (thousands)	Revenue (millions)	Sales per Retiree (thousands)
GM	358	$74,726	$209
Ford	130	55,398	426
Chrysler	92	30,973	337

Sources: Company annual reports and Bernstein & Co. estimates.

Question and Answer Session

Joseph G. Paul

Question: How should investors react to the big declines in net worth as a result of accruing for retiree health care and other costs? With respect to the changes in accounting methods that may lower the quality of earnings, what are the implications for stock prices?

Paul: The biggest change came last year with FAS No. 106, which is the accounting standard for retiree health care. I have for a long time recommended that we incorporate these changes in earnings forecasts, and that incorporation is essentially what has happened. The industry experienced a brief period in which companies wanted to adjust their numbers and exclude the accounting change, but they have relented, so analysts look at earnings on a post-FAS No. 106 basis. From an accounting point of view, the changes associated with FAS No. 106 have led to much more conservative accounting for health care than in the past and, essentially, a return to the matching principle. That is, the expenses associated with an employee are matched with the revenue he or she is generating. Because such a substantial portion of total compensation now takes the form of retiree benefits, companies should be accruing for that expense when they generate revenue.

The accounting changes have been incorporated into earnings estimates and obviously are influencing stock prices. The big question for the future is whether the market will take into account the changes in the companies' balance sheets. If I had been asked this question 18 months ago, I would have said that the appreciation of General Motors would be substantially restrained by the fact that its balance sheet is in worse condition than its competitors', but the market seems to be more interested in how quickly the earnings are changing than in the structure of the company's long-term liabilities. One reason may be that stockholders do not think they will own the stocks when the company actually has to pay off the retirees.

Question: How do the national contract negotiations with the UAW affect the local contract negotiations?

Paul: The national negotiations provide an umbrella that governs the local agreements. The local agreements are different in the sense that they govern the way work will be done at each individual bargaining unit. The biggest problem remains at GM, where 50–60 locals have yet to sign.

At the local level, the issues concern political and control issues within the union more than problems with the national contract. There have been and will continue to be a series of strikes at the local level related to the settling of these agreements. They are driven primarily by two factors: first, the need of certain people in the UAW to garner support from the locals for elections that will come up later and, second, local factions within the UAW who are disappointed and believe they were sold out. Those factions are attempting to resist GM's efforts to reduce its level of UAW employment. The issues are complicated and vary by local, but the primary problem at the local level is that the workers are angry about jobs disappearing. They are doing everything they can to resist that trend.

Question: According to the union income-security provisions, what happens after the 36-week period?

Paul: Employees are paid until the money runs out or until the contract is renegotiated and the fund recharged. After the benefits of the 36-week period have been consumed, every covered employee receives full pay and full benefits as long as the employee is out of work or until the company has met its ceiling. The cap on spending varies by company. GM's is about $4.6 billion, the upper end of the range.

Question: Once a company reaches its dollar limit, does the company's leverage with respect to outsourcing increase?

Paul: At the dollar limit, the company's legal obligation ends, but keep in mind that the income-security arrangement involves a marriage between organized labor and management. A company's strategy is considerably more complicated than it might initially appear; the strategy of using a big club is limited. For example, during 1993, GM actually ran out of money in the JOBS (Job Opportunity Bank Security) Program. The company transferred most of those people into a lower paying subfund, so everyone got to stay on the gravy train but they had to move to coach from their first-class seats. This circumstance provided an incentive for many people to retire early.

The passage of time is what truly gets a company out of this problem. The contracts do not require companies to replace people who leave; therefore, over time, a company will experience substantial attrition. As time passes, people quit, people die, people retire. In our lifetime, GM, for example, will not hire another hourly employee. This attrition will lead to a change in its sourcing structure, and more work will be done outside than inside GM. It will be a gradual process, however.

Question: Did the GM pool of laid-off workers who were collecting 100 percent of salary under the preceding contract continue to collect 100 percent under the UAW contract signed in the fall of 1993, or did that benefit end?

Paul: The benefit rolled over. Directly prior to the new contract, however, the number of people pulling full income security was significantly reduced; this reduction was somewhat forced because the fund ran out of money. Many people left. They were probably induced to leave by the risk that a contract transition poses; they never know, if they are getting paid for doing nothing, whether the national union will sell them out in exchange for something else. Those that did stick around were paid. In fact, because they had been paid at the sublevel, their pay increased.

Question: How do the original-equipment manufacturers (OEMs) and their suppliers hedge their exposure to commodity prices?

Paul: There is not much the OEMs can do to hedge that exposure. They can buy forward contracts, but that step merely postpones the inevitable. Hedging possibilities for the suppliers vary by industry. For example, the aluminum wheel industry is completely insulated against changes in the price of that commodity; all of that risk has been transferred to the OEMs.

Question: Is the pace of amortization of tooling increasing because of the increasing frequency of changes in styling and rapid model turnover?

Paul: Such a development would be logical, but Ford, for example, just switched from an accelerated depreciation method to a straight-line depreciation method, which is really moving in the other direction. The industry is investing in more flexible tooling rather than in dedicated tooling.

Question: What are the best information sources for the domestic and global auto industries?

Paul: We develop the detail in our analysis of the North American automotive cost structure primarily by beginning with public information and then working backward. We know how much money is taken in and how much money is made or lost in any given region. We also know the asset bases and the employment levels associated with those regions, which helps allocate some of the global and aggregate costs.

A broad array of industry publications is available. In addition, the UAW is a good source of information on salaries and employment levels. Analysts should also spend as much time as they can talking to people in the companies about specific issues. Think tanks and universities are good sources of information, not only here, but also in Europe and Japan.

Question: Are the credit card programs that Ford and GM have undertaken had any effect on the balance sheets, or will they cause surprises in the balance sheets?

Paul: The answer depends entirely on the assumption investors make about how much new business will be brought in by these credit card companies. A Gold Card from GM allows a buyer to earn up to $7,000 off a vehicle, so if the buyer catches GM on a good day, he or she can get a Chevy Cavalier for free!

Should the company be accruing something for all these charges? The airline industry has not been required to accrue for frequent-flyer miles, but airlines are not giving away something that costs them anything. The airlines control how many frequent-flyer seats are given away; if they can sell out the plane, they will not give away any seats. The marginal cost of a consumer getting on a plane with a free ticket is basically zero.

The issue is different for the auto companies' card programs because they give something away that actually costs something. The marginal cost may not be great in the case of GM, where the cost structure is largely fixed, but it is still at least several thousand dollars.

So the issue is whether the companies will sell more vehicles as a result of the card than they would have sold otherwise. Are they locking in a buyer they would otherwise not have been able to lock in? It is far too early to tell.

Another piece of information analysts would like to have about this issue is how the people who own these cards are behaving. Based on the experience gained from frequent-flyer programs, people who have such cards are very different from the people who have a regular credit card. The frequent flyers do not have extremely high charge volumes, and they do not revolve their balances from month to month, so an issuing company does not make any money on the cards. In fact, it basically loses money on the frequent-flyer cards. So, the question will be: Is the holder of an auto card more like the holder of a credit card for an airline program or more like a traditional cardholder, on whom companies can actually make a fair amount of money?

Question: Can manufacturers control their currency risk in an economical fashion, or should they simply try to keep production and sales in balance geographically?

Paul: Ideally, companies should have production and sales in balance geographically. Hedging is only a short-term and imperfect solution, and it can be expensive. One of the big trends

with the Japanese companies is to keep this balance. They manufacture in the United States partly because they have a large U.S.-dollar exposure in terms of revenues. During the next couple of years, analysts will see the Japanese automakers buying a lot more parts here because the fall of the yen has obviously hurt them.

The Art of the Automotive Interview

David Healy, CFA
Vice President
S.G. Warburg & Company

Michele Heid
Vice President, Investor Relations and Planning
Cummins Engine Company, Inc.

Interview questions may have to be carefully crafted, on the basis of the analyst's familiarity with the company and what the company is likely to answer, in order to collect all the legitimate information the analyst wants. The investor relations staff, for their part, are trying to make sure that shareholders and investors have the facts. The interviewer and interviewee in this presentation give guidelines to attain their objectives, and the mock interview illustrates their advice.

The Interviewer (Healy)

My part of this presentation emphasizes what an analyst can hope to find out from interviewing an investor relations (IR) contact in an automotive company. It includes questions to ask and not to ask, ways of implying questions without asking them, and issues related to inside information. The questions differ according to whether the analyst has been following the company for a long time or is just initiating coverage.

Questions to Ask Familiar Companies

Most of the questions I ask companies that I have followed for a long time deal with feeding my "monster," an auto industry earnings forecast model. The model follows a top-down method that starts with the broad economy, interest rates, used-car prices, the number of two- to six-year-old cars on the road, and unemployment percentages. The model allows me to use the economic and industry variables to forecast car and truck sales. For example, today's forecast generates 15.2 million vehicle sales in the United States for 1994, including heavy-duty and medium-size trucks.

To convert an industry forecast to a company forecast requires some judgments about market shares. I collect information about new products coming out, what company has what, what will sell well, and what will not sell well. I then forecast unit sales for the particular company.

The earnings sector of the forecast model is based primarily on the change in unit volume times the incremental profit per vehicle (currently, $4,000 for Ford and GM and $5,000 for Chrysler), which equals the change in earnings. The model is set up for quarterly forecasts through 1994 and annual forecasts through 1996. It generates each line of the forecasted income statements for the individual companies, then generates a line-by-line cash flow statement. The result is a 464-line spreadsheet that begins with interest rates and winds up with each company's cash balance.

The numbers provided by the trade press are often useful in developing the monster. *Ward's Automotive Reports* provides production schedules for GM, for example, that are more reliable than the ones the company provides. *Automotive News* provides new-product information and advance spy photos of the new models, which is more than the companies will reveal about their new products.

Cummins Engine Company is an exception to the rule in the auto industry that an analyst can get better information from the trade press than from the companies. Cummins is a good source of industry data—on diesel-engine numbers, market shares, orders, backlogs, inventories, production schedules, and so forth—for both North American and overseas companies.

The unit sales and production figures are important drivers of earnings in the model, so talking to the companies helps keep the model up-to-date and accurate. The companies can provide production schedules, for example.

Industry pricing is a major adjustment to the profitability line in my model. Therefore, I specifically ask the companies about their variable profits on new models. They will not necessarily tell me, but they may give some hints as to the profitability of the models. The companies can also be helpful regarding trends in selling, general, and administrative expenses (SG&A). I also ask about future and past sales incentives; for example, I want to know how much sales incentives will add or detract from profitability in this quarter and the next quarter.

Analyzing the North American auto companies involves some complicated issues regarding tax rates. General Motors and Ford are particularly complex because they have several overseas operations with varying tax rates and a lot of tax loss carryforwards. In addition, a number of recent accounting changes have affected the industry—Financial Accounting Statement (FAS) No. 106 on accounting for health care for retirees, FAS No. 112 on disability income, and FAS No. 109 on income taxes. Given the complexities, the companies can help analysts assign the correct tax rates for a forecast model.

Capital spending is an important part of the cash flow model; analysts like to know the expected level of capital spending as well as the projects the companies are pursuing. Two important questions are: Where are the dollars being spent, and what operations are receiving the increases?

I always ask companies whether they are considering seeking any new financing. Generally, they will give no direct answer, but the nuances in the answers they give are usually helpful. For example, a company may say in January that it "will not seek any new financing," the implication being that it does not need the money. If in July it changes the response to say it "has no immediate plans to seek financing," the implication is that the company may need some cash.

Simply adjusting the model to obtain an accurate dilution calculation can involve complicated issues related to the number of shares outstanding. Cummins is a good example. Since October 1993, Cummins has split its stock two for one, had a common stock offering, and called two convertible issues. Every analyst who follows Cummins asks about net income, because nobody knows what the per-share figures are any more.

Finally, I like to ask about the company's dividend policy and dividend plans. Again, I will not get a direct answer. The usual answer is, "Well, dividend policy is the prerogative of the board." If I

remain silent, however, the IR contact may talk a little bit more and give a hint as to whether the general expectation is a raised dividend or perhaps the risk of a cut, or may state a target payout ratio.

The result of the questions to these companies is a detailed model of the industry and of company income and cash flow statements for the next four quarters and the next three years. The purpose is to determine whether Wall Street is right or wrong in its consensus view of the company. For example, if my model indicates Chrysler will earn $9 a share this year but the Street thinks Chrysler will earn $7 a share this year, either I am wrong and must return to the drawing board, or I have seen something that is not in the stock price. The model may provide an opportunity to make some money or avoid losing some money if my forecast is correct and the rest of the Street is not.

Questions to Ask New Companies

The kinds of questions I ask a company that I am just beginning to follow—a new automotive parts company, for example—are different from those I ask the familiar companies. First, so as not to waste time in the interview, preparation before the interview is important. I read all the company annual and quarterly reports, the 10-K, the 10-Q—everything I can get my hands on. I also read the reports provided by various brokerage houses and the data available from the several data services, such as One Source or FactSet.

The intention is to assimilate all the general knowledge that Wall Street has on that company. In other words, the analyst wants to determine what is in the price of the stock based on what some of the major brokerage houses have been saying about that stock.

Armed with this background information, the analyst can choose useful questions to ask a new company even if the company provides good public information. For example, Eaton Corporation, a major producer of truck transmissions and related products, publishes its sales broken down by product and by geography but not both. Suppose an analyst noticed in the reports on Eaton that its third-quarter sales of passenger-car components declined 12 percent from year to year even though passenger-car production increased 12 percent during that time. One possible explanation is that the company lost market share, and the analyst can query management about that possibility. The actual verbal explanation provided by management was that, of Eaton's passenger-car component sales, 40 percent came from Europe, which is experiencing a big decline for the industry. Thus, the analyst can glean more information from the interview than is provided even in detailed reports.

Analysts can learn about the company's business by asking questions that search deeper than the company's public statements. Auto parts companies, for example, do not like to talk publicly about sales to major customers, but they will often discuss such information in an interview. During interviews, analysts can sometimes obtain information on product shares, market shares, and labor costs.

Labor costs are a particularly interesting subject. Two auto parts suppliers who sell parts to GM have told me that their all-in employment cost—wages, fringes, everything—is $13–$15 an hour, compared with the $46-an-hour wage and benefit cost GM has in its in-house parts-making operations. Those numbers indicate that the in-house parts manufacturing at the Big Three automakers (GM, Ford, and Chrysler) is uneconomical and that, if outsourcing is possible, some of these outside suppliers will win new business.

Questions Not to Ask

One question analysts should not ask management is, "What are you going to earn?" Inevitably, the answer will be, "We do not forecast earnings." Instead, the analyst should ask, "What is the consensus of analysts' earnings estimates for your company?" The answer to the question phrased this way is likely to detail what the high analyst says, what the low analyst says, the average, and the range. The answer could be straightforward—the actual consensus of analysts' earnings estimates—or it could be what the company thinks the analysts' consensus should be. What the company thinks the consensus should be is one of two things: its own estimate of its earnings or what the company wants Wall Street's estimates to be, which is often, in fact, less than what the company thinks the earnings will actually prove to be.

Many companies try to lower Wall Street's expectations, because the companies and their IR people are reluctant for any negative earnings to surprise the market. Only experience talking with a company over time will show an analyst how a particular company likes to play the consensus game.

Occasionally, of course, the company itself truly does not know what earnings will be; surprises can occur. Company managers are probably 95 percent sure of what the next quarter's earnings will be, but the farther in the future, the less the company will know about earnings.

Do not ask about valuation; companies are not good at valuing their own stock. Most companies think their stock is undervalued in the market. Finally, asking the company about its corporate philosophy or mission or something like that is useless.

Questioning by Inference

One way of prying information out of companies without asking direct questions is to send the draft of a report or an earnings model to a company for comments. It does not hurt to put in a couple of outlandish numbers or comments; the company will probably correct you, and then you have the right information.

Inside Information

The issue of insider information always comes up when analysts are interviewing companies and asking for nonpublic information. In general, however, analysts rarely hear a piece of nonpublic information that is material—that is, information that, if known, could cause a significant move in the stock's price. In judging materiality, the "broker test" is useful: The information is inside information if you get the urge to call your broker when you hear it. If that is your reaction, watch out. Trading on the basis of material nonpublic information is illegal. In summary, if the inside information is any good, you cannot use it.

The few times I have received material inside information, the information has come from either investment banking work on a company or from talking to someone at a company who is unsophisticated about talking to analysts. Material nonpublic information rarely comes from an IR contact.

Conclusion

The basic intent of all the research and interview questions is to collect all the legitimate information you can about what is in the market today and what could affect the stock price. You may be collecting all the information to build a simple financial forecast or, as in my case, to feed a monster.

The Interviewee (Heid)

My part of the presentation offers interviewing tips from an IR perspective. The objectives of the IR group, guidelines for answering questions, vehicles to communicate information, and characteristics of an effective IR person are discussed.

Objectives

IR people have two important objectives. The first is to make sure that every shareholder or investor has the facts. We do not want them to rely on hearsay or industry rumors. The second is to respond to each contact on a timely basis. Cummins, for example, has a rule to respond to investor or analyst calls within a maximum of 24 hours. Obviously, we try to respond to all calls as quickly as possible, usually within an hour. With only two people in the IR Department, however, timely response can sometimes be difficult.

Guidelines

When answering questions, I follow three general guidelines. First, keep all the information consistent. I do not want to give any analyst or investor an unfair advantage, so I make sure to give everyone the same information. Some analysts or investors may think they are getting more information than others, but they are not, because we concentrate on being consistent.

Second, eliminate surprises. I cannot give analysts an exact earnings estimate, but I can calibrate their forecasts to avoid surprises in the future. I can tell them if they are wrong in one direction or another, or if their gross margin figure is way out of line, or if a trend is incorrect. I do such calibrations for most of the analysts who contact me. In fact, I see most of their models before they are published.

Third, be fair to all investors and analysts. Regardless of whether they have issued buy, sell, or hold recommendations, I want to be objective when I am giving analysts information. This guideline is not always easy to follow, but it is important for maintaining long-term relationships with investors and securities analysts.

Vehicles of Communication

Cummins sends information directly to all the analysts who follow the company as well as to investors. Whenever a press release goes out, it is faxed immediately to analysts; they do not have to pick it up off the wire. Analysts also receive all annual and quarterly reports, 10-Ks, and 10-Qs, so when that information is available, the analysts receive it as early as possible.

In this industry, analysts can subscribe to what we call "truck numbers," which identify monthly orders, retail sales, and so on. We fax this information monthly to those analysts who follow Cummins, and to major investors, to clarify truck trends and buying patterns.

We also periodically send out a fact book on Cummins. The fact book compiles ten years of history into a single document. Although analysts have all that information if they have kept ten years of historical documents, the fact book is a lot more convenient than rifling through annual reports.

Another useful method of communication is the teleconference. At the end of each year and following each earnings release, or any major press announcement, we host a teleconference for 80–100 people. We use an outside service and schedule the conference for about an hour. Following an earnings release, for example, the teleconference will discuss the current quarter in comparison with the previous quarter and with that same quarter for the previous year. The conference might also discuss factors affecting the earnings results, the outlook for the market, and any significant event that transpired during the quarter. We will also review the balance sheet and statement of cash flow so the analysts can construct their models for future earnings projections.

The teleconference begins with a one-way presentation from the company, and then we open the forum for questions. Participants can listen to the questions other analysts ask and hear all responses.

Another vehicle of communication is the annual meeting. Most people consider annual meetings mundane, but Cummins' annual meeting is two days of activities geared to meet the needs of the investment community. It starts with a dinner with senior management and a session the next morning, prior to the annual meeting, to cover specific topics of interest to analysts and investors. Following the annual meeting, we host an analysts luncheon. All the officers of the company attend the luncheon, and it provides a forum for the investment community to ask any questions or raise any concerns about the company.

Plant visits are a useful communications vehicle. We encourage analysts to visit our manufacturing facilities, technical centers, and the corporate office building and to meet with senior executives. Cummins hosts several visits each year for any analyst/investor who is interested.

The final important communications media are the phone conversations and the faxes that are regularly exchanged between the company and analysts. We talk on the phone with most of the analysts at least twice a month; if they are preparing a report, depending on what type of report it will be, we may exchange many phone calls. These calls provide the opportunity to review their information, ensure that they do not have factual errors, and offer suggestions.

Prerequisites for an Effective IR Contact

To fulfill his or her role in the most effective manner, an IR person must have three critical characteristics. The first is to be knowledgeable about the company and the products. The second is to be extremely familiar with the financials of the company. The people who contact an IR group—the investors and analysts—are financially savvy. Therefore, an IR staff person needs to know every intimate detail of the balance sheet, the cash flow statement, and the profit-and-loss statement.

Third, IR people must have credibility. They are the primary contacts between the company and the investing world. In order to make their decisions, analysts and investors must be able to rely on the information they obtain from the IR staff.

The Interview

Healy: New orders for heavy-duty trucks were extraordinarily strong for the industry in December. What was going on? Was a lot of prebuying going on to beat a price increase, or was there one big order?

Heid: [*What Healy really wants is the definitive answer to why December truck orders are so high.*] The fact is that nothing unusual was going on—no pricing changes, no prebuy. The strength that we have seen during the past year and a half has simply continued. December is normally not a strong month because of holidays, thus fewer work days than in other months. This December happened to be a record month for truck orders, however, and the ordering was strong across the board—from owner/operators in the high-horsepower segment, the fleets in the middle category, and the smaller, vocational trucks at the lower end of the horsepower range.

Healy: What are the implications of these strong orders for your business in 1994? How good is this huge, growing order backlog, and what percentage of your sales is in the area of U.S. heavy-duty trucks?

Heid: [*Healy is really asking several questions here. First, he wants to get a handle on the quality of the order backlog, and second, because he is recommending Cummins, he wants me to reconfirm that the backlog is very strong, which it is.*] The backlog is at an all-time high, 96,000 units. That equates to ten months of backlog, which may be normal in the auto industry, but in the diesel-engine business, is very strong. The diesel backlog usually runs between three and four months, so this ten-month backlog is extremely bullish.

[*The next issue—how important is the heavy-duty truck market to our business—shows Healy's savvy about Cummins and the diesel-engine business; we have been communicating to the investment community that the North American class 8 business is now a much smaller portion of Cummins' revenues than previously because of diversification.*] At one time, heavy-duty trucks were more than 50 percent of our business, but today that class represents only about 23 percent of our revenues. [*Healy actually knew the answer to this question, but by asking such questions, he can communicate to the rest of the investment community that the heavy-duty market is not as important to*

us as it once was.]

Healy: Outside the heavy-duty area, how important were your sales of the small and mid-range engines to Ford and Chrysler last year, and what is the outlook for that sector? There is a fair amount of interest in the new Chrysler pickup truck because it has a Cummins engine as a popular option. Are you limited by capacity on that engine?

Heid: [*In this question, Healy is actually trying to determine the growth potential in the mid-range truck market.*] From our perspective, entering the mid-range truck market has been a very good move. It was our entrée into the market for lower horsepower engines. We have two large customers, Ford and Chrysler, with which you are very familiar. We just completed our first full year of the Ford contract; we sold Ford about 35,000 units for its mid-range truck. For Chrysler, we provide the diesel engines for the Dodge Ram pickup, which has been a real success. It was chosen as *Motor Trend* magazine's "Truck of the Year." The fourth-quarter 1993 and first-quarter 1994 orders for the Chrysler pickup were very strong.

Are we capacity constrained? No, happily, we are able to meet any customer demand!

Healy: How important were overseas engine sales to Cummins last year, and is there any sign of a recovery in Europe and Mexico, which seem to be in pretty deep recessions right now?

Heid: Overseas sales represent about 44 percent of Cummins' sales. Europe is a depressed market, but Cummins' presence in Europe is small. We have a large presence in the United Kingdom, where sales are recovering. In fact, in November and December of 1993, the United Kingdom has had the highest vehicle registrations that country has seen in the past 18 months. So we are seeing a trend upward, which is very positive for Cummins.

Mexico has been going through a lot of tightening of credit and a lot of apprehension over the North American Free Trade Agreement. Volumes really dropped for the diesel-engine business in Mexico, but since the passage of NAFTA, we have seen some increase, and we hope to see continued strengthening in that market in 1994.

Healy: What percentage of your business—what percentage of sales—do you think the power-generation segment will account for in 1994? Are this area's relative margins equal to those of the rest of the company? What sort of overseas growth do you foresee for this segment?

Heid: [*I want to give some background to this question because, although Healy knows that the power-generation market is one of our growing markets, some people do not know much about it.*] Power generation is very much a growing area for the company. It is our second largest market, representing about 18 percent of our sales volume. If you add in the parts sales associated with power generation, it probably represents more than 23 percent. We believe it ultimately will become our largest market.

Power generation, unlike our other segments, is largely an international market. In fact, this market is more than 50 percent international, whereas several others are heavily weighted toward the domestic side.

Power-generation margins are in line with other market segments. In fact, our margins across the company are pretty balanced.

Healy: If you were modeling earnings, would Cummins' gross margins during the past year be a good guide to the immediate future?

Heid: [*I often hear this question from analysts because they are trying to feed gross margin improvements into their models and analyze what kind of trend and what kind of leverage they can get. From the company's perspective, I have to be careful when I answer this question because I want to calibrate people's information without giving them too much information.*] We have seen substantial growth in our gross margin during the past two years. We will continue to see volume leverage, but the growth that we see in the future probably will not be of the magnitude we have seen in the past two years, during which we have moved from breakeven to profitability.

Healy: Would it be a good technique to estimate your SG&A by extrapolating its historical percentage of sales, or do you expect increases beyond that percentage? What about for your research and development expenses?

Heid: SG&A is an expense in which we should have some volume leverage; that is, a portion of it is fixed, but a portion varies with volume. So, we will benefit from increased sales volume in SG&A.

Expenses for research and engineering are a somewhat different story. We have had high technical expenses to meet the emission standards for 1994, and such expenses will certainly continue in order to meet the standards for 1998. So despite sales volume increases, I expect that R&D expense as a percentage of sales will not change significantly.

Healy: Why do you have such a low effective income tax rate, and what will that look like in 1994?

Heid: [*Healy knows how to word this question. Most people would say, "When will you fully utilize your tax credits?" I will not tell them when I am going to utilize the tax credits fully, of course, because doing so will give them an earnings estimate.*] Cummins' income tax rate for 1993 averaged 13 percent exclusive of a $5.5 million tax credit because of the Clinton administration's tax bill. Our tax rate in 1994 should be somewhere around 15 percent.

Healy: Cummins has split the stock and sold new common shares and retired or called two convertible issues. Please tell me the proper number of shares.

Heid: [*Trying to gather analysts' earnings-per-share estimates for our board of directors meeting next week has been somewhat humorous. Traditionally, I've just had analysts give me their EPS estimates, but as Healy mentioned, with a stock split, a stock offering, and the calling of the convertible debentures and now the preference stock, analysts are using a variety of denominators to calculate EPS, so I need to find out what denominator each is using.*] As of today, we have 38.4 million shares outstanding. Assuming that the preference stock converts, this number would increase to 41.6 million shares outstanding by February.

Healy: Would you talk a bit about your capital spending budget for 1993 and 1994—not only the amounts, but where the spending is concentrated?

Heid: We will not release results until Thursday, but capital spending in 1993 will end up somewhere in the $165–$175 million range, which is consistent with the estimate we gave analysts earlier in the year. As we continue to invest in new products, and because we must invest in new fuel systems to meet the 1998 emission standards, we do not see that number decreasing, at least in the next couple of years. In fact, that number will increase.

Healy: Talk a little bit about the outlook for Cummins' overseas joint ventures. Why is this area attractive for the company?

Heid: The main attraction of the joint ventures for Cummins is an entrée into country markets that we previously could not access. For example, we just recently signed a joint venture with TELCO, the largest truck and bus producer in India. We have been in this country for 30 years, and we have done a lot of work with off-highway engine applications, but we have never been able to penetrate the on-highway market. In this joint alliance, TELCO will produce our B-series engine in India.

Healy: Can you talk some about your dividend policy? Cummins recently increased the dividend following the stock split. Do you have a target pay-out ratio or cash flow requirement that controls the dividend?

Heid: The dividend policy is up to the discretion of the board. It is reviewed on a regular basis and is adjusted when the board determines that doing so is prudent.

Question and Answer Session

David Healy, CFA
Michele C. Heid

Question: Chrysler has been earning good money, and it has been consistently beating estimates. Is this outcome something Chrysler is managing?

Healy: In my earnings model, I plugged in the change in volume from the last quarter, plugged in $5,000 for the variable profit instead of $4,000, and came up with an estimate of $1.85 a share for Chrysler's fourth quarter. The company had been saying that it was comfortable with estimates in the $1.55 range, but I have found in the case of Chrysler that my monster provides better information for forecasting earnings than does talking to the company. So, I stuck my neck out and published a $1.85 forecast. The actual figure was $1.91.

I do not know whether Chrysler was just being cautious or whether it was surprised—by the tax rate, for example. Chrysler will probably beat Wall Street expectations for this year. Over time, however, it will have more and more difficulty performing its "earnings miracles," beating estimates by 30 cents a share every quarter, because analysts learn. They raise their estimates.

Question: How do you handle a company that does not give you much guidance and then disappoints you in earnings?

Healy: You have to do your own work and make estimates as best you can with or without guidance from the company. It is certainly a company's prerogative to say nothing about its outlook before it releases earnings figures. There is no excuse, however, for the company not giving an expla-

nation after the numbers come out. In other words, I can't be mad at a company if it does not forecast earnings, as long as it gives a good breakdown afterward of why the quarter was better or worse than expected. A company may be devalued in the marketplace if it is not communicating well with analysts.

Question: How long is too long for a telephone interview?

Heid: Because every investor and every analyst is a valued customer, I should answer that no telephone conversation is too long. In reality, what I do with all investors and analysts, but particularly new ones, is encourage them to visit the company, see the facilities, meet with senior management, and get background information in that way. I try to keep phone conversations under an hour, but many people need more time, and we are willing to spend whatever time it takes.

Question: If an analyst says, "Gee, what did I miss? What should I have asked you?," how do you answer?

Heid: I'm convinced that people are told to ask that question in Analyst Class 101, because I get that question at least five times a month. I think quite honestly about what they did ask, and if they missed asking about key things that they should know, I may suggest, "Have you considered this aspect?" or "Are you familiar with this?" It is important to Cummins that analysts have a comprehensive picture.

Question: How do you handle

an IR person who is consistently not helpful?

Healy: Not many of that species exist. I have more problems when a company has constant turnover. If analysts do receive little help from an IR person, however, they must rely on their own work. They must make outside projections. For consolation, keep in mind that if you are not getting any help from that particular IR person, presumably, no one else is either; so, at least the playing field is level.

Question: Why have GM and Ford stopped reporting ten-day sales? Does this development bother you?

Healy: Although the stated reasons for dropping the ten-day numbers were that they contained a lot of statistical noise, the reasons given were not very persuasive. The numbers were helpful in revealing trends. Now, analysts are going to overanalyze the monthly numbers as they come out. Actually, I thought the ending of ten-day sales reports would simply require laying off a lot of analysts and reporters because of the drop in numbers to crunch! Seriously though, I am not going to grieve over the loss of the ten-day sales figures.

Question: For the types of companies you cover, what do you consider an acceptable margin of error in your estimates? Are you happy to be within 5 percent or 10 percent?

Healy: I would be delighted to be within 5–10 percent—particularly for estimates far out in time.

The auto industry has an awful lot of earnings leverage, and analysts generally overestimate how good things will get when business is rising and underestimate how bad things will get when the industry is falling into a recession. I am happy if I get within 10 cents or 15 cents for a quarter, but if I am within 50 percent of a number five years in the future, I am happy. Considering all that can happen, if I turn out to be within $3 or $4 a share of what GM can earn in 1996, I will be delighted.

Question: Do IR people worry about litigation? Has this concern changed any of your practices?

Heid: We are always cautious about what we say to the external investment community, because we want the information to be factual and we want to ensure consistency throughout. Our move to teleconferencing has been a great help in maintaining consistency.

Valuing the Automakers' Securities

Richard B. England, CFA
Vice President and Analyst
Putnam Investments

The most important aspect in valuing the U.S. automaker stocks is timing the stocks' probable periods of outperforming the market. Among the varied valuation methods, the recommendation made here is a matrix approach—using several methodologies to come up with target prices and then overlaying on those targets a consideration of the subjective issues.

No hard-and-fast rules exist for buying and selling automotive stocks, so analysts should be skeptical of anybody's decision rules, including mine. Trading auto stocks is an art, not a science. Also, in North America and other developed markets, this industry is highly cyclical. Understanding that aspect, and realizing that an analyst's purpose in life is to outperform the market, I would suggest that "Timing the Automakers' Securities" might be a more appropriate title for this presentation than "Valuing the Automakers' Securities."

Stock Performance over Time

The cycles for the automotive industry generally coincide with those of GDP, but they are much more pronounced than for the economy as a whole. The U.S. auto industry's cyclicality is evident in **Figure 1**, which shows light-vehicle sales from 1963 through 1992 and estimates through 1996. As the industry matured, the sales cycles became more pronounced. The industry is now mature and depends for its growth on discretionary spending by consumers, businesses, and governments.

The cyclicality in earnings is even more pronounced than it is with sales, as seen in **Figure 2** for the Big Three (GM, Ford, and Chrysler). The figure shows a classic case of leverage. With the 1990 UAW and CAW (Canadian Auto Workers) labor agreements, labor became much more of a fixed cost than previously, which is largely the reason earnings in the most recent industry trough were generally worse than they were in the 1981–82 recession, despite higher unit sales.

Thus, analysts are dealing with an industry and companies in which the sales and earnings oscillate

sharply around a slowly growing trendline. The stocks also behave in a very cyclical fashion, as shown in **Figure 3**. Graphing relative performance would not change the picture much, except that the GM line would change from generally flat to a 28-year downward slide with a few bumps in it.

Like any cyclical industry, the auto stocks are not long-term, buy-and-hold stocks, which makes them interesting investments. Investors can make huge amounts of money if they play the stocks correctly, and they do not have to be too precise about picking the tops and bottoms in order to do it.

The relationship between these stocks' outperformance and the sales cycle varies, and the stocks show precious little consistency. The performance of the stocks of the Big Three during various automotive sales cycles are examined in detail in **Figure 4**, **Figure 5**, and **Figure 6**. As shown, the outperformance had no consistent magnitude or duration. The auto stocks never began or ceased outperforming at the same time, although they generally started to outperform before a sales trough and stopped before a peak.

The sales data are three-month moving averages of light-vehicle seasonally adjusted annual rates of sales (SAARS). (The top panel of Figure 4 shows GM's auto sales alone rather than light-vehicle sales.) The figures show the stock performance of each of the Big Three companies and the S&P 500, each indexed to be 1.00 in the month that outperformance began for each of the cycles; the distance between the lines represents the outperformance. Thus, a widening gap indicates the stock has outperformed the S&P, and a narrowing gap indicates it has underperformed. Generally, the trough in light-vehicle sales will be evident on the graphs, but many of the sales

Figure 1. Light-Vehicle Sales
(units)

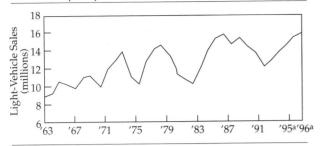

Source: Putnam Investments.

[a]Estimate.

peaks do not appear because the outperformance often stopped well before the peak.

As shown in the top panel of Figure 4, outperformance began for GM stock in December 1966 and stopped five months later, in April 1967. Auto sales troughed in March 1967; the company began outperforming four months before that and quit one month after the trough with an almost not-worth-the-effort outperformance of 14.3 percent. During the next period, shown in the middle panel of Figure 4, the outperformance was once again anemic. The sales trough was not until December 1970, and GM stopped outperforming in August 1970, before sales ever turned up. GM's best effort, shown in the bottom panel of Figure 4, was in the 1982–84 period, when it managed to outperform by about 104 percent.

Ford stock's outperformance for three periods is shown in Figure 5. Ford did not sustain any outperformance during the 1967–68 cycle. The interesting thing about the cycle shown in the middle panel of Figure 5 is that, although the peak in outperformance came about three years after it began in May 1975, most of the relative gain was accumulated in the first 11 months of the cycle, which is unusual. The bottom panel of Figure 5 helps illustrate why some sell-side analysts referred to Ford in this period as "the stock that wouldn't die." From late 1981 through mid-1988, Ford's outperformance amounted to almost 1,250 percent.

As shown in the three panels of Figure 6, Chrysler's performance has also varied considerably in magnitude. The middle panel shows a very short-lived burst of outperformance for Chrysler in the 1975–78 cycle, similar to that of GM. If Ford in the 1980s was the stock that would not die, Chrysler in the 1980s was the Energizer Bunny of auto stocks. When Chrysler began the run shown in the bottom panel, the company was in the early stages of emerging from bankruptcy, so the stock price was extremely depressed, but the run was impressive nonetheless. Ford was good, but Chrysler, outperforming the S&P 500 by 2,700 percent, nearly doubled Ford's performance.

Note that in a substantial number of cases, the outperformance began in December. One possible explanation is that, at the end of a recession, with terrible stock performance, investors get to November or December and say to themselves, "We have had two terrible years. Next year must be an up year." So, people pile into the stocks at the end of the year, and sometimes the end of the year turns out to be the bottom.

The length of outperformance varied from stock to stock and cycle to cycle. A summary of the relationship between outperformance and the sales cycle

Figure 2. Trailing Fourth-Quarter Earnings of the Big Three

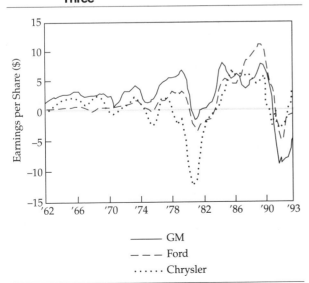

Source: Putnam Investments.

Figure 3. Indexed Stock Performance of the Big Three

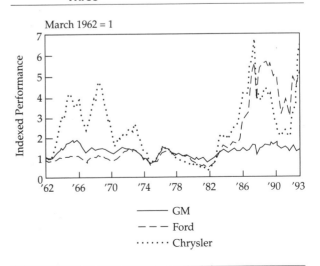

Source: Putnam Investments.

Figure 4. GM's Outperformance during Three Sales Cycles
(sales in units)

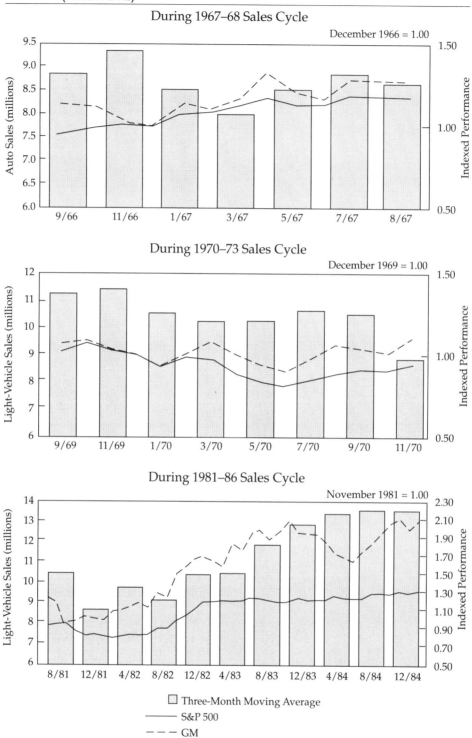

During 1967–68 Sales Cycle

December 1966 = 1.00

During 1970–73 Sales Cycle

December 1969 = 1.00

During 1981–86 Sales Cycle

November 1981 = 1.00

☐ Three-Month Moving Average
—— S&P 500
– – – GM

Source: Putnam Investments.

Notes: For 1967–68 cycle, outperformance started December 1966, stopped April 1967, and had a magnitude of 14.3 percent; for 1970–73 cycle, outperformance started December 1969, stopped August 1970, and had a magnitude of 18.2 percent; and for 1981–86 cycle, outperformance started November 1981, stopped October 1984, and had a magnitude of 85.1 percent.

Figure 5. Ford's Outperformance during Three Sales Cycles
(sales in units)

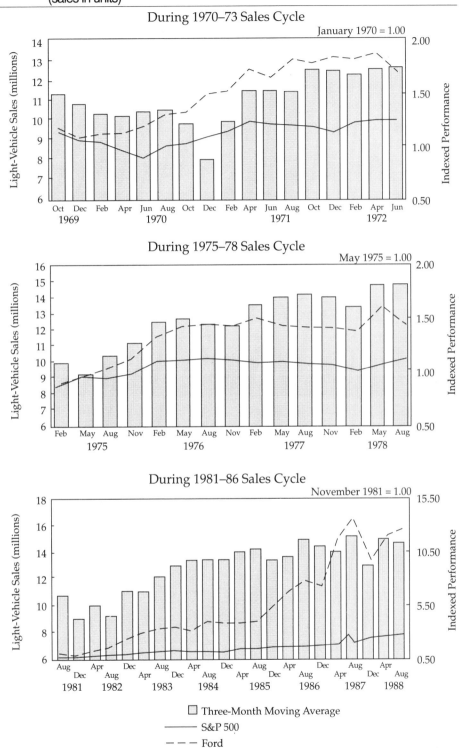

Source: Putnam Investments.

Notes: For 1970–73 cycle, outperformance started January 1970, stopped January 1972, and had a magnitude of 76.4 percent; for 1975–78 cycle, outperformance started May 1975, stopped April 1978, and had a magnitude of 66.5 percent; and for 1981–86 cycle, outperformance started November 1981, stopped June 1988, and had a magnitude of 1,246.9 percent.

Figure 6. Chrysler's Outperformance during Three Sales Cycles
(sales in units)

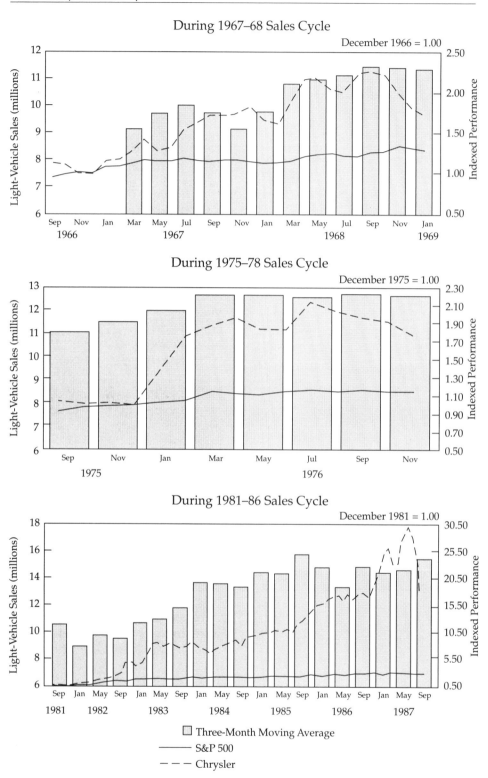

Source: Putnam Investments.

Notes: For 1967–68 cycle, outperformance started December 1966, stopped September 1968, and had a magnitude of 98.6 percent; for 1975–78 cycle, outperformance started December 1975, stopped July 1976, and had a magnitude of 98.9 percent; and for 1981–86 cycle, outperformance started December 1981, stopped August 1987, and had a magnitude of 2,713.9 percent.

appears in **Table 1** and indicates no consistency in duration. In the first sales cycle, for example, 1967 through 1968, GM's stock began to outperform 4 months before the sales trough and stopped outperforming 18 months prior to the peak. Chrysler also began to outperform 4 months before the trough, but it stopped outperforming just 1 month before the peak.

Table 1. Auto Stock Outperformance and Its Relationship to the Sales Cycle
(months)

Sales Cycle	GM	Ford	Chrysler
1967–68			
Outperformance vs. trough	–4	—	–4
Outperformance vs. peak	–18	—	–1
1970–73			
Outperformance vs. trough	–12	–11	–6
Outperformance vs. peak	–33	–16	–6
1975–78			
Outperformance vs. trough	–2	+4	+11
Outperformance vs. peak	–18	–2	–23
1981–86			
Outperformance vs. trough	–1	–1	0
Outperformance vs. peak	–23	+21	+11
1991–			
Outperformance vs. trough	–1	–2	–4
Outperformance vs. peak	—	—	—

Source: Putnam Investments.

Notes: A negative number of months implies that the outperformance started or stopped *before* the trough or peak in sales. Inflection points in light-vehicle sales are based on a three-month moving average.

Based on these observations, auto stocks are difficult stocks to trade. They are perfectly liquid, but investors are better off buying once they have concluded that things have turned up and holding until they have concluded that the stocks are not worth owning any more, rather than trying to move in and out of the stocks on the basis of relative moves within a cycle.

The Current Cycle

The current cycle began in 1991. Figure 1 showed that 1993 was the second year of the current recovery in light-vehicle sales. In 1992, 12.9 million light vehicles were sold, and in 1993, 13.9 million, but sales are still modestly below trend, so barring some sort of economic shock, this auto cycle should have at least a couple more years to go.

As in previous cycles, the Big Three's stock performance for the current cycle varies. As shown in **Figure 7**, GM got off to a pretty good start in early 1992 and then gave nearly all of that outperformance back as its boardroom turmoil unfolded. Perform-

ance turned back up again about November, when Bob Stempell left and Jack Smith was installed as head of the company. GM, as of mid-January 1994, had outperformed the market by 97 percent.

Ford has been steadier than GM, as **Figure 8** shows. It underperformed in the fall of 1992 in the face of significant concern about European profitability, but through mid-January 1994, Ford had outperformed the market by 168 percent.

As in the 1980s, Chrysler has been the big stock in this cycle, as demonstrated in **Figure 9**. Through mid-January 1994, Chrysler had outperformed by 489 percent. Chrysler has had a very hot product hand during the past two years.

Valuation/Timing Techniques

Today, the industry is well off the bottom, and therefore, the following discussion of valuation methods will be geared toward picking an exit point, although it is not necessarily too late to buy. The goal with these stocks is timing rather than pure valuation. A wide range of techniques is used to call the peak, and this discussion will cover several of them, but the list is by no means all inclusive.

Ratio of Price to Book Value

In the past, the price-to-book ratio was of some use and, in particular, had some popularity as a way to call a trough, but the Financial Accounting Standards Board and various and sundry write-offs have significantly diminished its usefulness.

Relative Yield

The analysis of relative yield is not a widely used technique but merits a look. Because yields and prices move inversely to one another, investors look for the point at which the yield reaches a relative low and try to coordinate that point with the peak in relative performance.

Choosing an exit point implies setting a target price, and analysts must make several assumptions or projections to arrive at that target price. The primary one is a dividend forecast. A reasonable assumption is the peak dividend in the preceding cycle, because it seems rational that a company's managers would like at least to match what it has paid in the past. From that point, the forecast can be adjusted up or down based on projections for peak earnings and the company's likely cash flow requirements. Then, analysts should make an assumption as to market yield at the time the stock is expected to peak. The final variable in the equation is what relative yield to use.

The performance peaks of GM stock relative to the market, shown in the top panel of **Figure 10,** are

Figure 7. GM's Outperformance during Current Cycle
(sales in units)

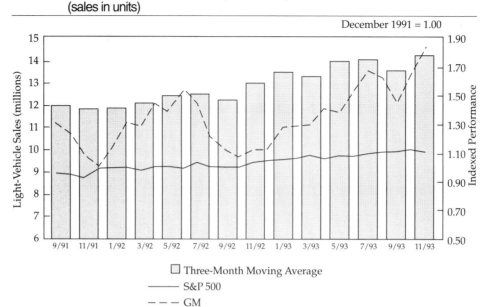

Source: Putnam Investments.

Note: Outperformance started December 1991.

difficult to judge, because the stock was in a secular relative decline for most of this period, but it peaked four times at relative yields ranging from 105 percent to 161 percent of the market. Ford's stock performance, in the middle panel, shows more consistency; the three peaks came at 127 percent, 127 percent, and 138 percent. Chrysler, in the bottom panel of Figure 10, has not typically been regarded as a yield play, but nonetheless, the four relative peaks ranged from 75 percent to 102 percent.

Analysts can set target prices through the use of relative-yield analysis, as shown in **Table 2**. Using the relative performance peaks, the relative yields that the stock had at the time, and projected divi-

Figure 8. Ford's Outperformance during Current Cycle
(sales in units)

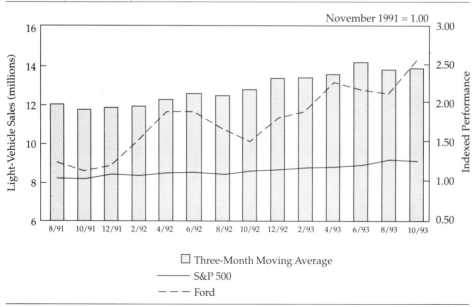

Source: Putnam Investments.

Note: Outperformance started November 1991.

Figure 9. Chrysler's Outperformance during Current Cycle
(sales in units)

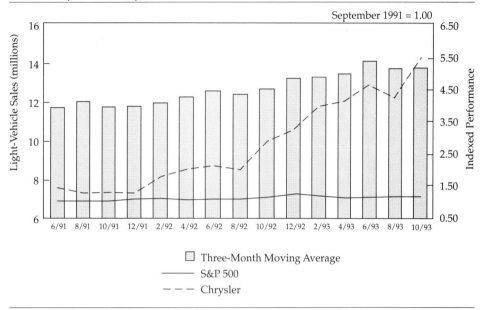

Source: Putnam Investments.

Note: Outperformance started September 1991.

dends, analysts can apply the information to the current cycle to find a target price. The assumed dividends are similar to the dividends paid in the prior cycle, with slight adjustments based on cash flow and earnings projections. Dividing the forecasted dividend by the product of the market yield and the relative yield produces a target price for GM somewhere between $52 and $79.

This information is not particularly useful, however, because a sample size of three or four observations is probably too small to set any dependable parameters and the ranges tend to be too wide to be informative. In fact, Chrysler is already off the charts; its stock is well over $56.

Ratio of Price to Peak Earnings

Calling a target price based on an expected multiple of peak earnings per share (EPS) is by far the most common valuation or timing methodology analysts and portfolio managers use. As a starting point, the method entails forecasting what earnings will be at the peak. The next, and more controversial step, is to pick an appropriate multiple to attach to those earnings.

Historically, the stocks' absolute multiples on peak earnings at the time outperformance ceased have varied significantly. **Table 3** reveals no consistency whatsoever in either the magnitude of the multiples or even the relationship between the three multiples in a given cycle.

A more satisfactory result emerges for relative

Table 2. Price Targets Using Relative-Yield Analysis

A. Historical relative yields

Company	Peak	Historical Relative Yield
GM	6/67	161%
	9/70	148
	12/76	105
	12/84	137
	Average	138
Ford	3/72	127
	6/78	138
	6/88	127
	Average	131
Chrysler	9/68	102
	12/72	91
	12/76	75
	9/87	86
	Average	89

B. Price target during current cycle

Company	Assumed Dividend	Historical Yield	Price Target
GM	$2.50	161%	$52
		138	61
		105	79
Ford	3.00	138	72
		131	77
		127	79
Chrysler	1.25	102	41
		89	46
		75	56

Source: Putnam Investments.

Notes: Assumes a market yield of 3 percent. Price targets are given for the historical high, average, and low yields.

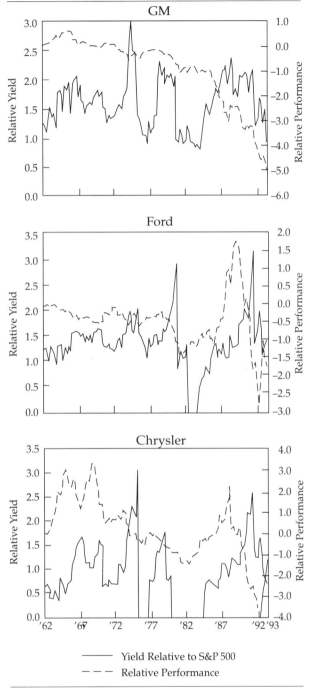

Figure 10. The Big Three's Relative Performance versus Relative Yield

GM

Ford

Chrysler

——— Yield Relative to S&P 500
– – – Relative Performance

Source: Putnam Investments.

multiples: The ranges tighten up considerably, although rank ordering of the stocks is still not terribly consistent. Note that the range is generally 40–60 percent of the market, and probably because of its greater consistency, GM tends to garner the highest multiple.

The data in Table 3 highlight two aspects of using price to peak earnings as a valuation method. First,

and probably not surprisingly, higher interest rates generally imply lower multiples. Looking at Table 3, however, investors might conclude that the impact of higher rates is on the absolute multiples, not the relative ones. Thus, the interest rate environment must be considered when forecasting the market multiple used to arrive at a target auto company multiple.

Second, expectations play a role. The flaw in this analysis is that the historical peak P/Es are based on a price and actual peak earnings, whereas the earnings usually peaked after the stock price. So, the more relevant information to determine would be the P/E based on expected peak earnings when the outperformance stopped. Unfortunately, however, solid expectations data do not exist for dates prior to the mid-1980s.

One anomaly of Table 3 is that, in the most recent cycle, Ford produced the most consistent and loftiest earnings among the Big Three but peaked at the lowest multiple. This phenomenon may have occurred because Ford achieved or exceeded expected peak earnings and GM and Chrysler came up short.

Table 3. Multiples of Peak Earnings

Sales Peak	GM	Ford	Chrysler
1973			
EPS	$ 4.17	$ 1.62	$ 2.13
Price	36.875	13.156	18.222
Date	8/70	1/72	12/72
Earnings multiple	8.8	8.1	8.5
S&P 500 earnings multiple	15.3	16.2	14.5
Relative multiple of earnings	58%	50%	59%
1978			
EPS	$ 6.12	$ 3.15	$ 2.42
Price	39.25	11.361	9.611
Date	12/76	4/78	9/76
Earnings multiple	6.4	3.6	4.0
S&P 500 earnings multiple	9.9	7.3	9.8
Relative multiple of earnings	65%	49%	41%
1986			
EPS	$ 7.17	$ 10.96	$ 6.31
Price	40.063	53.25	44.75
Date	10/84	6/88	8/87
Earnings multiple	5.6	4.9	7.1
S&P 500 earnings multiple	10.3	10.4	13.2
Relative multiple of earnings	54%	47%	54%

Source: Putnam Investments.

Note: S&P earnings multiple is four quarters forward at time of outperformance peak.

Ratio of Price to Trailing Earnings

A less often used valuation technique involves the price-to-trailing-earnings ratio. As shown in **Table 4**, this technique lacks consistency because the spreads are too wide to be useful. It does offer something of value, however. As shown in **Figure 11**, simply buying and selling Chrysler and Ford when the direction of trailing earnings changed would have proved to be an effective and profitable technique. The relationship cannot be seen for GM, perhaps because of the company's secular decline. For Ford and Chrysler, the timing of the turn in trailing earnings and of relative performance is remarkably close, even in the mid-1980s when the economy slowed. In 1985 and 1986, for example, Ford's relative performance rolled over slightly, but when the trailing earnings turned back up, the stock took off again. Earnings and performance peaked almost simultaneously in 1989. Analysts could have used a similar method to call the trough in late 1991 when trailing earnings and performance turned at about the same time.

Table 4. Trailing P/Es when Outperformance Stopped

Sales Peak	GM	Ford	Chrysler
1973			
Date	9/70	3/72	12/72
Trailing P/E	16.4	10.3	8.8
S&P 500 P/E	15.2	18.2	18.0
Relative P/E	108%	57%	49%
1978			
Date	12/76	6/78	9/76
Trailing P/E	7.4	3.5	4.5
S&P 500 P/E	10.5	8.6	10.9
Relative P/E	71%	41%	41%
1988			
Date	12/84	6/88	9/87
Trailing P/E	5.4	5.0	7.3
S&P 500 P/E	9.8	11.4	18.2
Relative P/E	55%	44%	40%

Source: Putnam Investments.

As amazing as it seems, this method certainly makes intuitive sense: The stocks stop outperforming when the earnings stop going up. But who would have thought that something so simple could actually be predictive? This method is rather disconcerting, therefore, because it does not involve any forecasting or fancy analysis whatsoever. If it works, nobody needs analysts!

"Normal" Earnings and the Dividend Discount Model

One of the classic valuation methods is to use a dividend discount model (DDM). This model has a wide range of options and variations, but the garden variety DDM relates a dividend stream to the difference between a required rate of return and the company's growth rate.

In the DDM approach, analysts typically make

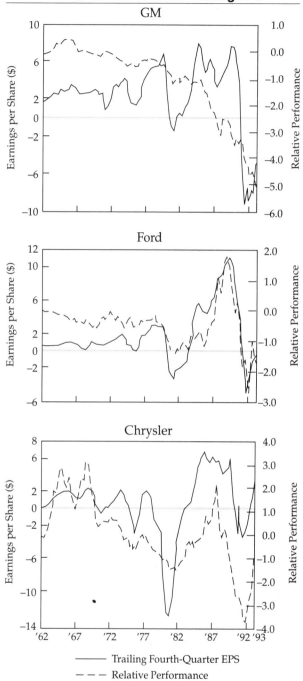

Figure 11. The Big Three's Relative Performance versus Fourth-Quarter Trailing EPS

Source: Putnam Investments.

explicit forecasts of earnings and a payout ratio, or dividend, for the next three-to-five years, followed by a normalized earnings estimate—all discounted back to the present. The normalization process can be as simple as taking average earnings over a cycle or as complex as making the wide range of assumptions necessary to produce an earnings estimate in a so-called "normal" year based on adjustments for market share and degree of vertical integration, disadvantages such as health care cost, differentials, and so forth.

The beauty of this methodology is that it is designed to put all stocks and all industries on an equal footing in searching for those that are most attractive. One challenge, particularly in a mature industry such as the automotive industry, is choosing the growth rate. The nominal secular growth rate for this industry for profits or dividends is probably anywhere between 4 percent and 7 percent. Which number is selected has a meaningful impact on the fair-value figure that the model spits out.

How the Subjective Affects the Objective Valuation

The duration and magnitude of outperformance and the valuations that these stocks receive vary widely for a number of reasons. In addition to the presumed effect of interest rates and expectations, an ever-changing list of many other issues has played a role in all this variability. Not all of these factors are subjective, but analysts treat them as such because, in many cases, the impact of the factors on the financial statements was not felt until long after the factors occurred.

Market share is one such factor. GM, for example, has had a secularly declining market share since at least the late 1960s, which is a likely factor in the company's secularly declining relative performance. Nevertheless, GM's best cyclical outperformance came in the 1975–78 sales cycle. Perhaps not coincidentally, during that period, GM managed to gain back several points of share from a low point in 1974.

A hot product hand is related to market share but is not exactly the same issue. Ford transformed itself into the styling leader with the debut of the Taurus in late 1985. Similarly, Chrysler created a sensation when it invented the minivan in 1983, and since 1992, the company has been absolutely red hot. These perceptions of leadership helped the stocks long before they translated into earnings. GM is in precisely the wrong position as regards the hot-product factor. The company has not established any kind of product momentum in a long time.

Earnings quality has also played a role in outperformance, or the lack thereof. GM was most egregious in the mid- and late 1980s in changing accounting methodologies for the express purpose of propping up earnings. The market did not seem to want to pay for that strategy, not surprisingly, and the stock had a hard time outperforming. It stopped outperforming in 1984, when the sales cycle still had two years to run, but Ford and Chrysler ran three or four more years after that.

Another factor that affects stock prices is acqui-

sitions. The market has not looked kindly on companies spending money outside their core operations. GM's relative peak in 1984 roughly coincided with the acquisitions of Electronic Data Systems and Hughes. Chrysler stopped outperforming almost coincidentally with its American Motors Corporation acquisition in 1987; less than a year previously, it had bought Gulfstream. In both cases, the companies were clearly trying to buy firms outside the auto industry for the presumed benefit of smoothing out the cyclicality in the auto business. The efforts were not beneficial to the stocks, however.

Many other factors, such as Pinto gas tanks and management turmoil, could be listed as affecting stock performance. It should be evident that non-earnings-specific items—whether some nagging deficiency, perceived trend, or sudden event—can significantly alter stock performance.

Performance in this industry does not have enough real consistency to permit formulation of a rule that will call the top with any accuracy. Given that constraint, what is an investor to do? My recommendation would be to take a matrix approach; that is, use several of these methodologies, and perhaps some others, to come up with target prices. The closer the spread produced by the various valuation techniques, the more credence one can put in the target. The next step would be to overlay the subjective issues on the target, in recognition that because of them, a stock may never reach the price target or may go well beyond what the investor believes the stock can achieve. All of this discussion of valuation methods is discouragingly imprecise, but an investor who follows the matrix approach can get out of these stocks close enough to the top to do better than most other investors—and certainly better than the market.

Troughs and Peaks in Foreign Stocks

I do not formally follow the foreign auto stocks, but because the European and Japanese auto markets are both mature like the North American market, the foreign stocks, at least on average, are probably going to begin to outperform before the country's car sales turn up and cease to outperform before the sales turn down. Investors should adjust their earnings forecasts for accounting differences, however. The P/E differences in the markets and their subsequent impact on relative P/Es certainly should be considered in deciding when to get into and out of the foreign auto stocks. Although P/E levels probably will not be the same as U.S. P/E levels, outperformance should generally lead the trough and stop ahead of the peak.

Picking an Entry Point in the Next Cycle

Investors are up against a significant challenge if they try to own or trade these stocks; they do not want to own the Big Three's stocks between the peak and subsequent trough. The numbers, as shown in **Table 5**, are amazingly consistent: Each company underperformed three out of four quarters and by an average, although the range is wide, of about 70 percent.

As the yields rise, the stocks become tempting, but such an effort can best be analogized as attempting to catch falling daggers. Investors should currently avoid owning these stocks until they can conclude that the stocks have turned up again—1998, 1999, or 2000.

Imagine moving forward to, say, 1998, when the industry has nearly completed the automobile cycle, the economy is in a recession, and auto sales are in the dumps. How does an investor know when to buy? Two types of information that are often used to decide are dividend cuts and vehicle sales data.

Dividend Cuts

One of the more common beliefs is that these stocks should be bought on a dividend cut. The evidence for this belief is mixed, as shown in **Table 6**. Note that, on average, GM and Ford outperformed the market and Chrysler lagged slightly in the two months following the cuts.

In only two instances among the three stocks and during three sales cycles did the dividend cut approximately coincide with the beginning of the outperformance. In every other case, the cut was at least 4 and as much as 37 months too early. The modest average outperformance investors would pick up by

buying on the cut would be more than given back before the outperformance truly began.

Vehicle Sales Data

The other information tool many analysts use to call the trough is light-vehicle sales. Analysts can look at a variety of signals: the first positive year-over-year comparison in SAARS, the first positive year-over-year comparison in three-month moving-average SAARS, a substantial narrowing in negative comparisons, or the first uptick in the SAARS series. Given the experience described here in searching for consistency, however, investors should not be surprised to learn that I found no useful relationships.

Recommendations

Investors cannot rely on either the dividend action or the industry selling pace to call the trough, but I would like to offer the following advice:

- Getting in close to the bottom will require buying the stocks when the industry outlook and company profits look worst, which will take a lot of guts.

- Remember December. If the past two or three years have been tough, and the season is late summer or early fall, investors might save themselves some aggravation by waiting until December to get into these stocks.

- The evidence on trailing earnings for Chrysler and Ford suggests that waiting until the earnings turn might be the least stressful way to pick an entry point.

- The magnitude of the outperformance for these companies, on average anyway, is

Table 5. Peak-to-Trough Performance of Auto Stocks

Company	Stock Relative Performance		Underperformed Quarters	Relative Performance
	Peak	Trough		
GM	6/67	12/69	8 of 10	−14.5%
	9/70	12/74	14 of 17	−42.7
	12/76	12/81	15 of 20	−68.6
	12/84	12/91	18 of 28	−157.1
		Average	75.0%	−70.7
Ford	3/72	6/75	10 of 13	−33.6
	6/78	12/81	11 of 14	−94.3
	6/88	12/91	10 of 14	−95.4
		Average	76.0%	−74.4
Chrysler	12/64	12/66	6 of 8	−40.3
	9/68	6/70	7 of 7	−44.0
	12/72	12/75	6 of 12	−50.6
	9/76	12/81	15 of 21	−100.5
	9/87	12/91	12 of 17	−93.8
		Average	73.4%	−65.8

Source: Putnam Investments.

Table 6. Performance Following Dividend Cut

Company/Date	Company Performance	S&P Performance	Relative Performance
GM			
11/74[a]–1/75	+26.2%	+10.0%	+16.2%
2/75–4/75	+10.3	+7.0	+3.3
5/80–7/80	+17.0	+9.4	+7.6
2/91–4/91	−9.5	+2.3	−11.8
11/92–1/93	+17.0	+1.7	+15.3
Average			+6.1
Ford			
4/75[a]–6/75	+14.2	+9.0	+5.2
7/80–9/80	−3.1	+3.1	−6.2
1/82–3/82	+13.7	−7.0	+20.7
4/91–6/91	+10.8	−1.1	+11.9
Average			+7.9
Chrysler			
2/70[a]–4/70	−7.4	−8.9	+1.5
2/75–4/75	−1.2	+7.0	−8.2
11/78–1/79	+9.1	+5.5	+3.6
8/79–10/79	−13.2	−6.9	−6.3
3/91–5/91	+3.5	+3.9	−0.4
Average			−2.0

Source: Putnam Investments.

[a]Month of the dividend cut.

such that investors can do very well with these stocks even if they do not call the bottom or top precisely. The stocks' cumulative outperformance typically builds fairly slowly, because the consensus that the recovery has begun or will begin soon takes a while to form. This period affords some margin for error in buying the stocks.

Concluding Comments

Several valuation mistakes are common in this industry, including the following:

- relying too heavily on one valuation method or one analyst's opinion;

- thinking you have found a good reason, such as the yield, to own these stocks between a peak and the next trough;

- underestimating the power of expectations and momentum;

- using the price action of the stocks to decide whether they have gone up enough—for example, reaching the conclusion that "Chrysler has doubled off the bottom, so the outperformance must be over." In the current cycle, Chrysler stock traded as low as 9⅞. A lot of people got out at 20 because the stock had doubled; now it is over 60. Do not pay too much attention to how much the price has changed from the trough.

The leverage in this business will continually surprise investors. Most analysts' estimates of peak earnings will be too low, and the converse will be true of trough earnings. When the industry is moving away from those troughs and peaks, continual revisions in estimates will play an important role in driving the industry's stock prices.

Although the automotive group is exciting—and a tremendous amount of money can be made—this presentation should instill a healthy dose of skepticism toward anyone who purports to offer tight rules for investing in it.

Question and Answer Session

Richard B. England, CFA

Question: Do product recalls affect automotive stock prices?

England: Probably less than investors think. Looking at the timing of recall announcements and at the stock chart, analysts would be hard-pressed to find any impact at all. Often, the cost of a recall is not particularly significant, and the auto companies have also been able to shift some of the cost back to their suppliers. The important factor has been how the company has handled the recall. Shortly after Lexus was launched, every LS-400 model had to be recalled, and not for trivial problems. The company handled the recalls remarkably well. Saturn has had some recalls, but it has also treated its customers very well. The companies have all discovered that how they treat their customers is paramount.

Question: In terms of cycle-to-cycle P/Es, can you make an appropriate adjustment for the accounting changes that have recently affected the industry?

England: You can, but you may be treading on thin ice in doing so. The difference is about $2 in earnings for GM and about $1 each for Ford and Chrysler. Unless every other investor is making the same adjustments, you will be disadvantaged in calling the appropriate P/E if you make the adjustments.

Question: What kind of valuation parameters would you use to value an automotive supplier? Although they are cyclical, they also have a growth profile because of outsourcing.

England: The automotive supply industry is a tough one to call. Many original-equipment suppliers are trading at lofty multiples, certainly relative to what their past has been. I analyze them as I do auto stocks—that is, look at the stocks on the basis of a multiple of peak earnings to establish some sort of price target. A lot of things that are going on in the supplier base may cause them to be less cyclical than they were in the past. Magna International, for example, would argue that its earnings will not decline in the next cycle. That may prove to be optimistic, but with the considerable new-product flow and geographical diversification, earnings may hold flat for a year or two even as the North American market turns down. If that is what happens, investors could see a revaluation in the multiples. At this point, however, I am taking a don't-fight-the-tape approach with the suppliers.

Competitive Factors in a Manufacturing Setting

James C. Rucker
Executive Director, Industrial and General Assembly Engineering,
  North American Operations
General Motors Corporation

The critical factors in modern manufacturing operations are related to the need to wed technology to profound process knowledge and to the importance of people's know-how. Factors that investment analysts can examine to evaluate auto manufacturers' competitiveness from the standpoint of manufacturing are (1) the company's use of technology to achieve its quality and customer-satisfaction goals, (2) whether product and process are developed concurrently, and (3) whether the company structure results in process knowledge residing where it is needed.

Several years ago, the Massachusetts Institute of Technology's Commission on Industrial Productivity published a book titled *Made in America*, in which the introduction's first line reads, "To live well, a nation must produce well."[1] The book builds a convincing case that the manufacturing sector is critical to the United States' economic well-being and ability to generate wealth.

Nations create wealth in only three ways: They can farm it, mine it, or manufacture it. The functions that take place after those creations merely move wealth around; they do not add to it. Manufacturing is the primary creator of jobs and wealth in every economy of the modern world.

The United States seems to be waffling, however, in its commitment to manufacturing and is apparently willing to evolve into a service economy. In 1991, for example, Dow Jones dropped steel manufacturer USX from the DJIA and replaced it with the Walt Disney Company. But the manufacturing sector, not the service sector, is the only realistic place to create wealth to eliminate the U.S. trade imbalance; hospital rooms, payroll systems, and dinners at Trader Vic's cannot be exported. Services arise to follow manufacturing, and if the United States loses its focus on manufacturing, it will pay a price.

Unfortunately, manufacturing is not very glamorous. It does not have the image of an exciting or provocative place to spend a career. The best and

brightest managers now often go to Wall Street instead of Detroit—partly, no doubt, because of the three D's associated with manufacturing: dark, dangerous, and dirty.

In light of the importance of manufacturing in the U.S. economy, the health of the automotive industry is vital. It is the largest segment of the U.S. manufacturing sector. The automotive industry accounts directly for more than a million jobs and has an impact on about one out of every seven jobs in America. According to the U.S. Department of Commerce, the auto industry uses 40 percent of the machine tools, 20 percent of the semiconductors, 20 percent of the aluminum, 20 percent of the glass, and 12 percent of the steel consumed in the United States, and it represents about 10 percent of all consumer spending.

This presentation discusses the critical factors in modern manufacturing operations and suggests how investment analysts can use insights about those factors to evaluate companies' competitiveness. The explanations and examples come from the General Motors Corporation, but the concepts and evaluation approaches are applicable to any manufacturing company.

Manufacturing: The Marriage of Knowledge and Technology

Manufacturing was responsible for the U.S. rise to

---

[1]Cambridge, Mass.: MIT Press, 1989.

global economic leadership in the first half of the 20th century. The reason the United States was so successful is that Americans understood and excelled in the manufacturing paradigm of the time: mass production. This expertise, not technology alone, gave the United States a competitive advantage for decades. The United States excelled at mass production because it invested in the necessary scientific base, research and development, and education to support the advanced methods and technologies of mass production.

Many people today think technology is the key to reducing costs and improving productivity. Technology, however, is not enough for modern competitiveness. The fact is that such manufacturing technologies as robotics, computer-aided design (CAD) and manufacturing (CAM), and artificial intelligence are merely tools. They cannot in and of themselves increase a company's productivity. In fact, to use technology alone as the measure of a company's likelihood of success is to miss the point and to risk poor investment decisions.

A narrow focus on technology is not unusual, however, in the automotive industry. The entire industry made that mistake in the 1980s: Companies rushed into state-of-the-art technologies such as robotic welding, automated guided vehicles, and so forth, in the belief that they were the panacea for improving quality and efficiency. Some people actually went around counting robots in the plants as a measure of the plants' competitiveness.

Today, the auto industry has learned that technology by itself does not provide the *knowledge* needed to manufacture safely, efficiently, and at a high level of quality. Knowledge and technology are totally interdependent. Of the two, however, knowledge is the key. It tells companies how to apply the technology to improve human productivity.

The late W. Edwards Deming was one of the most influential quality management gurus of the 20th century. His philosophies are in practice all over the world, and they reflect this emphasis on knowledge—specifically, "profound knowledge," which is Deming's term for knowledge of the entire system and how it works. That profound knowledge is what gives a product, a company, or a nation a competitive advantage.

Anybody can go out and buy a piece of technology. In fact, world trade and international communication capabilities have made the diffusion of technology around the world quicker and easier today than ever before. What determines whether that technology results in growth and wealth is how it is applied, and the competitor that has the profound knowledge of the system will know best how to apply the technology.

Maintaining economic leadership requires profound knowledge of new manufacturing paradigms. The manufacturing paradigm is changing, and it is changing quickly. Industry has been moving out of the mass-production paradigm and into the paradigm of lean production. The key to lean manufacturing is not technology; the key is to use human knowledge and understanding of the production system to identify sources of waste and eradicate them. Furthermore, lean manufacturing is being overtaken by yet another paradigm, agile production.

Agile systems are designed to deliver unique products made to customer specifications but without the cost or waiting. A real-world example is the bicycle shop. A customer can enter a bicycle shop in Japan and order a bicycle. The order is then electronically transmitted to the plant, which changes the setting of the machine tools, makes the tubing (which is the primary factor differentiating the size of the frame), assembles the bike to the customer's wishes, adds the components that were ordered, and finishes the bike—in a day. The kicker in this example is that the company then holds on to the bike for six days—to build the customer's anticipation. The customer is astounded because a one-week bike is a wonderful marvel of technology.

Agile enterprises include the capability for rapid reconfiguration of the production process. Ultimately, the goal is to increase the range of what is buildable and to achieve the flexibility to produce in a lot size as small as one, at a moment's notice, at a high level of quality, and at the lowest possible cost. Just as the United States invested in the enabling technologies and scientific base of the mass-production paradigm, it will have to invest heavily in the enabling technologies and knowledge required for the lean and then the agile manufacturing paradigms. Moving from mass to lean to agile is not wasted motion. Companies cannot switch to agile from mass. They have to get lean first.

Manufacturing know-how and process excellence are at least as important as product R&D in 20th century success. U.S. manufacturing leadership and economic growth during the first half of this century were largely based on technologies invented by somebody else but applied and improved upon by Americans. The automobile industry is a good example. The Big Three (GM, Ford, and Chrysler) did not invent the automobile; the Europeans did. U.S. automakers, however, invented a mass-production system to produce common products at low cost that shattered the European system, the old paradigm, of craftsmen building one custom-made car at a time.

Now consider this example from the second half of the 20th century: The three most successful new consumer products developed in the past 20 years—the VCR, the fax machine, and the compact disc and player—although invented by Americans and the Dutch, are produced primarily by the Japanese. The reason may be simple. In the United States, about 80 percent of all R&D is on products and only 20 percent is on process. Japan, and some other countries, emphasize process, the science of manufacturing, because the creation of lots of new products does not guarantee a long-term, sustainable advantage. Products can be copied, and patents eventually expire. Only process innovation gives a country the know-how to be the low-cost, high-quality, high-value producer.

Manufacturing know-how provides a country or a company room to maneuver in the marketplace. Any company that wants to be competitive will have to reflect the priority of manufacturing know-how in its management systems, its structure, and its behavior.

Evaluating Automotive Manufacturers

The three recommendations given here for analyzing companies in the automotive industry, or in any modern manufacturing industry, reflect the philosophy that technology must be combined with know-how in order to manufacture safely and at a high level of quality. Analysts should look at whether the company uses technology to achieve its quality and customer-satisfaction goals; look at how the company develops the product and process; and look at where in the company the process knowledge resides. GM's experiences will be used in the following sections to illustrate this kind of analysis.

Technology

How technology is used is more important than simply the existence of up-to-date technology. Technology needs to be used to improve cost, quality, and customer satisfaction.

GM applies advanced technology in several areas of manufacturing in order to meet customers' needs.

■ *Cutting and welding.* Laser technology is an important tool for both cutting and welding metal. Laser blanking of steel, for example, allows the combination of various grades or thicknesses, even different types of steel, into a single blank. (A blank is a big sheet of steel that is placed into a die system to make a part.) Laser blanking thus allows a manufacturer to have a heavy gauge where the vehicle needs the extra structure (e.g., around the door hinge) and a lighter gauge where that weight is not necessary. This technology helps reduce parts, saves money on die costs and tooling maintenance, and improves the

ease of vehicle assembly, which ultimately reduces variations in the dimensional accuracy of the vehicle's body.

GM has used laser blanking on several cars to achieve the dimensional stability customers want and need through a process that is totally invisible to customers. In the 1994 Cadillac DeVille and DeVille Concours, for example, the entire body side ring is made of a single piece containing three different thicknesses of metal.

GM is also using laser technology to cut metal, which expands the build capability for GM product designs. On the new Cadillac Seville, for example, one distinctive feature is the deck lid, which has a small lip and an integrated, high-mounted stop lamp. The lamp is unique; it is longer and thinner than anything else on the market today, and it is built directly into the deck lid itself, not on the spoiler or some other plastic add-on part. This deck lid is a challenge to manufacture. The length and width of the stop lamp prevented stamping the deck lid in one piece using a conventional die-cut opening. We could not simply punch out the lamp opening without distorting the deck lid. Laser cutters, however, allowed us to create the opening and give the Seville its unique look.

The deck lid on the Seville also uses laser welding to attach the reinforcement to which the center high-mounted stop lamp is mounted. The reinforcement is behind the lamp. Because of the thinness of the stop lamp, workers cannot get into that part with a spot-weld gun. Also, the surfaces and flanges inside are not large enough to support a spot weld. So, GM turned to laser technology for the process and laser-welded the reinforcements to the inside of the deck lid.

The objective of today's welding technology is to develop processes that minimize distortion of the metal and require little reinforcement (because reinforcement adds unwanted weight to a vehicle). Welding needs to do more than simply make the car stick together; the goal is to produce a smooth-looking car. Another objective is a welding process that does not require large access holes, which can compromise structural integrity.

In addition to laser welds, GM uses another non-conventional welding process—arc spray brazing. This technique has several advantages over conventional silicon bronze welding: It requires less heat, thus is less likely to distort metal and produce unwanted variations; it does not require large access holes behind a panel, which improves the body's structural integrity; and it results in a much cleaner, smoother look to the joint, which gives a car the high-quality appearance customers expect. GM uses robotically applied spray brazing on several models, including the Pontiac Bonneville, the Oldsmobile Ninety-Eight, and the Oldsmobile Aurora.

In all cases of technology choice in cutting and welding, the decision to use a particular technology is driven by the product characteristics required to meet the demands of a target market.

■ *Metal forming.* GM is applying such advanced technology as multibending, roll forming, and hydroforming to optimize the basic structure of its vehicles. These technologies allow the manufacturing of more complex bends, or shapes, than previously and thus widen the possibilities for new-vehicle designs. The new technologies also reduce the weight and number of parts in a vehicle, which improves dimensional integrity and quality and reduces investment cost and waste.

GM used advanced metal-forming technologies to create the body-in-white and other large components for the Aurora and the Buick Riviera, which are due out in spring 1994. For both cars, the product team set its goals for the car structure based on market research, competitive data, and the voice of the customer. The team constructed capable manufacturing processes early in the development of these cars and also turned for help to the Manufacturing Center of North American Operations (NAO), which develops advanced technologies.

Together, these groups designed a numerically controlled multibender that can bend large parts on more than one axis at a time. The windshield header, for example, which is a boxed section made by roll forming and then seam welding, is put in the multibender and sculpted in three dimensions to match the contours of the car. The header is one piece; the process entails no dies and no spot welding.

GM also developed in house the technology to design, engineer, and manufacture hydroformed pieces, technology in which water actually forms the part in a high-pressure die set. The Aurora's front subframe was manufactured in this way, and the process reduced the part count from 40 to 18, reduced the welding operations from 73 to 45, and saved GM $5 million on the program.

■ *Paint.* The appearance of the paint is a big part of a customer's first impression of a vehicle, and the durability of the paint has a great impact on the customer's overall satisfaction during the vehicle's life. GM was one of the leaders in the application of basecoat/clearcoat paint. This process is used on all GM passenger vehicles and, by 1995, will be used also on all truck models.

Several paint technologies and processes have recently been or are being developed to improve the paint itself or to lessen the effects of paint or the painting process on the environment. GM is implementing etch-resistant clearcoats, for example, that

have superior durability against the elements, even acid rain. The company is also using water-borne basecoat paint, which has much lower solvent emissions but still gives the high-quality appearance of high-solvent-emitting paints. In addition, GM has made a significant investment in several plants to change to a powder primer that has a dry, nonhazardous by-product and sends no harmful emissions into the environment. This process is used in the plants that produce GM's compact pickup trucks, and it will be used in the new-generation compact sport/utility vehicles, such as the Chevrolet Blazer and the GMC Jimmy.

Product and Process Development

In order to apply new technologies such as those discussed in the preceding section, the product engineers must know the manufacturing systems and must design the vehicle with the *process* and its requirements and capabilities in mind. Thus, an important factor in evaluating a manufacturing company's competitiveness is the emphasis it gives to process requirements in developing a product.

Smart companies will develop the product and the process concurrently to reduce and control variations and achieve a precision build. Design typically accounts for only about 5 percent of total traditional product cost, but decisions made during the design phase can influence 70 percent or more of the ongoing manufacturing costs.

The need for concurrent product and process design is the reason most automotive companies now use cross-functional platform teams, in which product engineers, manufacturing engineers, and marketing representatives work together to bring out a new vehicle. The Aurora and Riviera are examples. Those models were developed on the same platform by the Cadillac–Luxury Car Engineering and Manufacturing Division. Process control and capability received heavy emphasis in the earliest phases of development. The product team performed a technique called decision and risk analysis, in which decision makers look at the trade-offs in the car program and try to understand how to connect marketing to engineering to manufacturing so as to optimize the vehicle as a system, not just a collection of parts. The team adopted a total-vehicle focus and developed the product and the process concurrently, taking responsibility for both from the concept stage right up through the start of regular production in the plant.

People from the assembly plants work with the platform team while the car is still in the concept stage to evaluate the build process and improve it before the vehicle reaches the plant for a pilot build. They look at the timing, the sequence of build, and the ergonomics of the assembly function, and they make whatever design modifications are necessary to reduce variation and improve process control. The process is fine-tuned in the pilot build, so when regular production begins, we have a highly capable process producing high-quality vehicles. The key is knowledge of the process—up-front knowledge—applied to the earliest phases of product design.

Company Organization and the Site of Process Knowledge

The third recommendation for automotive industry analysts goes hand in hand with studying how a company develops its products. The analyst can tell a lot about a company's priorities by looking at the way it is organized. Where does the process knowledge reside? How closely linked is it to the product? What is the background of those in charge? Do they understand the importance of the process?

Executing quality is a complex, demanding process. It requires a total-systems perspective and a well-integrated organization. In the past, GM thrived on variations or differences between the internal organizations. Not much outside competition existed in the Oldsmobile market segment, so the competition was Buick. That attitude seemed to be ingrained at GM, but today, a great deal of competition exists in every part of the market. Interdivisional competition is changing. From now on, GM will have one stress-analysis tool, one common flow of math data through the company from beginning to end of a product program, and one process for all vehicle development. This change has not been easy, but it is the right thing to do.

The experience of GM in reconfiguring NAO to achieve integration illustrates the streamlining goals: GM consolidated the NAO passenger-car platform teams down to three, plus Saturn, and implemented a single, common process for vehicle development across the entire operations. The company also aligned the NAO Technical Center to be an operating, rather than a staff, function. The major organizations in the Tech Center—design, R&D, manufacturing, and engineering—are now focused to support the platform teams directly in their efforts to satisfy the final customer. The operating divisions intersect with the Tech Center through work on advanced projects, direct divisional support, and the new NAO Vehicle Launch Center.

To facilitate learning, the Launch Center will be the repository for knowledge of the system that all the platforms will use and that will apply to all new car and truck programs. The Launch Center will draw in people from the four functions in the Tech Center and align them with the product development team. The Launch Center is intended to assure

that GM leverages its resources in the most efficient and effective manner possible through the use of best practices. It is intended to increase the diffusion of knowledge across the platform teams as it works with multiple programs each year.

The Manufacturing Center directly supports the Launch Center and the vehicle platforms. Together with the platform teams, it develops the common process model that will be used for everything on the vehicle from the sheet-metal tool and die work, to the stamping, body assembly, paint, and general assembly. At the Manufacturing Center, the focus is on the science of manufacturing and building a professional team of people who act on the belief that manufacturing matters.

The resources saved by consolidating organizations will be applied to differentiate the vehicle features that should be unique—the features that customers see and feel, such as styling, the instrument panel, the ride and the handling, the seats, and so forth.

Building Profound Knowledge of the System

One effective way for manufacturers to build profound knowledge is to apply knowledge-based rather than technology-based tools and methodologies. A good example is the method called design for manufacturability (DFM), which requires product designers to maintain a manufacturing focus and consider the requirements and capabilities of the process in the beginning of the design phase.

At GM, DFM has helped reduce part count and assembly time, improve the ergonomic design of the process, reduce costs, and improve quality. GM is now using DFM to accomplish lean manufacturing, the replacement for the mass-production paradigm, by wiping out waste. The next step, agile production, will use the improved quality of the lean system with the provision for variety to meet customer demands.

Knowledge, in the forms of real and artificial intelligence, is critical to the new production paradigm. The first step in being agile is knowing where the action is. This knowledge must be in the hands and minds of the production people who are trained and empowered to take appropriate action. All workers, not just the engineers or managers, need to understand the jobs they are doing and how they fit into the overall system. Whereas the success of the mass-production paradigm was based on renting people's hands and brawn, strength or dexterity, the agile-production paradigm is based on optimal use of people's brains and knowledge. The productivity of the work force in the new paradigm is not so much a function of the amount of technology at their disposal as it is of the knowledge and skills the workers have to add value to the process. Human capital—knowledge, the ability of the work force to make the best of new technologies—is as important as physical capital in determining productivity. The manufacturing firms that develop profound knowledge of the manufacturing system and invest in their human capital will soon have the upper hand. A company's human capital is the one competitive advantage that cannot be quickly copied or acquired.

This development has definite implications for U.S. educational systems and for the kind of education and training the manufacturing companies themselves may need to supply. For this reason, GM has developed into one of the largest private educational institutions in the world. GM spends hundreds of millions of dollars every year on continuing education and training of its work force.

Today's manufacturing firms must be people centered; people provide the true distinguishing character of companies. Indeed, the manufacturing plants of tomorrow may be even less automated than the plants of today. Toyota's new plant in Kyushu, Japan, for example, is a $1.5 billion plant that has only ten robots in its final assembly shop, and only 6 percent of its final assembly processes are automated. Why would the company move in that direction? Because Toyota must believe that simply replacing people with machines does not work.

The goal of any change in manufacturing systems is to help people do their jobs more effectively. Sometimes that goal requires automation and technology; sometimes, redesigning the work flow; and sometimes, education and training to improve the skills of the operator. The goal is met today by creating smarter processes and smarter people. Companies are training workers to serve both the internal customer, the person who has the next job in the process, and the external customer, the person who purchases and drives the vehicle.

Conclusion

The recommendations on how to analyze an automotive (or any) manufacturing company can be summarized as follows:

- Look at how the company views technology—as an end in itself or as an enabler.
- Look at the way the company develops products and whether it balances product and process requirements.
- Look at how the company is organized and where the process knowledge resides. No matter how automated the processes are, if all the knowledge resides at the top of the organization, that company is not going to do well in the future.
- Look also at the means used to apply human capital. Interview the people who get the job done—not only in manufacturing, but in all aspects of the business.

These factors will define long-term success, but none of these factors will show up on the current balance sheet; nor will analysts find them in the annual report. Analysts will have to do some digging.

Finally, remember the quotation cited earlier: "To live well, a nation must produce well." Manufacturing matters to our economy and to our national security. If we, as a nation, want to continue to live well, then we have to reestablish manufacturing as a national priority.

Question and Answer Session

James C. Rucker

Question: Of the major manufacturers in Japan and Europe, which has the best manufacturing process, and how do each of those companies compare with GM's NAO?

Rucker: Of the Japanese, we take a close look at Toyota's manufacturing. First, the company is large. Also, GM considers Toyota very successful at manufacturing; in fact, we have several partnerships with Toyota. We are also watching Honda. At Honda, engineering does manufacturing engineering and manufacturing has a respected place in the scheme of things. We have spent some time examining that manufacturing model.

The European companies are still shaking out. BMW seems to know what it's doing in manufacturing. You cannot discount Mercedes-Benz, but I am not as familiar with how it does business as I am with some of the Japanese companies. I do know that some of GM's European operations are actually the most efficient in Europe.

Most U.S. industries are reaching out to analyze and understand what works and what does not work in manufacturing—not simply to look at what is going on, but to learn why it is going on. Why are new Japanese plants so much less automated in general assembly than, for example, some European plants? There is probably more than one reason, and understanding the reasons is the key to understanding the best approach. What is best may not be the same for all organizations because they start from different bases. Home countries' industrial climates are

different. The markets served are different. If a company understands each competitor, however—where it started and why it is doing what it is doing—then the company can judge what its own manufacturing strategy should be.

Question: Why does designing and building a new platform take so long?

Rucker: This process does take a long time, and the times vary by manufacturer. The automotive manufacturers are probably giving you different numbers for product-development cycle times but calling them the same things. So, for comparisons, analysts need to make sure that their metrics are right and consistent. For example, GM has a four-phase vehicle process. Others might have five or six phases. Analysts need to spend some time aligning what is included in those phases. For example, most companies define the first stage of the development cycle as lasting to the point at which concept approval is given for the product program. That period is generally before giant expenses start because concept approval typically refers to a financial as well as market go-ahead. It follows some initial work, which GM would call Phase Zero. From that point, the question to ask in comparisons is: How soon can the company get to market? All the automotive assemblers want to get to market faster now because the market is harder to predict than previously; it has more variety than ever before.

A lot of reasons account for the lengthy development times.

What I found in GM when I worked on our four-phase process some years ago was a fair amount of variability in terms of how we do early vehicle development. Oldsmobile might do it one way, Cadillac another way, and Buick yet another. So, one way to speed the process at GM is to standardize common processes. Doing so will let us take advantage of learning curves. GM does more product programs than most companies. That factor does not give us an advantage, however, unless we learn from all of them combined instead of concentrating on single operations. Trying to learn from, say, Buick, then Oldsmobile, and then Cadillac is like trying to learn from five different Chrysler companies; it is not as fast as learning from one GM.

One GM goal is to be as quick to market as anybody on the globe, and we are not far from that goal. The GM vehicle on the road today is typically the result of a 36–42-month cycle (defined as the period from concept approval to market). Our aim is for something much shorter, because customers are demanding a change. They want the product to be up-to-date, sharp, and we want the same thing. All the North American companies are working hard to be quick to market—not at any cost, however. Simply throwing money at the task is not going to work. The approach has to be well thought through.

The issues involved in shortening the time are much more complicated than whether the CAD/CAM system connects from beginning to end. What is needed, and what GM is working toward, is a cultural connection from beginning to end. Other companies may have different approaches.

Question: What are you doing to make the most of your human capital, particularly on the shop floor?

Rucker: What GM is doing involves three aspects. First, as for the human capital—the employees who are out there building cars, trucks, alternators, transmissions, and so on—we have some fairly intensive education and training programs for hourly employees that we use a lot, including paid-leave programs for education. Also, when we start up a major new product or a new plant, we spend lots of money training people. We have spent as much as $80 million training people to work in new plants. That sort of expenditure is par for the course in this business. We believe that if we do not have our employees off the floor at least two weeks a year for learning, we are not doing the job right. These programs are the most visible part of training.

A part that is less visible to outsiders is the meetings held once each week in the half-hour before the line starts, in which we talk about what is new, what is happening, what is coming, what are the measures, what makes one method work better than another, and who to go see about questions. These efforts, formal and informal, are all important; they are all aimed at trying to make everybody in the company a part of the system and have them understand the system.

Finally, our agreement with the UAW is to take care of those people who are displaced because of the company's efforts to become leaner and more productive. Redeployed people are a big item on our agenda. We have

many things that need to be done. We are in the process of examining the size of this issue at the assembly plants in NAO, for example, and analyzing whether the magnitude of the plans to deal with the situation equals the magnitude of the people involved. We have not solved the problem, but we are close.

Question: Is there an optimal degree of vertical integration in the automotive industry, and if GM is not at that level today, what would be required to get it there?

Rucker: The popular belief today is that vertical integration hurts the company. I don't know what an optimal degree of vertical integration would be for the industry or for GM. Historically, GM started with a great deal of vertical integration but less than Ford. Ford used to make such elements of its vehicles as glass and steel. Today, whereas Ford has exited many of the businesses it was in, GM has stayed at the level of integration with which it began. European and Japanese competitors are typically not nearly as vertically integrated as GM.

GM has two efforts under way that are related to reducing vertical integration. First, our components group is striving to change itself from making about 25 percent of its sales outside GM to making 50 percent of its sales outside. That goal is ambitious, but the achievements it has made in the last couple of years suggest it will reach that goal.

Second, GM's approach today to the component divisions or smaller business units is in some ways similar to Jack Welch's approach at General Electric. We told them they had to be competitive, which means using benchmarking to emulate the best in the world and become the top

one or two in their market segments. If a group cannot become a top competitor, then, like GE had to do, we will have to consider exiting that business. That decision, however, will also rest to some extent on whether a business is part of our core competency. For example, one of Honda's core competencies is engine design and manufacture. It is an engine company; it makes lawn mowers, motorcycles, outboard motors, and so on, in which the common denominator is engine technology. Even if Honda knew that for some reason it was not making money in some engine process, I seriously doubt that it would declare that process unnecessary vertical integration. So, we are also looking at each business to determine what part of our core business it represents.

Question: Could you evaluate your domestic competitors, Chrysler and Ford, with respect to the design process?

Rucker: Some things coming out of Chrysler today are testimony to the integration of vehicle engineering and process engineering. Chrysler integrated some small, well-energized product teams to design some of its new vehicles, including the Neon, with great success. Chrysler may have used teams because it did not have the resources to do it any other way, but whatever the reason was, the effort worked. At issue will be whether the company can replicate the approach. It probably can in the short term because the knowledge is still in place. The people are right there, and the organization is small enough that such knowledge does not have to go very far to get to the next person.

What is going on at Ford is confusing. It has apparently not been able to duplicate Team Taurus. Team Taurus was the watershed team program and also a very good program. The new effort, the midsize World Car, has apparently not followed that learning pattern. So, Ford may not have a flow of knowledge from one program to the other like Chrysler seems to have.

Question: The *Harbour Report* suggests that GM uses 40 percent more labor hours to assemble a U.S. vehicle than Ford.[1] How did this differential arise, and what are the chances that the gap can be closed? Also, please comment on the number of sales cycles it will take for GM to reach the long-term cost benchmarks implicit in the new paradigm.

Rucker: The number varies in different reports; 40 percent is typically cited when analysts look at a Ford Taurus versus a midsize GM car. The figure is probably different if other products' costs are being compared. Ford is leaner than GM on the factory floor in terms of hours of labor per car. We are struggling not only to catch up to but to surpass Ford in this respect. We are leaner than Ford in some areas of the production system, such as inventory processes, how many buffers are in the plant, and so forth.

All of us at GM are working on the whole system, not simply labor, as hard as we can. The big question is how soon the differential can be eliminated. We *think* the gap will be closed soon, but the predicted differential with any of our competitors depends on what they will be doing as well as what we are doing. Our projections are based on the best knowledge we have at the time.

The question of labor-hours is related to the sales-cycle issue and the new-car programs. Re-

[1]Troy, Mich.: Harbour & Associates, 1993.

member that engineering casts a 70 percent cost shadow. A plant manager has to work hard to get 10–15 percent productivity improvement in one year. That is a lot for ongoing operations, but the manager can get that in a flash with a new-car program. We can get significantly greater productivity improvements with a new-car program. So, the timing of reduction in labor-hours will depend somewhat on our programs for new cars, which investment analysts can follow. GM believes it can and must close the gap in the near future and that it must make improvements through both new-car and ongoing systems.

In general, GM believes it does not have time to waste. We cannot afford to wait around; we do not have the money to not reach the benchmarks. We know that we cannot be competitive as the high-cost producer, and we do not intend to stay that way. Stiff requirements have been set for the company from the top, and we know we must become competitive.

Question: With respect to components manufactured by your suppliers, how will you project your knowledge base to them and assist them in their operations?

Rucker: We deal more closely today with suppliers than we did even two years ago. We have long-term contracts with some suppliers.

One of the tools we use is called a PICOS (purchased input concept optimization suppliers) team. In this approach, we go to a supplier and talk about a part, which may be for a current or a new car. We have a target price, a target quality, a target mass—all kinds of targets to make the car turn out right. We explain the targets to the vendor and discuss

how the vendor can reach them. To help the vendor, we may bring in some of our people who know something about the vendor's process, and they and the vendor's people form a PICOS team. Generally, we will send in engineers, and they can usually make a substantial improvement in that part of the process they investigate. Moreover, the effort doesn't take long; it happens in a week. PICOS represents a high level of cooperation with suppliers on a basic engineering level, and it is paying dividends.

The increasing work with suppliers is a two-edged sword, however. We have been accused of using approaches like the PICOS teams to pressure suppliers, but we do more studies inside than outside GM. The team is not simply a way to put pressure on suppliers. What's good for our suppliers is good for us as well.

Question: Do any of the manufacturing processes on the horizon look particularly challenging to develop and implement?

Rucker: Some 100 or 200 possible new processes are on the horizon. The technology is dazzling, but the important part is: What will the manufacturers do about it; how can they use it? We have had new machines come into plants that we could not even start up. The technology was wonderful; it would have been nice if somebody had told us how to make it run or how to fix it. One of the changes GM is making is that we have begun to take a much more active role in the development of our manufacturing equipment so that we can have more say in the maintainability, uptime, quality, capability, and so on, of the machine tools, of the technology, we buy. The Big Three are probably all following a similar approach.

All the automotive companies are looking at the cutting-edge technology every day trying to figure out what will help them. In the past, GM has been in and out of lasers and in and out of all kinds of machine tools. Some of the processes multiplied the speed of the usual kinds of turning, cutting, and grinding operations we do by a factor of ten. Lots of them worked, and some of them did not work. GM has learned in the last ten years that great technology will help us only if the poor soul who has to pick it up and use it understands and can apply it. We used to run after technology, hardware; now we run after *some* hardware but a whole lot of "humanware"—the human knowledge and support systems required to be successful.

Question: Is the structure of your compensation consistent with the objectives you are trying to achieve as a manufacturing executive?

Rucker: Yes, it is hooked to the results that we need right now, to one or two major issues related to the turnaround. GM made the hard decision not to pay bonuses even after we began to make money for a good reason. The worst thing we could have done is turn the company around (and we have made a $10 billion turnaround) and then say, "Man, fantastic, largest turnaround in the history of America!" and relax. It has been a tremendous turnaround, but we are only halfway to where we want to be. I do not want to break even; I would like to make $10 billion. I do not want to go through this kind of struggle again, ever.

So, despite the fact that incentive compensation or bonuses are necessary in the long run to make a company competitive in attracting people, the tack we are taking in compensation today is necessary to get the message across inside our organization. Today we need to concentrate on: Are we turned around? Are we winning or not? Until we are winning, compensation will remain the way it is.

The UAW Perspective on the U.S. Auto Industry

Owen Bieber
President
United Automobile, Aerospace, and Agricultural Implement Workers of America
International Union

The UAW has always functioned as an instrument of economic change but also a means of industrywide perspective, stability, and problem solving. The union views its emphasis on job and income security and on improving work conditions as underlying corporate drives for productivity, quality, efficiency, and customer satisfaction. The UAW expects continued joint labor–management programs to increase the U.S. industry's competitiveness.

Because financial analysts and the UAW represent different constituencies with somewhat different interests, they do not always see the world the same way. At the risk of oversimplification, analysts may be said to think that what is good for unions and workers is often bad for companies. More often than not, when unions seek or make gains, they can expect to read a gloom and doom blast from some analyst somewhere.

Is the analyst attitude short-sighted? I think so, and I think that both the current condition and the prospects of the domestic auto industry provide a good argument for my position.

Quality, productivity, and sales are up for the U.S. auto producers. A turnaround has clearly taken place. Indeed, if there has ever been an industry that has made more changes under more pressure during peacetime than the U.S. domestic auto industry since 1970, I do not know what that industry might be.

Has the turnaround come about in spite of the union, or has the UAW contributed significantly to it? My answer, which will not surprise you, is that the UAW has been and will continue to be a major contributor to meeting the challenges the industry faces. The UAW has contributed stability, perspective, leadership, and innovation during a time of intense change.

None of this contribution should be surprising. The UAW is, by its very nature, a change agent. It began as a change agent nearly 60 years ago, and that is what it remains today. The idea of change is neither alien nor frightening to the union. Of course,

the UAW is a mature institution now. The UAW—and its members—have more than a few things to protect today that we did not have when the union started in the 1930s. Nevertheless, I assure you that we in the UAW still see the union, first and foremost, as an instrument for social and economic change.

Ironically, the UAW is, at the same time, a rock of stability. For instance, during the time I have been UAW president, I have seen nine individuals come and go as CEOs at the Big Three (GM, Ford, and Chrysler). Furthermore, unlike the auto companies—and unlike the unions in Japan—the UAW brings an industrywide perspective to the change process. Keep in mind that the UAW represents workers throughout the Big Three and at three of the transplant operations—NUMMI (New United Motor Manufacturing, Inc.), the Toyota–GM joint venture; AutoAlliance, the Mazda–Ford joint venture; and Diamond Star Motors, now wholly owned by Mitsubishi. While the companies are focused on gaining at the expense of one another, the UAW negotiates for and represents its members with the aim of balancing the needs of all—not merely those of any one company.

Keep in mind also that, through the decades, the union has seen companies come and companies go. We have seen companies at their weakest, at their strongest, and at points in between. We know that the company on top today may not be on top tomorrow. For instance, in 1990, some analysts predicted that, by forcing Chrysler to accept the terms of the Big Three pattern agreement, the union was playing

Dr. Jack Kevorkian to Chrysler's corporate suicide. Yet Chrysler recently announced that it had broken all kinds of records for sales and profits, and its stock price shot up.

Beyond the perspective it provides, the UAW also provides experience, structure, and organization. As a result, the union offers an orderly and rational means of problem solving. That is true both when it comes to contract negotiations and when it comes to solving the day-to-day issues that inevitably arise all the way from the shop floor to the highest levels of the union–corporate relationship. Specifically, the job- and income-security provisions the UAW has negotiated through the years provide an indispensable foundation for the Big Three's dramatic quality and productivity improvements.

Now, there is a school of thought that believes in terrorizing workers with the threat of job insecurity as a means of imposing change. There will always be those who take that path, and that is one reason there will always be unions. But intimidated employees are not the most motivated employees.

The evidence is also growing that the knee-jerk solution to improving productivity by simply throwing half the work force on the scrap heap is no magic bullet either. Last year, U.S. businesses announced plans for the elimination of 600,000 jobs. Labor Secretary Robert Reich, however, and a growing number of others have recently cast doubt on the assumption that fewer jobs automatically mean healthier companies. Academic studies, not to mention practical experience, are calling into doubt the payoff that companies get from slashing the payroll. *Fortune* magazine reported in the January 10, 1994, issue that only about one-third of downsized companies reported increases in productivity; fewer than half reported increases in profits. In other words, managing smaller is not necessarily managing smarter.

Moreover, trying to sustain a consumer-driven economy by having one company after another relentlessly cut jobs and wages is self-evidently crazy. In such a scenario, where, after all, are the consumers supposed to come from?

As obvious as preserving good jobs and good wages is, however, it has often been a lonely battle these last few years. Nevertheless, I am proud that the UAW has practiced what we preached when we said that "American jobs are worth fighting for." Had we not done so, I don't know who else would have.

Today, it is fashionable to at least talk about a high-wage, high-skill road to prosperity, but that wasn't always the case. In fact, it is not going too far to say that, if not for the UAW's struggles on this issue, the loss of good-paying U.S. manufacturing jobs would have been far worse than it has been.

A few years ago, I served on the Commission on the Skills of the American Workforce with, among others, Hillary Rodham Clinton and former Labor Secretaries Ray Marshall and Bill Brock. The title of the commission's report summed up the alternatives the United States faces; it was called "America's Choice: High Skills or Low Wages." The point is that, unless the country commits to competing in the world economy on the basis of high skills and high productivity, the United States will wind up in a brutal wage competition with the developing nations—a competition that none of the competitors will win. Some people did not even want to look at the commission's report when it was first published, but now a growing number of policy makers are coming around to the idea that building a high-skill, high-productivity, and high-wage economy is in everyone's interest in the long haul.

The UAW's innovative fight for job and income security is not the only element of its contribution to the reform of the domestic auto industry. The "people" programs the union put in place have also contributed significantly to productivity and quality gains. The union has always believed that people are the key to success, both in the public and the private sector. By getting the broadest possible involvement in solving on-the-job health and safety problems, by relieving parents of anxiety through providing access to good child care, by helping workers deal with substance abuse and other problems, the union is accomplishing three things.

First, we are helping create the good life. Second, we are providing critical support to the quality, productivity, and customer-satisfaction practices that generate prosperity for the many. Third, by protecting the jobs and incomes of its members industry-wide, the UAW is doing more than simply supporting a good climate for change. We are creating the healthiest and best conditions for competition. Why? Because when unions protect wages and benefits, companies are then motivated to improve their business by concentrating on quality, efficiency, and customer satisfaction, which is good for everybody—including stockholders.

The role the UAW has played in quality improvement is particularly admirable. Before most people, here or in Japan, had even heard about the late W. Edwards Deming's theories for improving quality, the UAW knew that the workers had to be involved if the automakers were to produce quality products. Unfortunately, management did not share that view.

In the early 1970s, then UAW Vice President Irving Bluestone, who directed the UAW's General Motors Department, sent a memo titled "Quality is our concern, too" to all UAW-GM locals. He noted that, although much of GM's quality problem was tied to engineering and to supervisors' push for production, the quality of workmanship had also slipped.

Bluestone urged every UAW-GM worker to "pay close attention to the quality of his work" because declining quality "may well be followed by declining sales." He added, "Dissatisfied GM customers don't necessarily turn to Ford, Chrysler or AMC [American Motors Corporation] products. They often turn to foreign imports."

The response? Around the country, UAW locals were enthusiastically putting Bluestone's quality memo on their bulletin boards. But then a GM vice president called Bluestone and demanded that the memos come down because, he said, quality is management's job—not the union's!

Well, quality is the union's job. It always has been. That is why, in 1984, we insisted that quality be put on the table as a bargaining issue at Ford and GM. Ever since then, the industry has been making steady progress on quality. Moreover, today's quality programs are joint management–union programs. Everybody is interested in quality.

The UAW has also steadily increased its involvement in company decisions about sourcing, an area that involves both quality and job security. I have always been troubled that whenever a Big Three product is recalled, most people think the cause is sloppy UAW workmanship when, frequently, the culprit is some small piece of equipment, some gadget, and not workmanship. In many cases (particularly at Chrysler, which buys about 70 percent of its parts from outside suppliers), that gadget was made outside the United States in one of the very low wage countries. UAW workers had no control over that little gadget.

Finally, the UAW is not now, nor have we ever been, the enemy of productivity gains. That is why, contrary to the impression created by what some analysts say about the cost of UAW settlements, unit labor costs at the Big Three during the past ten years have gone down substantially—not up. In fact, no other U.S. industry has made greater productivity gains than the auto industry.

The union's contribution is not limited to what happens in the factory. In stabilizing the change process for workers, the UAW has also brought a measure of stability to the economy of scores of communities, providing support for retailers, service providers, and the tax base.

Moreover, job and income security for auto workers also shore up consumer confidence and give people the money to spend that keeps the economy in motion. As badly as the U.S. economy has performed in recent years, I shudder to think how much worse it could have been had wages and employment fallen even more than they did. In that sense, trade unions serve as a critical thermostat in an economy, especially when the economy gets too cold. Unions are there to try to keep things stable.

Unions serve a comparable role in their capacity as advocates for public policy. The Chrysler bailout, health care reform, and trade policy are examples in which the UAW's basic position has been vindicated.

The turnaround of the domestic auto industry is an encouraging and continuing development. It reminds the country that Americans are indeed a resourceful people, fully capable of rising to a challenge. I am proud of the role the UAW played in the process and confident that we will continue to make a major contribution.

I am also mindful, however, of the price paid in lost jobs, broken families, diminished communities, a frayed social contract, and lowered expectations for millions of U.S. workers—especially those not protected by membership in a union. And as a trade union leader, citizen, parent, and grandparent, I worry deeply that our society is far from being out of the woods.

While the new post-Cold War world economic order is being born, the danger is not small that the restructuring will take our society not in the direction of greater democracy and prosperity but in the direction of oligarchy and inequality. Trade unionists never forget that societies that distribute wealth unfairly soon start to create far less of it. I hope all financial analysts will keep that truth in mind.

Question and Answer Session

Owen Bieber

Question: Are the labor relations in the UAW-represented transplants—the NUMMI, Diamond Star, and Flat Rock (Mazda) plants—materially different, on average, from relations in the Big Three plants?

Bieber: No, the difference is not great. At each of them, although the Japanese certainly have input, and they sit at the negotiating table, Americans have been moving into the operation of the companies. The labor relations representative at Flat Rock, for example, is a former member of the UAW. He was a committeeman in Bay City Chevrolet, then went to work for Volkswagen, and subsequently worked for Mazda.

Today, labor relations in the Big Three have changed a great deal from what they were 15 years ago. Hard times have been a harsh, but in some ways a good, teacher—especially, I believe, for management.

Question: Has the new management at the Big Three affected relationships with the UAW?

Bieber: Relationships between labor and management have changed drastically since I've been in the industry. When I first started servicing local unions in the GM system in 1964, the world was different in all these plants. No one looked to shop floor employees for any input. As a matter of fact, most supervisors resented such input because if somebody found out a suggestion did not originate with the supervisor, the worker who made the suggestion was looked upon as a challenge to the supervisor. In the plant where I worked, super-

visors came and went fast. So, the threat of being challenged was not an idle threat to the supervisors. That situation has changed a great deal.

The structure and the people have changed at the Big Three. Jack Smith's demeanor and the way he approaches people is much different from what I found the first time I walked into the GM building. Workers were striking at a seat plant in GM, and the two sides decided to meet. The GM people sat there, dressed in blue pinstriped suits. The managers were rigid, and the pecking order was obvious; the top manager spoke, and the rest of them said nothing unless he asked them.

Meetings are much different today. Pinstriped suits are no longer the mode. At GM, for example, no one wears a tie on Fridays.

In summary, the individuals have changed. The times have changed. A lot of input comes now from the shop floor.

Question: Will future contracts with the Big Three contain any two-tier wage or benefit structures?

Bieber: No, and they should not. Two-tier wage structures are a ridiculous way to try to take care of problems. Under two-tiered wage structures, two people standing next to each other doing the same job can earn different wages. For example, one may earn, say, $12 an hour and the other may earn $7.

By using such a structure, companies are driving wages down to the lowest common denominator around the world. U.S. workers have always had to compete against low-wage work-

ers in other countries, but the technology made available to those workers was only what a low-wage economy provided. U.S. workers had an advantage in superior technology. That is not true today. Analysts do not have to go far to confirm this change. Go to Mexico and look at the *maquiladora* operations. Some of those plants have later and more sophisticated technology than some similar U.S. plants. So, the non-U.S. plants have the top technology, and the workers are earning, on average, $4–$5 a day versus an average hourly wage of $18 for U.S. autoworkers. This situation makes the competition today very, very tough.

The first major negotiation after I was elected in June 1983 was in Dallas, Texas. At that time, the union had a problem that was somewhat brought about by government influence. The staff person for military procurement in the Reagan administration sent a letter saying that he would support the company to the extent of taking strikes but that the company had to lower its costs. The company said that to lower costs meant going to a two-tier wage system. In the system, for some classifications, it would have taken a new person 20 years to get to the top of the wage rates. Something was out of line: Either the wage rate was way too low (if 20 years were needed to learn the job), or the structure was unfair.

The UAW has fought the two-tier structures but finally acquiesced in some. At General Dynamics' Electric Boat Division, for example, when the strike was nine months long, we finally had to agree to two tiers. About midway through a three-year agreement to that effect, I received a call from management requesting a meeting. I thought they were after the union to make more concessions. What they said, however, was, "This two-tier wage thing is not working. It's just not going to work." In the middle of that contract term, we went in and negotiated out the two-tier system.

Two-tier wages will not work. Common sense tells us they will not work. Furthermore, companies should not pursue such a strategy. If one worker is just as efficient as the next, he or she should earn the same wage for doing that work.

Question: What is the historical foundation for the attrition rule, and how important is it to the UAW in the future?

Bieber: The attrition rule requires the Big Three automakers to hire one new worker for every two workers who leave through normal attrition—retirement, death, and so on. It is important to us. People objected to my theory of guaranteed income and job security, but one of the things that we have to analyze is how to slow down the reduction in jobs. Protecting the basic industry of this country is the only way to have a decent living standard and increase the economy. You can go back to the beginning of time, and you will realize that a country must produce some product; services alone will not keep that country's living standard and economy going. It never has in the history of the world, and it will not now.

The union had to devise some way of halting the loss of manufacturing jobs. Now, we did not say, "You have to give us a job whether we can compete or not." We said, "You cannot just, wholesale, do away with this industry. People who have provided for you have a right to

expect some security in return. We want an opportunity to build these products. To give us that opportunity, you have to make some investment. You cannot take all your investment to the *maquiladoras* in Mexico, or Malaysia, or someplace else. You must invest something here."

Question: Was the size of GM's unfunded pension liability a factor in your negotiating strategy, and how do you judge GM's progress in becoming a better competitor?

Bieber: The unfunded pension liability was a big problem because GM was worried about what Wall Street would do to its credit rating. People at GM said that adding to the fund would lower the credit rating, and they could explain how a change in one point up or down would cost them X millions of dollars. Everybody is on edge and very concerned about Wall Street's reaction to the issue of GM's unfunded pension liability.

As to how GM is doing in terms of competitiveness, the profit report for the fourth quarter 1993 will show North American operations doing much better than previously; those operations will report before-tax profits for the first time in a long time. There are a lot of reasons; one is that GM has a good product line. In that sense, GM is in the kind of position Chrysler was in during 1990. GM also has some great new products coming out in the future.

Question: What are some of the benefits and drawbacks of having labor representation on corporate boards?

Bieber: There are advantages, but a single representative cannot do much. I chair the UAW board meetings. We have quarterly

meetings, and they usually last three or four days. Our meetings are long; everybody says their piece.

I followed another UAW president onto the Chrysler board and served on it for seven years, and the experience was very different. The meetings were short. The first time I went to a Chrysler meeting, I was given an agenda that laid out 1 minute for item so and so, 1.5 minutes for item so and so, and so forth. I soon found out how they could be so precise: The designated person reports, and boom, that's it. At my first meeting, I asked one question. I kept pushing for more discussion, however, and was finally successful.

The major drawback to labor representation on the boards is that the labor representatives do not win any arguments there. They never win a vote at the board meeting. Those votes are all won in the committees that make the reports.

At one Chrysler board meeting, I remember other people saying in some respects the same thing I was. When the vote came, however, I was the only vote for that view. As we left the room, several other board members (not just those who had spoken favorably) told me I had been right! The size of the Chrysler board increased and decreased while I was on it, and sometimes I could say that my vote was worth more; instead of the votes being 21 to 1, they were only 19 to 1.

One advantage is that the labor representative has an opportunity to shape how things are going to come out on the board. Lee Iacocca was a strong character. He accepted some criticism but not much. When the company was considering selling Accustar (Chrysler's parts division), I asked Iacocca for a private meeting. I asked not just as president of the UAW but as a member of the board. I told him that if he proceeded he would destroy the company because the union workers would not accept the sale. They had paid a dear price to help bring the company back and would not break up the family at this point. Chrysler was being offered a lot of money, but after some debate, Iacocca realized I meant what I was telling him. When I left there, I knew the sale was not going to happen. The union was able to avert this sale, and previously had been able to avert several plant closings, by being in a position to steer matters before a board vote.

My preference—and what would be better for the industry in the long run—would be a system like the German joint councils. In them, labor has far more input, and public attitudes and opinions get far more weight, than through small representation on boards.

That preference does not mean the UAW will stop fighting to have people on boards. In America, however, the only time companies want to push labor representation on the board is when they are in deep trouble.

Question: What is the relationship between the UAW and the CAW (Canadian Auto Workers)? Are wages and benefits different between the two?

Bieber: Well, after Buzz Hargrove became president of the CAW, I spoke at its conference on political action and contract preparation. I received a warm reception, and although I saw a lot of new faces, I also saw people who had been part of the same organization I have for many years. The relationship between the un-

ions is much better than it was when Bob White was president of the CAW. White had ambitions to become prime minister of Canada, and he used nationalism to separate the unions.

The economic disadvantage the UAW has is that workers in Canada are covered by a national health care system that assures a substantial savings for Canadian operations. In fact, one of my arguments in the debate on health care coverage in the United States is that universal, publicly funded health care is not only morally right for this country—that is, depriving people of it is wrong—but the lack of it puts U.S. industry at a big cost disadvantage. Other factors in the Canada–U.S. competition include, of course, the currency differences and shipping costs.

Question: How do you assess the chances of President Bill Clinton's health care plan being passed?

Bieber: It will be a terrible fight. Although the plan does not have everything we would like to see, nor in the long run is it the most economical plan, the UAW will fight hard alongside President Clinton. The Clinton plan has the basic things that it should, such as universal coverage, employer mandates, cost containment, and consumer choice. It also gives the states the option of setting up single-payer plans.

The most economical plans and the ones with the slowest rates of increase in insurance costs are the single-payer plans. Someday, I assume we will have such a system.

I favor universal coverage. To develop medical science to the

extent that we have but somehow only for those who can afford it is morally indefensible. It is improper and inefficient to leave people out there on their own, not give them preventative care, and maintain a system in which their primary access to medical care is the most expensive—through the emergency room.

Question: What is the UAW doing to make its membership aware of how many manufacturers are competing for the sales dollar in the automobile market?

Bieber: That kind of competitive pressure is not new. The UAW does not lack information. Our research and engineering department prepares our negotiators. The purpose is to sit down with management before jobs are taken out of the plants. Increasingly these days, we have the information necessary to help determine whether the company can build a particular product competitively.

President Clinton's approach has helped change some attitudes about international competition by saying to some of our trading partners, "Now listen, this is going to have to be a two-way street, or we are going to put some brakes on this stuff. You cannot have trade as a one-way street." The laws do not necessarily have to change; jawboning, if used properly, can be very successful.

The auto industry is not the only U.S. industry having problems with Japanese imports, but it is the biggest. Unless the country does something about the imbalance in the auto industry, we will never bring the trade balance in line.

The Automotive Parts Industry, Part I

Philip K. Fricke
First Vice President and Senior Auto Analyst
Prudential Securities, Inc.

Structural changes affecting the auto parts industry range from proliferating customers in North America to the importance of systems supply to rising opportunities in the worldwide after-market. Certain characteristics will separate the winners from the losers: proprietary technology and processes, design and prototype capability, manufacturing efficiency, systems capability, cost-saving products and products for high-growth models, and superb cost structures.

Automotive parts manufacturers supply both the original-equipment manufacturers (OEMs) and the after-market. Understanding the automotive parts industry requires an understanding of the structural changes that are dictating the criteria for future success as well as the current status and outlook for the market segments. With this understanding, analysts will be able to assess individual companies' competitive advantages, cost structures, and probable futures.

Structural Changes

As a result of automakers' needs for parts and systems that will provide their customers with ever-improving performance at greatly lowered cost, the auto parts manufacturing industry has undergone five major structural changes.

New Customers

The customer base that the parts companies supply is changing and will continue to change. No longer can General Motors, Ford, and Chrysler alone be referred to as the traditional customers in the North American auto parts industry. Today, the industry is home to Japanese transplants, and tomorrow, it will be home to the Europeans also.

Japanese production in North America could increase in the next five years, with more facilities and 500,000–600,000 more units of production output. As can be seen in **Figure 1**, production in the United States is rising relative to production in Japan for the first time in a decade. The number of vehicles Japan exports to the United States will probably fall significantly. North America—the United States, in

particular—should gain share in world auto production during the 1990s.

Supplier Base

The second structural change is a slowly shrinking supplier base. Automakers today are going more and more to one manufacturer for parts. Many suppliers act as a sole source. For example, MascoTech supplies all of the connecting rods for Ford's new engines. This situation holds risks for the automakers but is widespread. Shrinking the supplier base is a money-saving strategy for the automakers. The effect of the contraction differs according to parts categories, but it is a significant trend today, and it is a huge source of incremental sales for the surviving companies.

Outsourcing

Outsourcing by automakers evolved over a long period. Ford and Chrysler are less vertically integrated companies than GM, and outsourcing at both today is substantial. It may increase even further, however. The UAW would like to prevent its spread, but outsourcing is inevitable. In the case of GM, for example, the question is not *whether* GM will outsource but what the magnitude and timing of the outsourcing will be.

Japan and U.S. Parts

About 75 percent of the U.S. trade deficit with the Japanese involves the automotive industry, and this problem has been a sticking point in trade negotiations between the two governments. The Fair Trade in Automotive Parts Act of 1989 mandated that Con-

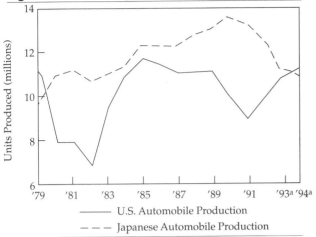

Figure 1. U.S. and Japanese Auto Production

Units Produced (millions)

——— U.S. Automobile Production

− − − Japanese Automobile Production

Source: James R. Crate and Richard Johnson, "US to Regain Output Crown," *Automotive News* (December 20, 1993).

[a]Estimate.

gress and the U.S. Department of Commerce study the issue of automotive parts trade with Japan, and it established the Automotive Parts Advisory Council. APAC and the Clinton administration are now putting genuine pressure on the Japanese to buy parts from North American parts companies.

Generally, the Japanese automakers based in Japan and in North America are buying and will continue to buy more North American parts than in the past. Analysts, however, should not believe some of the numbers being suggested. Do not believe that the Japanese will increase U.S. parts procurement from $12 billion in parts purchases in 1992 to $19 billion by 1994 as they promised. Such an increase will take longer.

The motivation today for the Japanese to purchase parts from North American suppliers is economic as well as political. One type of parts made in North America that may be particularly attractive for Japanese automakers is drivetrain parts, such as engine and transmission parts. To date, the engines and transmissions actually assembled or built in the United States have been assemblies of parts from Japan, but the industry is expected to evolve toward local purchase of these parts. APAC data indicate that the typical well-run North American parts company has a 20–30 percent price advantage, depending on the part category, over the comparable Japanese parts supplier. To increase transplanted Japanese companies' use of locally manufactured parts, North American parts suppliers must be included at the concept and design stages.

Focus on Systems

The fifth major structural change, and perhaps the most important, is a trend toward the supply of

systems rather than isolated parts. The typical U.S.-based auto assembly plant has anywhere from 3,000–3,500 workers, depending on the assembly process done on site. Five to eight years from now, these assembly plants will have 1,800-2,000 people, mainly because suppliers will be providing whole systems.

Some of the new GM plants have already cut down to about 2,000 people for this reason. Magna International is supplying the whole front-end fascia assembly to Chrysler for the LH cars. Magna makes the composite material fascia, the energy-absorbing structure behind the fascia, and the structural steel beam; puts these elements together; and ships the system to the Bromelea plant in Ontario. Magna also supplies automakers with seat assemblies. In the future, the parts manufacturers will provide whole door modules, dashboard modules, sections of the interior, and so on.

The most important aspect about the trend to systems is that systems give parts manufacturers an opportunity to maximize profitability. The auto parts manufacturer that supplies a system prices by the system. It does not price each component. Magna, for example, priced the fascia system, not the components, that it was providing Chrysler. Chrysler gave Magna a target price for the entire system; it was not a matter of negotiating profit margins based on component prices.

The After-Market

Changes in the parts after-market will provide attractive opportunities for companies prepared to exploit them.

▧ *North America.* Interesting structural changes are occurring in the after-market in North America, principally in the United States. In the traditional U.S. after-market distribution system, a manufacturer produces a part, such as a gear or bearing, at a factory cost of, say, 50 cents and sells the product to an OEM for about 55 cents. The parts maker might sell the part to a warehouse distributor (WD) for $1; the WD then sells it to a jobber; and the jobber to a professional installer. By the time a car owner buys it, the part costs $8. The retail value of after-market parts in this system is believed to approximate $120 billion, but the value of those parts sold to the WD is $35 billion. The difference between those two figures represents a lot of waste, a lot of inefficiency in the distribution system.

This distribution system evolved and is necessary mainly because so many different kinds of vehicles are on the road and because, when a customer's vehicle needs repair, the customer wants it fixed immediately. The professional installer has no idea who is going to drive in next or what must be inventoried and, therefore, depends on access to the large inventories of middlemen. So, this three-layer system between manufacturer and customer—WD, jobber, and installer—evolved, and U.S customers became somewhat spoiled by the usual rapid repairs they can expect.

An increased share of the after-market, however, is going to retail parts supply stores, such as Auto Zones and Pep Boys, instead of through the middlemen. These retailers buy directly from the parts suppliers and sell to customers at steep discounts. The WD is thus losing share, and the trend is toward a two-step, even a one-step, system. This structural change has major implications for parts manufacturers because, the farther down the distribution channel they can sell, the more profits they can make.

■ *Latin and South America.* Latin America and South America have no organized distribution of auto parts. The likelihood of having an engine rebuilt or almost any kind of repair work done in a short time by a professional installer in, say, Santiago, Chile, is small. In South America, and in most developing countries, local importers who do not have a great deal of expertise in importing and matching inventory to end-user needs order the parts. The importers tend to import very high volumes of parts infrequently—every six or nine months—so they are sitting on huge inventories that do not necessarily match what is needed.

Federal-Mogul, a global after-market company, is the first of the parts companies to take advantage of this gap between supply and demand and develop a retail system in Latin and South America. Its 80 distribution centers worldwide allow it to sell in Europe, Central America, South America, Australia, and the Middle East. Most interesting is the strategy that the company is pursuing in developing countries—particularly in such Central and South American countries as Mexico, Puerto Rico, Panama, Chile, and Ecuador. Federal-Mogul's strategy is to ship parts to company-owned stores that will distribute after-market parts to anybody who walks in, professional installer or do-it-yourselfer. (In Central and South America, the buyer is most likely to be a professional installer.) Resupply is weekly.

The change to retailing in the parts after-market of Central and South America is only in its infancy. Ten years from now, more parts retailers will probably have followed Federal-Mogul's lead south of the border.

■ *Europe.* Parts distribution in the European after-market has traditionally been through new-vehicle dealers. In Europe, most vehicle owners have been going back to the dealer for service and parts. The European national markets have become increasingly heterogeneous, however; the percentage of non-German cars sold in Germany, for example,

has increased immensely in the past five-to-ten years, and this trend will accelerate during the next five years. Therefore, a traditional U.S.-style distribution system is growing throughout Europe. More and more vehicle owners in Europe are going to independent professional installers instead of vehicle dealers, which provides opportunity for companies like Federal-Mogul.

Analyzing the Parts Companies

In the past, forecasting the earnings of the parts manufacturing segment in cyclical upturns was fairly straightforward. The automakers typically performed design and engineering themselves and then took the specifications to parts companies for bids. So, an analyst could look at the traditional customers (Chrysler, Ford, and GM), look at the expected change in production over the course of X number of years, factor in operating leverage, and determine earnings.

When making earnings estimates for parts suppliers today, the analyst cannot rely on the approach used in the past. Today, there are new customers, and extraordinary opportunities exist to gain dollars per unit. Research, design, and engineering (RD&E) is more often handled by the parts supplier.

Analysts can segment auto demand into two time spans: very near term and longer term. Very-near-term demand is a function of variables such as consumer confidence, consumer income, and vehicle prices. Analysts can develop a car and light-truck sales forecast from these factors. Secular or structural variables determine longer term demand.

The year 1993 marked the second year in what should be an upturn that continues through 1996. The trendline in **Figure 2** represents the number of cars and trucks that must be sold by the system to accommodate growth of the vehicle population and replacement needs. According to this chart, although sales rose in 1993 by about 1 million units— from about 12.9 million units in 1992—the deficit to trend (sometimes called pent-up demand) increased rather than decreased. Such an outcome had never happened previously. Generally in the past, by the time the U.S. economy moved into the first year of a recovery, sales were typically already above trend.

According to my calculations, however, a deficit to trend of about 3.8 million units had already been established when the industry entered 1993. My analysis indicates that 1993's trendline was about 14.6 million units. This trendline is lower than those of economists at the automakers, which have trendlines above 15 million units. Even with the lower trendline number, because the industry delivered only 13.9 million units, the deficit to trend increased.

Figure 2. U.S. Light-Vehicle Sales
(units)

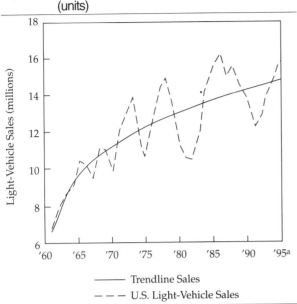

Source: Prudential Securities. Data sources are *Ward's Automotive Reports* for 1961–93 retail sales and Prudential Securities estimates for 1994–96 retail and trendline sales.

Note: Trendline retail sales for 1961 through 1993 are regression-calculated data points.

[a]Estimate.

The deficit to trend is 4.5–4.7 million units today, a huge deficit that the industry is only beginning to correct. If the industry delivers 15.5 million units in 1994, the deficit will have already been cut by 800,000 units. Subsequently, the industry should experience several more years of above-trend sales. Eventually, the entire deficit to trend will be corrected, but it will take years.

The industry should thrive until at least 1996, with delivery of at least 16 million units, but the recovery will be slow. Sales of 16 million units would put the industry about 1 million units above trend. In prior cycles, the peak has represented about 2 million units above trend. The cycle should peak in 1996 or 1997—possibly later but probably not sooner. Thus, production and earnings are likely to rise significantly through 1996 and maybe through 1997.

Analysts need to determine who will win (i.e., gain share in the marketplace) and who will lose, given the evolving structure of the parts manufacturing industry. Five critical characteristics will separate the winners from the losers.

Proprietary Technology

First, a winning company will have proprietary technologies and processes. It will be able to do something that other parts suppliers cannot do, or are unwilling to do, and that the automakers cannot do. MascoTech, for example, is a supplier of forgings and stampings with superior technology and thus has the potential to sell additional parts to the Japanese automakers.

In addition, the specific nature of the proprietary advantage is important. Does the company's proprietary advantage lie in the product, in the manufacturing process? Is the process and control equipment used in manufacturing proprietary in and of itself?

Design and Prototype Capabilities

Second, the best parts suppliers will have excellent design, engineering, and prototyping capabilities. Prototyping is particularly important to Japanese auto companies. When a part prototype is submitted to the Japanese for assessment, the Japanese engineers quickly assess it and provide feedback to the parts maker. Then, the prototype must be quickly redone. Thus, the ability of the parts maker to combine engineers and designers working together and to produce the successive prototypes will be critical to success in the business.

Efficient Manufacturing

The auto parts industry has a tremendous range of capabilities in terms of manufacturing processes. In attempts to improve productivity and manufacturing ten years ago, many parts companies focused on the manufacturing cell (measuring the time from cell one to cell two, for example) rather than on total throughput (the time from order to taking in cash). Maximizing throughput is the critical criterion, however, and the term the industry uses to describe it is "lean manufacturing." Lean manufacturing minimizes the time from the point when a part is started to the point it is actually delivered or sent to a customer and payment is received. Lean manufacturing maximizes inventory turns, and most importantly, lean manufacturing allows a company to be flexible. Automakers demand changes, sometimes very quickly. The ability of a parts company, whether supplying the OEM market or the after-market, to react quickly is critical to success. Federal-Mogul is an example of a company that has successfully revamped all of its manufacturing processes and moved all of its North American plants into the category of lean manufacturing.

Systems Capabilities

The most successful of the winning companies will have systems capabilities. This characteristic has not previously been a prerequisite for profitability. MascoTech, for example, does not provide systems but has been profitable.

Magna is a noncaptive auto parts supplier with superior systems capability. The primary characteristic that sets Magna apart from its competitors is the breadth of its product line and technologies. Magna's expertise is in metals processing. It can stamp almost any piece of metal on a car or truck—from common trim to class A body panels. It does the stamping with world-class precision and quality.

Magna also has great expertise in a broad spectrum of composite materials and plastics. In addition to vertical and horizontal body panels, Magna can produce interior composite systems such as seats, dashboards, and entire dashboard modules.

Magna has deep vertical integration, which can be extremely important because parts suppliers are now required to ship defect-free products. Inspection is no longer carried out at the final assembly plant; it is the responsibility of the parts supplier. If an assembly plant finds one defect in a batch of parts during assembly, it sends the whole batch back to the supplier. The supplier is responsible for resupply and bears all the costs. The more vertical integration (as opposed to reliance on outside vendors), the more control the parts supplier has over the quality of inputs to its products.

Cost-Saving Products

Analysts should also determine whether the product the process yields saves the automaker/customer money and gives the automaker/customer an improved product. A good example of such a product is MascoTech's forged gears. MascoTech forges many gears that are used for transmissions, engines, axles, and so forth. MascoTech uses a technology that forges to "net form"; that is, the forging that comes out of the process and is delivered to the customer needs little if any final finishing. Rather than needing a dozen or more expensive finishing or grinding steps, it can go right into the engine or right into the transmission, which saves the customer an immense amount of money.

Parts for New Customer Models

Winning companies will supply the parts for the best and newest models—parts that are likely to undergo changes. The worst thing that can happen to a parts supplier is to supply a part that never changes, because the supplier loses all pricing flexibility. Federal-Mogul's OE side, for example, supplies engine gears to the automakers, and in some cases, the gears have not changed in ten years. So, Federal-Mogul's pricing flexibility is zero. If a part changes, the manufacturer can price from a new basis. Thus, changes in parts provide pricing flexibility and pricing leverage.

Analysts should know not only who the customer is but also which model will use the particular part and what the projected production of that model

is for the next five years or so. Is the model reaching its maturity or just starting to grow? At first glance, having a lot of content on the Chrysler minivan or the Jeep Grand Cherokee, for example, might seem great. Those models are very solid. If one looks at the course of production over the next three to four years, however, the rate of increase in production of the minivan and the Grand Cherokee will probably be a lot less than that of many other models because the minivan and Grand Cherokee plants are near full capacity. Some capacity will be added, but those models do not offer much potential for growth. Growth comes from content on brand-new models. Even Chrysler's LH is not as beneficial as the Neon today.

Superior Cost Structure

Finally, winning companies will have superb cost structures and, as a result, the potential to capture new business or make good returns on investment. The analyst needs an understanding of which costs are variable in order to understand where the leverage is and where margins can go. The tremendous earnings surprises in this industry have been a result of analysts not examining variable margins and, therefore, not realizing the amount of margin expansion that was possible.

When talking about their earnings, about what is going on with their gross profit margins, or the ratio of selling, general, and administrative expense to revenues, managers may indicate, for example, that SG&A "will be going down" as a percentage of sales, but they do not elaborate. The next questions an analyst should ask, therefore, are: What percentage of the selling price will drop to the gross profit line? What is the variable cost on the marginal dollar? What is in the variable cost? Is it all raw materials?

An analyst must factor into an earnings forecast the percentage of variable margins and then determine how the profit margin can expand or not expand. Thus, analysts need to know the components of gross profit. They need to know which costs are really fixed and what is in the cost of sales. RD&E is typically part of cost of sales, but analysts will want to know trends in absolute, not relative, RD&E. They will also need to understand what is fixed and what is not fixed in SG&A.

The consensus today is that auto parts companies cannot make decent profits selling to the automakers; the automakers' power is too great. The auto parts makers that are pricing by systems or have proprietary products, however, and have good cost structures can make a lot of money. Parts makers with the lowest fixed costs and the lowest variable costs can realize extremely good profit margins.

With many of the products MascoTech supplies to automakers, for example, the variable cost is primarily raw material. Labor costs can be as low as 5 percent of each revenue dollar, and everything else is fixed. Thus, as unit shipments increase, margins expand. Many superior companies are in such a position; if all of the company's variable costs are in raw materials, a high percentage of sales price falls to gross profits.

Although customers can exert a lot of pressure, therefore, superior auto parts makers can expand margins and make significant profits. When examining the auto parts companies, analysts should look for the variable profit margin and consider what will happen to the gross profit margin as unit shipments increase. As auto production rises through 1996, unit shipments will rise significantly, and even though the auto parts companies will have to cut some prices, they can expand margins.

Examples of companies with attractive cost structures are MascoTech, Magna, and Dana Corporation. The incremental unit that MascoTech ships contributes about 30 percent to gross profits. Cost structure and technology suggest that MascoTech can expect to capture new customers, a high market share, and more content per unit than many competitors.

Question and Answer Session

Philip K. Fricke

Question: Should GM spin off its Automotive Components Group (ACG)?

Fricke: No, but GM needs to be extremely discriminating about what parts manufacturing it keeps and what portion it divests. Some portions of ACG are first class in terms of quality and cost, so it would be in GM's interest to keep them. Others aren't, and they are likely to be sold or shut down.

Question: Would the Big Three (GM, Ford, and Chrysler) buy or bail out a supplier that failed financially but was supplying them 100 percent of a critical item?

Fricke: They would likely bail out a supplier. Many years ago, Ford helped a troubled Magna by setting up joint ventures that were actually financed through Ford Motor Credit. In the future, if a company is the sole source of an important part and is in financial trouble, the customer will probably help. Even so, when the Big Three or the Japanese automakers are determining who will be a supplier—particularly, a sole supplier—they will go with the financially strong companies. This change is one reason Magna wants to have zero debt; the absence of debt puts a company in an excellent competitive position.

Question: Why is GM outsourcing more components today than in the past when it currently has so many employees in the JOBS (Job Opportunity Bank Security) Program.

Fricke: The JOBS Program has been whittled down and will be further whittled down through attrition and contract buyouts. Within a few years, if not sooner, the JOBS Program will be zero. GM strategy is dictated by a longer term view. In the long term, GM needs to source a part or a system on the basis of cost and performance. If the internal source is not providing the quality or if the quality–cost relationship of an outside supplier is superior, GM must go to the outside supplier. The JOBS problem will take care of itself.

Question: Please explain the difference between Tier I and Tier II suppliers. Will the small suppliers drop out of the supply chain, and if not, do the Tier II suppliers offer any investment opportunities?

Fricke: A Tier I supplier has design, engineering, and prototyping capability. It sells parts or systems directly to the OEMs. Tier II suppliers supply Tier I suppliers. For example, Magna, a Tier I supplier, when putting together a system, may have to buy certain system subcomponents parts from a Tier II supplier. In the future, Tier II suppliers will have the greatest difficulty because companies like Magna will exert the same, or perhaps more, pressure on them as GM, for example, puts on the Tier I companies.

The number of Tier II suppliers is thus likely to shrink considerably. Some Tier II suppliers will survive, of course, and be profitable. MascoTech, for example, a kind of hybrid Tier I/Tier II company, is expected to do well. MascoTech markets many of the products it manufactures to other manufacturers. It sells to a lot of Japanese parts makers, for example, and makes good margins on that business.

Question: Do the new North American plants for BMW and Mercedes-Benz offer a meaningful opportunity for U.S. parts companies? If so, how do the requirements of these plants differ from the requirements of the Japanese transplants?

Fricke: The BMW and Mercedes plants provide significant opportunity for North American-based parts companies. The plants themselves will not be much different from the Japanese plants, but North American parts makers should have easier access to the European plants.

The greatest difficulty North American parts companies have had in selling to the Japanese has been in getting in at the start of a new-product development program. If a supplier is not in at that stage, it has great difficulty getting a contract on that model.

The German companies are likely to erect fewer structural impediments than the Japanese and to provide the U.S. companies much easier access to the design stage. Thus, doing business with the Germans will probably be easier than it has been, or will be, with the Japanese.

Question: With respect to the 20–30 percent price advantage U.S. suppliers have over comparable Japanese manufacturers, at what level of exchange rate would that advantage be wiped out, or is some factor other than currency at work?

Fricke: When the yen was at 150, the price advantage was 10–15 percent. The yen would have to go much lower than that to wipe out the price advantage.

The political issue of trade is of incredible importance. Inevitably, the Japanese will have to come to grips with a Democratic U.S. Congress and a Democratic administration saying that the trade surplus with the United States has been too high for too long and needs to be corrected. It has to decline significantly, if not to zero, and the only way that can happen is if the Japanese lower the auto trade surplus by buying more auto parts from North American parts companies.

Question: How important is the North American Free Trade Agreement in your evaluation of these companies?

Fricke: NAFTA in and of itself is not a significant variable; I would not change any earnings estimates or any stock recommendations because of NAFTA. To the extent that NAFTA will in time allow rationalization of the entire manufacturing base in North America, however, it will help North American parts companies. The automobile industry—the automakers and, in turn, the auto parts manufacturers—is rationalizing manufacturing worldwide, and NAFTA will facilitate this process.

Question: When you look at a parts company, do you place more emphasis on its ability to increase the price of what it sells or on its prospects for higher volume?

Fricke: I place much greater emphasis on volume and the company's ability to control costs than on price. This business will not experience any price increases. I cannot conceive of

many companies that will be able to raise prices on products. Superior Industries International may be able to raise prices because it can pass along the cost of aluminum. Generally, prices will decline, as they did in the electronics industry. Therefore, the emphasis will be on units and the degree to which the parts company can lower its costs through productivity gains and improved manufacturing.

Question: Does the performance of the parts makers' stocks lead, follow, or parallel that of the auto companies?

Fricke: Historically, the stocks of the two groups have moved simultaneously, but investors can disregard history, because portfolio managers and analysts are recognizing the structural changes in the parts segment. The market has been very astute in recent years at identifying special conditions and circumstances. For instance, in the case of Superior, portfolio managers realized that, even though auto production was declining, Superior's earnings were increasing because aluminum wheel installations were increasing.

Since 1990, therefore, the performance of the auto parts manufacturers' stocks has been independent of the performance of the OEMs', and that situation is likely to continue in the future. Valuations and P/Es of the auto parts makers could be higher than they historically have been.

By the way, a review of 30 years or so of data will reveal no "typical" auto cycle, or P/E, or valuation, or set of valuation parameters. Every cycle has been different; every stock has been different. The only generalization analysts can make about this industry is that they can't generalize.

Question: If sales of U.S. parts to Japanese companies increase, what will be the impact on Japanese auto parts manufacturers transplanted in the United States?

Fricke: They are already having difficulty, and I suspect many will fail.

Question: What U.S. suppliers will benefit from increased purchasing by the Japanese auto transplants?

Fricke: The chief beneficiary will be Magna, but MascoTech, Dana, and TRW should also benefit.

Question: What is the future of suppliers of aluminum wheels?

Fricke: As installation rates of aluminum wheels peak, the earnings of these companies will become dependent solely on auto production; thus, they will become more cyclical.

Question: How does the consolidation of the OEM supplier base affect the cyclical nature of the companies' business?

Fricke: It could lessen the cyclical profile of earnings.

Question: What do the high-fixed-cost firms do in a downturn?

Fricke: They do very poorly—that is, suffer a substantial trend down in earnings and, in many cases, red ink.

Question: As the OEMs shift manufacturing risk onto those suppliers providing systems, how are these risks shared between the OEMs and the parts suppliers?

Fricke: Equally.

The Automotive Parts Industry, Part II

Michael P. Ward, CFA
Senior Vice President
Kidder, Peabody & Company, Inc.

Valuation of the supplier companies needs to begin with an industry outlook—U.S. demographics, market saturation, and the rise of light trucks. The next steps are to identify the company's business mix and its peer group, by size and opportunities. In the search for a company that is undervalued in its group, analysts need to consider particularly the outlook for the company's key products, how it compares with competition, and in some cases, key programs in growth areas.

This presentation focuses on the key factors to consider in forecasting revenues for the North American automotive parts suppliers. To prepare for that discussion, part of this presentation outlines some of the major trends in the industry, followed by one way of estimating revenues. Finally, the presentation lays out a recommended comparative approach to valuation.

Forecasting

Any forecast for the automotive suppliers should start with some long-term industry forecast for volume. The automotive industry is highly cyclical, and the parts companies react to that cycle. In examining the long-term trends in the industry, analysts need to take a long-term view of the cycle.

Demographics

Long-term vehicle demand trends in the United States will be a function of demographics, the most important element of which is the population of people 15 years and older, which is shown in **Figure 1**. Of this age group, about 86 percent have a license to drive, and the natural progression is to obtain a driver's license and then get a vehicle to drive. The population of vehicles in the United States grew from 0.55 vehicles registered per licensed driver in 1960 to about 0.91 in 1992. Today the United States has about 1.07 vehicles registered per licensed driver, which means that the U.S. vehicle market is saturated; it probably became saturated in the late 1980s or early 1990s.

Saturation has an obvious impact on an industry's cycle. In the appliance industry, saturation has

meant increased cyclicality. In the auto industry, the total effect is not known, but clearly, market growth will slow down in the future. The industry growth rate between 1960 and 1992 was about 3 percent and will probably be about 1 percent between 1993 and the year 2000. The U.S. vehicle industry has increasingly become a replacement-type industry.

The implications for the parts suppliers are significant. Their segment of the industry will probably not be nearly as cyclical or have as dramatic increases up or down during the next five to seven years as in the past. The result is that the parts suppliers will be able to manage their capacity and employment levels better than previously, which should lead to cuts in costs and increased efficiency.

Cars versus Light Trucks

The bulk of U.S. suppliers' sales go to the domestic original-equipment manufacturers (OEMs); therefore, analyzing the suppliers means looking at what is going on for the Big Three (GM, Ford, and Chrysler). From that angle, a significant industry trend is the increase in light-truck sales relative to cars. In the early 1980s, light trucks—a category that includes minivans, sport/utility vehicles, pickup trucks, and large vans—had under 20 percent of the overall vehicle market in the United States. As shown in **Figure 2**, as of year-end 1993, light trucks had almost a 40 percent market share. The change is all the more significant because the Big Three have an 85–86 percent share of the retail unit light-truck market versus a 66 percent share of the car market. The trend toward light trucks should continue. Therefore, a parts maker that is not supplying to light trucks domestically will lose market share to other

Figure 1. U.S. Population and Long-Term Trends in the U.S. Vehicle Industry

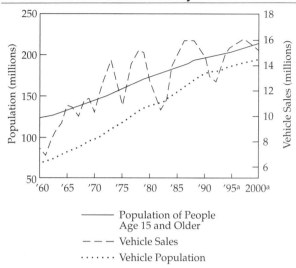

Source: Kidder, Peabody & Co.

Figure 2. U.S. Retail Light-Truck Market Shares

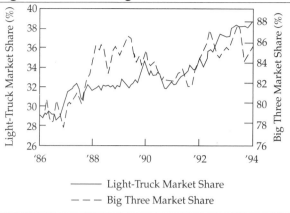

Source: Kidder, Peabody & Co.

Note: Unit sales; shares based on a three-month moving average.

suppliers.

As shown in **Table 1**, the Big Three's share of the car market decreased from about 71 percent in 1986 to 67 percent in 1993. Their share of the light-truck market increased from 79 percent to 86 percent during the same period. The Big Three's share improved in the overall market in 1993, therefore, primarily because of the extremely high growth of light trucks.

In the light-truck sector, the Big Three can prob-

ably maintain their shares in the future. They have a competitive advantage on the light-truck side because they are the innovators in the segment and because of the size of their home market; U.S. light-truck sales should total almost 6 million units in 1994, which is more than the rest of the world combined.

Imports

Another trend in the marketplace relates to "other imports"—that is, imports not coming from Honda, Nissan, Toyota, or the import transplants. Penetration of the other imports in the marketplace,

Table 1. Total U.S. Retail Car and Light-Truck Unit Sales
(in thousands)

	1985	1986	1987	1988	1989	1990	1991	1992	1993[a]	1994[a]	1995[a]
Retail sales											
Car sales	10,983	11,408	10,189	10,543	9,777	9,300	8,175	8,214	8,550	9,250	9,500
Light-truck sales	4,457	4,642	4,706	4,922	4,763	4,558	4,135	4,647	5,350	5,750	6,000
Total sales	15,440	16,050	14,895	15,465	14,540	13,858	12,310	12,861	13,900	15,000	15,500
GM											
Car share	42.7%	41.1%	36.6%	36.3%	35.2%	35.6%	35.6%	34.6%	34.3%	34.4%	34.6%
Light-truck share	35.7	33.1	31.6	34.3	35.0	35.7	34.0	33.3	32.5	32.0	32.0
Total share	40.7	38.8	35.0	35.6	35.1	35.6	35.1	34.1	33.7	33.5	33.6
Ford											
Car share	18.9	18.2	20.2	21.7	22.3	20.9	20.0	21.6	22.1	22.3	22.1
Light-truck share	27.2	28.5	29.7	29.7	29.3	29.6	29.3	30.1	31.0	31.3	31.3
Total share	21.3	21.2	23.2	24.3	24.6	23.7	23.1	24.7	25.6	25.5	25.7
Chrysler											
Car share	12.5	12.1	10.8	11.3	10.4	9.3	8.6	8.3	9.9	10.3	10.3
Light-truck share	17.7	17.3	19.5	20.7	20.7	18.4	19.5	22.2	22.7	23.0	23.0
Total share	14.0	13.6	13.5	14.3	13.8	12.3	12.2	13.3	14.8	15.2	15.2
Big Three											
Car share	74.1	71.5	67.6	69.3	67.9	65.7	64.2	64.5	67.0	66.8	67.0
Light-truck share	80.5	78.9	80.8	84.7	85.0	83.6	82.8	85.6	85.5	86.0	86.3
Total share	76.0	73.6	71.7	74.2	73.5	71.6	70.4	72.1	74.1	74.2	74.5

Source: Kidder, Peabody & Co. estimates

[a]Estimates, as of December 16, 1993.

Figure 3. Market Shares in U.S. Retail Car and Light-Truck Sales: Big Three versus Other Imports

——— Big Three Market Share

– – – Other Imports Market Share

Source: Kidder, Peabody & Co.

Notes: Unit sales; shares based on a three-month moving average. "Other imports" excludes Honda, Nissan, and Toyota.

Table 2. Volume Leaders in North America

Model	1991	1992	1993[a]
GM C/K pickup	613,237	627,905	745,000
Ford F-series	443,187	560,621	610,000
Ford Explorer	283,786	304,883	325,000
Chrysler minivan	486,326	554,678	590,000
Ford Taurus/Sable	427,567	551,172	570,000
GM W-cars	591,975	515,914	585,000
GM J-cars	371,472	298,236	405,000
Chrysler LH	0	50,645	290,000
Honda Accord	366,229	356,385	285,000
Toyota Camry	187,726	240,382	235,000

Sources: Industry data and Kidder, Peabody & Co. estimates.

[a]Estimates.

as shown in **Figure 3**, has been in a steady decline since 1987; so basically, the U.S. market is separating into dominant and subordinate groups of assemblers. GM, Ford, Chrysler, Honda, Nissan, and Toyota are rising above the rest.

In addition, since about 1992, the Big Three group has benefited from the price advantage resulting from the strengthening of the yen. The major Japanese companies have several transplant operations in the United States, however, so they are not as disadvantaged as some other, smaller, Japanese importers.

The Big Three have some opportunities to gain penetration. They gained share during the last several years, and they can probably gain more, primarily because of the trend toward light trucks.

Vehicle Volume Leaders

When analysts look at supplier companies, they should focus on vehicles that are the key volume leaders and on which supplier companies have penetration in those models. Obviously, the more volume leaders a company supplies, the better. Sometimes a supplier will have two or three different volume leaders in its lineup; the best suppliers will have seven, eight, or nine. As shown in **Table 2**, the top four North American volume leaders are trucks.

To put the matter of volume in perspective, consider that a supplier that provides a $50 product for every GM C/K pickup truck has a $35 million contract. That is a big program for any of the domestic suppliers, which generally range in size from $300 million to $1 billion in annual sales.

The Chrysler LH car jumped into the top ten list shown in Table 2 in 1993 following start-up volume in 1992. The Honda Accord and Toyota Camry re-

main on the list but at the bottom. The newest of the volume leaders in 1994 is expected to be the Chrysler Neon, which has received justifiable attention. Chrysler began producing the Neon in late November 1993 and should reach full production in January or February 1994.

Analysts can pick up information about the identity of key suppliers to the volume leaders from trade journals and from the suppliers themselves. The following list of key component suppliers for the Neon illustrates the range of suppliers:

Company	*Component*
Arvin Industries	Goodyear Tire & Rubber
Automotive Industries	Exhaust systems
United Technologies	Interior trim
	Mirrors, instrument
TRW	panels, trim
Masland	Air bags
Kelsey-Hayes	Interior carpet
Bendix	Disc and drum brakes
	Brakes (two-wheel
	antilock braking system)
New Venture Gear	Automatic transmissions
Motor Wheel	Wheel drums
Littelfuse	Fuses/circuit protection
Keeler Brass Lighting	Headlamps
Goodyear Tire & Rubber	Tires

To comprehend the importance of supplying the volume leaders, consider its effect on Arvin Industries, for example, which manufactures the exhaust system for the Neon. Supplying the exhaust system for Chrysler is a big program, as shown in **Table 3**, and supplying the Neon is much more important than was supplying the Sundance/Shadow, the Chrysler product that the Neon replaces. The Sundance/Shadow 1988–93 volume averaged about 185,000 units. The expected Neon production is about 300,000 units for the 1994–96 time frame. If the Neon is produced simply at the old level of the Sundance/Shadow, which is unlikely, Arvin's exhaust system on the Neon, about $75 a unit, will be a $15 million program. If the Neon hits its expected target, the program will contribute $23–$25 million

Table 3. Supplier Content for Chrysler's 1994 Neon

Company	Component	Dollar Content per Unit	Revenue Based on 185,000 Units (millions)	Revenue Based on 300,000 Units (millions)
Arvin Industries	Exhaust system	$ 75	$15	$23
Automotive Industries	Interior trim	40	7	12
Masland	Interior carpet	35	6	10
TRW	Air bags	250	45	75

Source: Kidder, Peabody & Co. estimates.

to Arvin.

The more complicated the component, the higher the dollar content. Thus, TRW's air bag on the Neon provides $250 in revenues for each Neon unit.

The Neon is also an important product to suppliers from an image standpoint. Supplier companies often concentrate on new programs because being on those products shows that they have the latest and greatest components. Chrysler has been very selective with its suppliers, so to be on the Neon is a coup for any supplier, just as it would be to be on the new Ford Windstar or to be supplying to the Saturn program at GM.

When forecasting, analysts should dig out as much of this type of product and volume information as possible. The automakers are not a good source because they do not like to disclose such information, but the auto suppliers love to disclose it if they have it. Analysts can pick up bits and pieces about the suppliers' content per vehicle over time, and that information provides a base for forecasting revenues.

Segments

Unlike the automotive manufacturers, 90 percent of whose business is cars or trucks, analyzing the supplier companies is complicated because no two suppliers are really the same. The impact the auto industry will have on a particular supplier depends on the supplier's business segments. For example, three well-known automotive suppliers are Arvin, Eaton Corporation, and TRW. As shown in **Table 4**, Eaton, practically a household name in the automotive industry, received only about 12 percent of its revenues from passenger-car components in 1993; Arvin and TRW each received about 50 percent of revenues from automotive supplies. Even though half of TRW's volume is automotive related, Kidder, Peabody has a defense and electronics analyst cover the company. Analysts get a mixed bag with the supplier community; investigating all the different segments requires being a quick study.

Valuation

Many different methods can be used to value an OEM supplier. In all of them, however, the analyst needs to consider the size of company, the mix of its business, some of its key products, and its competition. Often the analyst will find two, three, or four very large suppliers of certain components; in that case, the analyst should look at the key programs, particularly in growth areas, such as light trucks today.

Other criteria include management, the earnings history, and all the traditional financial measures, which provide an outline for valuation. Analysts can classify suppliers into different groups: large suppliers, smaller but well-positioned suppliers, and suppliers that are less well positioned. Suppliers in the first group have large sales, large market capitalizations, and very strong historical relationships, and all are well recognized. The consolidation of the industry and the suppliers will enable the big to get bigger. In the marketplace today, therefore, as the current sales cycle matures, investors may flock to some of the largest suppliers—the household names—possibly in a quest for liquidity.

Consensus estimates for the larger suppliers during the next three-to-five years are for earnings growth at about 10 percent annually. As shown in **Table 5**, the forward P/Es for 1994 are fairly consistent with expected earnings as a proxy. Magna International has been undervalued on that basis, however, which may be why it is the favorite stock

Table 4. Automotive Segment Revenue
(dollars in millions)

Item	1991	1992	1993[a]
Arvin			
Automotive OEM revenue	$ 745	$ 886	$1,000
Percent of total company	44%	47%	51%
Eaton			
Passenger-car components revenue	$ 477	$ 542	$ 515
Percent of total company	14%	13%	12%
TRW			
Automotive revenue	$5,117	$4,383	$4,520
Percent of total company	65%	53%	56%

Sources: Industry data and Kidder, Peabody & Co. estimates.
[a]Estimates.

for industry analysts who follow it. Magna is obviously a strong name, and the company has performed well.

As Table 5 shows, the well-positioned suppliers are a mix, but one consistency among them is that they are expected to have strong market positions as a result of new products or programs that will contribute to growing penetration of some market segment. Superior Industries, for example, supplies cast-aluminum wheels that are gaining penetration in the overall market, and the product is becoming standard on an increasing number of vehicles. Superior might also have growth prospects overseas. Arvin is one of the leading worldwide suppliers of exhaust systems and ride-control components. Automotive Industries manufactures interior trim; Donnelly, mirrors; Simpson Industries, precision machine parts; and Walbro, fuel systems. For one reason or another, all of these companies are well positioned in their different segments. They have new products that should push earnings-per-share growth rates to about 15 percent, which is slightly higher than the larger suppliers' 10.5 percent EPS growth rates.

In general, the P/Es for the well-positioned companies are consistently in the 15 percent range. Superior Industries, at 21 times earnings, is a high flyer. Superior's growth has consistently exceeded expectations, and it has a strong market position in the growing cast-aluminum-wheel market.

The term "less well positioned" is not meant to be a derogatory comment, but these companies are not considered well positioned for various reasons—because they are in very competitive segments or industry areas of very low growth, because they have products with high labor content, or often, simply because the stock market misunderstands them. The reason could also be that the company is highly capital intensive. As shown in Table 5, the earnings growth rates of the less-well-positioned companies are comparable to those of the large suppliers and slightly less than the growth rates of the well-positioned suppliers. Their forward P/Es make clear that the market is not paying much money for these stocks; the market may not believe the earnings expectations. Some of the best opportunities in the market might lie, however, in finding one of these less-well-positioned companies that is likely to experience a big upsurge in price—because it has a new product, for example, or is getting into a new area.

Conclusion

First, valuation needs to begin with an industry outlook, and the concentration should be on volumes and opportunities—new programs, for example, or redesigns by the major automakers.

Second, although the grouping presented here is

Table 5. Valuation Analysis of Automotive Suppliers by Category

	Market Value of Equity	Stock Price on December 16, 1993	EPS Growth Rate[a]	Forward P/E [a, b] 1993	1994
Larger Suppliers					
Dana Corp.	$2,489	$54.00	9.5%	19.6	14.6
Eaton Corp.	3,415	49.00	10.0	16.9	14.2
Johnson Controls	2,161	53.50	10.0	16.5	14.9
Magna International	1,727	44.50	14.0	13.7	12.7
TRW	4,147	65.00	9.0	19.1	14.9
Mean	2,788		10.5	17.2	14.3
Well-Positioned Suppliers					
Arvin Industries	660	30.00	12.0	17.1	13.0
Automotive Industries	459	28.00	20.0	20.7	15.6
Donnelly Corp.	142	18.50	15.0	16.1	13.2
Simpson Industries	217	18.25	12.0	22.8	15.9
Superior Industries	1,148	38.13	15.0	26.3	21.8
Walbro Corp.	225	26.50	16.0	15.1	12.6
Mean	475		15.0	19.7	15.3
Less-Well-Positioned Suppliers					
A.O. Smith	443	30.63	10.0	15.3	12.3
Douglas & Lomason Co.	74	17.25	12.0	6.4	5.6
O'Sullivan Corp.	150	9.13	10.0	11.4	9.1
Standard Products Co.	573	34.63	12.0	15.1	12.1
Mean	310		11.0	12.0	9.8

Source: Kidder, Peabody & Co.

[a] Five-year growth rate and forward earnings are based on I/B/E/S and Kidder, Peabody & Co. estimates.
[b] Fiscal year-end is calendarized to December.

not the only way to analyze positioning, positioning is important. In particular, analysts are often brought in to participate in private companies making their initial public offerings (IPOs), and an analysis of positioning is vital for determining the initial valuation of a company and gaining some idea of what the market will pay for the stock.

Third, supplier companies come in various sizes and positions. Therefore, for valuation purposes, analysts should compare one company with another. That is what an efficient market does; for example, analysts will often hear one supplier company described in terms of another, as in: "Well, it's not a Superior" or "It's not a Magna." One purpose of the comparisons is to find a company that sticks out in its segment, like Magna in the large group, which offers an opportunity to buy the stock at a discount to the price of its peers.

Question and Answer Session

Michael P. Ward, CFA

Question: The expected peak in U.S. vehicle sales of 16 million units in about 1997 (as indicated in Figure 1) is no higher than the 1986 peak. The implication is that growth will not be even 1 percent, or is 16 million units simply too conservative?

Ward: A peak is a hard statistic to estimate. The people who are best in the industry at such predictions, such as some of the Big Three's economists, can come up with better analyses than investment analysts can. Some of their numbers go as high as 20 million units.

Investors have to look at the overall market and, I believe, concentrate on demographics. The overlying trend in this country will be set by the Baby Boomers, who will have to confront major spending needs in the next four-to-five years and will thus, because of human nature, be more likely to save than spend. Their choices will have a dampening effect on demand. In addition, the quality of cars built today means that people will keep them longer than in the past, which will also push down demand somewhat.

I think the industry will not surpass the previous cyclical peak by a great margin. The 1986 peak was artificially inflated because of the change in the tax law. In the past, interest expense was tax deductible, but that provision was eliminated in 1987, so late 1986 brought an unusual surge in demand—by our estimates, about 300,000 units. In addition, we believe saturation will keep the growth rate of the industry low.

Question: How do you make your production and market-share projections?

Ward: I am not a car fanatic, but I do pick up as much as I can from reading trade journals and so forth. In a case like Chrysler's Neon, an analyst will predict it to be a strong model because of certain industry history and statistics. Chrysler has been extremely successful in the past when it introduced products that overlap marketing segments. For example, the LH car is basically an overlap; it is a standard-size product with an intermediate-type price. The Neon is a similar overlap; it is almost the size of the Honda Accord but is priced as a small car. Consumers will get very good value for their money with the Neon.

Another source of information is the dealership count and examining which dealers are successful. For example, the new Ford Windstar minivan, in our opinion, will do very well, primarily because of the fact that the minivan segment is rapidly growing and because of Ford's strong dealer network. Based strictly on those fundamental data, Ford will probably sell out the Windstar during the first two years.

The production and market-share projections are thus based on looking at historical trends in the segment market shares and at what the different companies have done in those segments, reading industry publications to determine which cars may be successful and which may not, and putting all the information together to make some reasonable assumptions for production.

Question: Is the information about who is supplying parts for the Neon meaningful for investment purposes?

Ward: The Neon, probably more than any other program, has several very important investment implications. The Neon, because of the entire process, should tell the investment community which suppliers are on the leading edge from the standpoint of product development and technology.

Chrysler has done more than GM or Ford to get along with the supplier companies, as the suppliers will confirm. One way is that Chrysler has turned over entire programs to the different suppliers. Ten years ago, the exhaust system on the Neon would have been split, say, 50/50 between Arvin and Tenneco. Today, Chrysler is saying, "Arvin, you have the Neon exhaust system. You design it, engineer it, and deliver it here to us." That approach allows the parts suppliers to operate very efficiently.

Question: Please explain why the valuation is so low in Table 5 for the Douglas & Lomason stock.

Ward: I can only suggest some reasons because I do know not Douglas & Lomason well. The market capitalization is only $74 million. Therefore, someone wanting to buy the stock in a meaningful amount would probably have a tough time with liquidity. That circumstance certainly has to be a drag on the company. Also, the company has two strong competitors in Johnson Controls and Lear Seating. Possibly, the company is simply misunderstood.

Question: The United States has the strictest emission regulations in the world, but U.S.-type standards are apparently spreading, certainly to Europe. Does this trend offer an opportunity for Arvin or any other suppliers?

Ward: Definitely. Overseas sales will provide a lot of opportunities for several companies. Europe has passed some emission regulations for calendar year 1993, and they pushed them back throughout the year for final implementation because of the recession. In Europe, Arvin has an opportunity to get 25 percent of the catalytic-converter business. Arvin's share of each catalytic-converter unit sale will probably be about $50. Arvin could thus add $150 million in incremental revenue and have about a $500 million revenue base in Europe on an annual basis by 1994.

Arvin and Tenneco dominate the catalytic-converter market in the United States, and both are positioned to get business in Europe. GM, however, has seven key component areas on which it will concentrate, and one of them is catalytic converters. As an independent, GM is not competitive in North America in that business, but it is very competitive overseas.

In addition to these opportunities are opportunities for the companies at the other end of emission control; Walbro, for example, manufactures an electronic fuel injector that enhances fuel economy in the performance of cars and controls emissions, and it has set up a joint venture in Europe to supply fuel systems in the European market.

A lot of peripheral companies will benefit from the move to higher emission standards throughout the world. It is a growth area.

Question: Are any important

parts for a vehicle bought on anything other than a contract basis—on a spot basis, for example?

Ward: Contracts are the norm, but some of the smaller companies will get "letters of intent to purchase," "purchase orders," or so forth, that can clearly be canceled week by week. Shiloh, for example, which makes small stamping components and steel blanks for manufacturers, has numerous purchase-order contracts. The understanding with these contracts is that they will be for a certain term—one, two, or three years—but they can be canceled at short notice. Such contracts certainly add risk to a company's profile.

Question: Considering Chrysler's dominance and Ford's entries, is market saturation a risk in the minivan segment, and will the profitability of this segment decline?

Ward: I think profitability will continue and the market has room to grow. The prime driver for minivan and sport/utility vehicles' sales has been demographics. In the United States during the past five-to-seven years, minivan and sport/utility unit sales have tracked the population of people 30–45 years old, and that population will continue to grow steadily into the 1996–97 period. Based on demographics alone, therefore, the sport/utility and minivan segments, which accounted for about 2.5 million units in 1993, should grow to about 3.0 million units.

That growth figure may be on the conservative side. Some industry economists would point out that minivan buyers are about 90 percent repeat buyers, which may mean that the 45–54-year-old group is also important and that demand figures could grow well above the 3-million level.

Chrysler has been producing minivans at capacity since Day One. Thus, as for profitability, even if Ford does gain market share, Chrysler will still produce 600,000 of these vehicles. Revenue is reported on factory sales or production, not market share, so Chrysler may lose some share, but that really doesn't matter.

The major risk is that a big marketing war will break out. For example, Chrysler recently introduced that risk by bringing out its 10th anniversary minivan with cash-back offers and incentives, which Chrysler hopes will defeat Ford from the start. This program is probably temporary, however; it will last one, two, or three months at most, and then Chrysler will back off a bit. Nobody but consumers wants to see a pricing war, particularly with the industry fundamentals in such great shape today.

Overall, profitability is not a worry in this segment; it has a lot of growth ahead. And Chrysler will probably continue to be the leader—because it has the best product.

Question: Will any particular supplier sector be filing IPOs?

Ward: Companies in any of the sectors could go public, but the focus should probably be on those with relatively larger capitalizations—the $2-billion-type companies. In the past two years, many small, high-growth companies have had IPOs, but larger companies will probably come into the marketplace. We can expect more, perhaps half a dozen, IPOs such as the recent United Technologies announcement during the first half of 1994. UT is certainly larger than most previous IPOs in this industry segment.

Question: What would be the reaction to a spin-off of GM's Automotive Components Group

(ACG)?

Ward: ACG is an amazing business; it is a $25 billion business today within GM, and it is literally the worldwide market leader in several different categories. It is a tremendously strong business going through a big revolution in production costs, momentum, and so forth.

ACG is a captive supplier of GM, but its goal is to get to 50 percent sales outside GM in the next couple of years, which it certainly can do. GM has not done a good job of selling ACG's numerous strengths outside the company. All GM small cars now have antilock brakes, for example, which is a big achievement and was made possible by ACG.

Wall Street would love to see ACG spun off. If GM had a general offering of the whole ACG (not another alphabet stock, such as an E- or an H-stock), it would be very successful. A $5 billion IPO for ACG would generate $250 million in fees, which is enough to make Wall Street dance anytime. I believe an ACG offering would be well accepted by investors. ACG stock would be a very large-cap, liquid place to put some money.

Question: Are some of the Japanese parts companies that have come into the North American market at risk of getting crowded out by U.S. companies?

Ward: I think they are. In the Japanese system, a supplier is often dedicated to a specific automotive company—Toyota, Honda, Nissan, or so on. The Japanese suppliers apparently came over here, in joint ventures with one of the major suppliers in North America or on their own, with the hope that they could simply overwhelm the North American suppliers and win business from GM, Ford, and Chrysler. They have not been successful.

Now, with Japanese market share declining and volume relatively flat, they are probably losing a ton of money. So, some of these supplier companies will likely fail and go back to Japan. Whoever owns chunks of the companies will stop putting money into them, will stop taking the loss, and will force them to go back.

Question: As quality improves in automobiles, will the demand for after-market parts go down? Is the after-market supply business thus less attractive in the future than it has been?

Ward: The after-market is certainly one of the slower growing segments of the industry. As quality improves, the after-market business should slow down. For example, now that all exhaust systems are essentially stainless steel, they do not corrode, so the exhaust business, which had grown at a 5–7 percent annual rate, is now down to 1 percent at best, and the segment is very competitive.

Other segments have also slowed down. Spark plugs used to be a high-growth area of the after-market, but when gasoline refiners stopped adding lead (which fouls up spark plugs) to automotive gasoline, the growth in replacement spark plugs dropped. Still other segments are likely to experience similar trends in the next four-to-seven years.

The structure of the after-market is one of the biggest blunders ever in corporate America. Technically, GM, Ford, and Chrysler should control that $100 billion industry, but they do not. Their penetration levels are very low in the after-market.

Question: How are manufacturing defects or product recalls as a result of component problems handled? Do the OEM and the supplier divide up the costs? For example, the gas tanks in GM

compact pickup trucks had a problem with the way the vent tube was attached to the tank, so in certain circumstances, the tank leaked fuel after a collision. Who supplied those tanks?

Ward: In most cases, the supplier has the liability. In the gas-tank example, GM did not disclose the gas-tank manufacturer, but it did say that the supplier would be paying for all the defects. Also, TRW basically shoulders the liability for its air bags. Supplier liability is part of the system, and the supplier companies certainly allocate any warranty-type expenses to the future and accrue them.

Question: What sort of a company is Lear Seating?

Ward: Lear, which is one of the two leading seat manufacturers—Johnson Controls is the other—is now registering for a bond offering. It has been covered in the various trade journals recently, which more or less telegraphed that it planned to do something in the public market soon. A recent *Business Week* article specifically mentioned a GM production facility in Germany and the fact that Lear set up a small, state-of-the-art plant to supply that facility. GM called it the best supplier plant in the world.

Question: What would be the signs that the industry is rolling over into its next downturn?

Ward: The first thing would be sales rising above what analysts are expecting. For example, the industry forecast for 1994 is about 15 million units; if the sales start to rocket above that figure by 15–20 percent, up to a range between 15.8 and 16 million units, that would be a sign to me that industry demand was rolling over and the end was near.

The Tire and Rubber Industry

Stephen J. Girsky
First Vice President
PaineWebber, Inc.

The low return of the tire and rubber business can be attributed to numerous structural problems. Two companies' approaches to dealing with high fixed costs, excess capacities, slow growth, and intense price competition associated with these commodity-like products are discussed. One has chosen product differentiation and an end-user focus, and the other, maintaining the lowest possible cost position. Analysts need to track the industry's price environment, rubber costs, demand, and the companies' quality of earnings.

The tire and rubber industry, in its characteristics, is a cross between the auto industry (one of its end markets), the consumer products industry (another end market), and the chemical industry (in relation to cost structure). This presentation begins with a description of the structure and operating characteristics of the tire industry—in particular, the structural problems that explain why it is such a low-return industry in the developed countries. Two solutions to the structural problems are then discussed, namely, the approaches of Goodyear Tire & Rubber and of Cooper Tire & Rubber. In spite of its difficult environment, the tire and rubber industry offers some worthwhile investment opportunities. This presentation offers a method of tracking the industry and a method of evaluating the stocks.

Industry Characteristics

In 1993, stocks of publicly held tire companies performed poorly relative to the MSCI World Index, as the following PaineWebber figures show:

Stock	Return
Bridgestone	–6.6%
Continental	+21.9
Goodyear	+14.2
Michelin Tire	–4.1
Pirelli	–17.5
Sumitomo	–3.9

For the first three quarters of the year, industry performance was even worse than these annual figures show. Continental performed the best, followed by Goodyear. Goodyear was the only company that outperformed the MSCI World Index; the European

stocks PaineWebber tracks (Michelin, Continental, Bridgestone, Sumitomo, and Pirelli) made most of their improvements in the fourth quarter of the year.

The low return of this business can be attributed to several structural problems that particularly afflict tire companies in the developed markets: low growth, a commodity product, the nature of competition, customer purchasing power, excess capacity, high fixed costs and low margins, and generally high debt.

Growth

Companies in this industry can grow only as fast as the vehicle population grows, and the North American, European, and Japanese vehicle populations are simply not growing rapidly. For example, consider the following figures for number of vehicles per 1,000 people in the developed countries:

United States	768
Germany	527
United Kingdom	461
France	504
Italy	519
Spain	369

When 768 vehicles are on the road for every 1,000 residents, as in the United States, the market is saturated. And a saturated and low-growth U.S. auto market means low growth for the tire industry. In Western Europe, the market is difficult to grow because of space problems and because the mass-transit systems are highly developed and popular. These vehicle populations are mature. Therefore, the secular growth rate of the worldwide tire industry is estimated to be 2–3 percent. The tire industry will grow faster than that percentage, however, in Latin America, Eastern Europe, and Asia, as discussed in the section on "Less Developed Markets."

Growth in both the original-equipment (OE) and replacement markets are driven by these mature vehicle populations. Demand for replacement tires in the United States is shown in **Figure 1**. The industry had a decent year in 1992, but 1993 demand in the replacement market will be flat to down from 1992 figures.

Figure 1. U.S. Replacement-Tire Demand

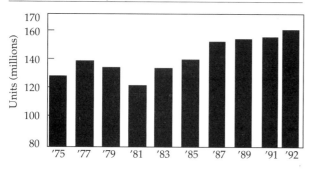

Source: PaineWebber.

On a worldwide basis, tire shipments from North America were strong in 1992, as indicated in **Table 1**. The result of the general market maturity, however, is that worldwide shipments will probably be flat in 1993 (the data are not yet complete). A strong OE market is expected to offset a weak replacement market. In Western Europe and Japan, sales will decrease 5–10 percent in 1993.

In such a basically mature, low-growth industry, competition is a zero-sum game: A gain in sales, earnings, or market share for one company comes at the expense of the others. And the competitors do not give anything away willingly.

Commodity Product

All tires are not necessarily equal, but a consumer's ability to substitute one product for another is high. Consumers can substitute a Goodyear for a Michelin, which they can substitute for a Bridgestone, and so forth. Competition, therefore, resembles that of a commodity business—driven by price and service.

Competitive Structure

The industry is an oligopoly with well-balanced competitors: The top six producers have 70 percent of the worldwide tire market. The tire industry does not behave like an oligopoly, however. The commodity nature of the product, high fixed costs, excess capacities, and slow growth come together to make price rivalry particularly intense.

The 1992 world market shares of the tire companies based on unit sales is depicted in **Figure 2**. Michelin has the largest slice of the pie, followed closely by Goodyear and Bridgestone. Ten years ago, Goodyear was the market leader. The rankings based on revenues, shown in **Table 2**, are similar, with fairly even matches at the top. Note that Firestone is now a Bridgestone subsidiary and that Kelly-Springfield is the private-label subsidiary of Goodyear; so to examine current corporate figures, some combining is necessary.

Since the early 1980s, the companies have been attempting to achieve some "critical" size in hopes of improving their returns. Michelin bought Uniroyal and BF Goodrich; Bridgestone bought Firestone; Continental bought General; Pirelli bought Armstrong; and Sumitomo bought Dunlop. This consolidation has not, however, improved returns.

Customer Purchasing Power

The auto companies account for 25–30 percent of

Table 1. Global Tire Shipments
(millions of units)

	1989	1990	Year-to-Year Change	1991	Year-to-Year Change	1992	Year-to-Year Change
North America							
Cars	224	219	–2.2%	217	–0.9%	233	7.4%
Trucks	16.8	16.1	–4.2	14.4	–10.6	15.9	10.4
Western Europe							
Cars	180	184	2.2	185	0.5	186	0.5
Trucks	12.1	12.2	0.8	11.7	–4.1	11.1	–5.1
Japan							
Cars	79	85	7.6	87	2.4	91	4.6
Trucks	5.5	5.7	3.6	5.5	–3.5	5.3	–3.6

Source: PaineWebber.

Figure 2. Worldwide Unit Market Shares, 1992

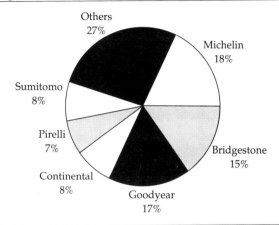

Others 27%
Michelin 18%
Sumitomo 8%
Pirelli 7%
Continental 8%
Goodyear 17%
Bridgestone 15%

Source: PaineWebber.

all tires sold. Therefore, they make the difference between a tire company running at 75 percent capacity utilization and one running at 95 percent utilization.

Unfortunately, because tires are a commodity, the auto companies can easily switch suppliers. In fact, tire suppliers are one of the easiest to switch. Therefore, tire companies are essentially at the mercy of their OE customers. Goodyear's CEO Stanley Gault has a famous quotation that illustrates the fundamental structural problem: "They are paying 1984 prices for tires. Are you paying 1984 prices for cars?"

Tire companies allocate capacity within the demands of the powerful automakers. For example, if a tire company has a capacity of 1 million units and GM wants 200,000, the tire company must give GM the first 200,000 tires because, first, GM is its largest customer and, second, it cannot shut GM down. Then the tire company can begin allocating tires to

Table 2. Worldwide Tire Revenue
(millions of dollars)

Company	1991	1992	Percent Change
Michelin	$10,020	$10,500	4.8%
Bridgestone	8,688	9,345	7.6
Goodyear	7,849	8,167	4.1
Bridgestone/Firestone	4,466	4,700	5.2
Continental	3,613	3,980	10.2
Sumitomo	3,050	3,276	7.4
Pirelli	2,756	2,875	4.3
Yokohama	2,320	2,432	4.8
UGR	2,300	NA	NA
General Tire	1,323	1,348	1.9
Kelly-Springfield	1,250	1,300	4.0
Toyo	1,194	1,263	5.8
Cooper	830	1,000	20.5
Kumho	703	844	20.0
Total industry	$50,400	$53,400	6.0%

Source: European Rubber Journal.

everybody else; it will allocate to one of its own brands, then to another, then to its private-label customers. If the company is running tight, at 95 percent, and GM suddenly hits a strong quarter (like the fourth quarter of 1993) and wants 400,000–500,000 tires, the tire company has to give GM those tires before filling any other firm's orders. As a result, the company will not be able to fill the orders of some private-label customers.

Another dilemma for the powerless, dependent tire companies is as follows: The OE automakers demand the product research, design, and innovation from their tire suppliers, but they do not want to pay for it. To get a tire approved as original equipment costs a tire company $3–$5 million. The tire manufacturers generally agree to provide the OE tires for free in hopes of gaining exposure for the new tire and recouping their investment in the replacement market. The belief is that the brand of tire the consumer takes off a car will be the brand the consumer puts on the car, which is not necessarily true.

Moreover, when a tire company launches a new product as OE, if the tire is on lots of cars, the competition will recognize that the new product may be a big one and can simply reverse-engineer the product. The competitor does not incur the R&D expense, or any of the $3–$5 million to get a product approved, does none of the testing, and yet is there in the replacement market—at a cheaper price. This me-too approach is essentially Cooper Tire's approach to the business.

Capacity

Capacity in this industry is typically added in large chunks, and the companies often build new plants without being sure of completely filling them with orders. Backlogs in this business are not large, so the companies build first and get business later.

Since the 1980s, the global tire industry has been experiencing excess capacity of roughly 20–25 percent, which has led inevitably to price cutting in order to use capacity and spread fixed costs. Sometimes the companies run at full capacity, but excess has been chronic in Europe and Japan. Note, however, that virtually every tire company in Western Europe is cutting capacity, as illustrated in **Exhibit 1**. These moves will not help in the near term, but when demand recovers, the companies' profitability should improve.

In general, the excess capacity has been moving east and west of the United States, largely because of currency and economic issues. The United States is the strongest economy in the world today, and the yen's problems are making imports from Japan uncompetitive.

Exhibit 1. European Tire Manufacturers' Capacity Reductions

Manu-facturer	Site	Reduction
Kleber	St. Ingbert	Phase out production of auto, light-truck, and agricultural tires by year-end 1994 (about 2.1 million units a year).
Continental	Sarrequemines	Phase out production of truck and bus tires by mid-1994 (900 units a day); transfer some production to other plants.
Semperit	Traiskirchen	Cut back production of truck and bus tires 20 percent to 320,000 units a year.
Goodyear	Philippsburg	Cut back production of auto tires about 16 percent (about 14,000 units a week).
Pirelli	Breuberg	Phase out production of truck and bus tires by mid-1994 (about 400,000 units a year); increase auto tire capacity 21 percent to 20,000 units a day.
	Burton-on-Trent	Phase out production of auto tires; absorb truck and bus tire production from Breuberg.
	Carlisle	Absorb auto tire production from Burton-on-Trent.
	Tivoli	Phase out production of auto and light-truck tires; plant to specialize in agricultural tires.
	Villafranca	Plant closed; primarily motorcycle tire output.
SP Reifen-werke	Wittlich	Shift production of truck and bus tires to Wittlich from Hanau.
	Hanau	Expand light-truck capacity at Hanau.

Source: European Rubber Journal.

Costs and Margins

Operating results for the major tire companies in 1992 are shown in **Table 3**. Goodyear's operating income would have been $1.1 billion without corporate expense, which was 40 percent higher than in 1991. The difference in Michelin's operating and net income reflects its huge financial leverage. (Note that Michelin's pretax income, not operating income, is used in Table 3.)

Goodyear's operating margins range from 7 percent to 8 percent; Bridgestone's are about 7 percent; Continental's, 2.5 percent; Pirelli's, 6.9 percent; and Michelin's, about 6 percent. Net margins are even worse.

Debt Levels

One of Goodyear's advantages is that it has been reducing its debt. As shown in **Table 4**, Goodyear's debt fell to about $2 billion at year-end 1992, and final figures for 1993 are expected to show even lower debt. In comparison, Bridgestone's debt is about $6.6 billion.

Michelin's debt would be a big disadvantage

except that its debt is primarily held by French banks, which are state owned. Technically, the company is not government subsidized, but in reality, it is.

The Prisoner's Dilemma

The problems of the tire industry have created a form of the classic Prisoner's Dilemma of Game Theory. In this context, the two "prisoners" each have two choices, as illustrated in **Figure 3**: They can "cooperate" by, in this simplified version of the game, raising prices, or they can "defect" by cutting prices. As shown in the figure, the game has four possible outcomes depending on each prisoner's choice. If both players cooperate, they both make a small but adequate return on investment. If both prisoners defect, they both lose money. If one player cooperates and the other defects, the defector, having cut prices, gains market share and makes money while the cooperator loses money.

Unfortunately for the tire producers, this game is the ongoing pattern in the industry. Usually, the companies start out cooperating. Then, some companies defect by cutting prices—in order to fill capac-

Table 3. Major Tire Companies' Operating Results, 1992
(millions)

Company	Operating Income			Net Income		
	Local Currency	U.S. Dollars	Percent Change	Local Currency	U.S. Dollars	Percent Change
Goodyear	$1,110.0	$ 815.0	41.7	$370.0	$370.0	283.1%
Bridgestone	122,800.0	1,098.4	4.9	28,400.0	254.0	278.7
Continental	DM244.9	140.9	85.8	DM133.0	76.5	NMF
Pirelli	DFL567.0	0.3	64.8	DFL(260.0)	(0.2)	NMF
Michelin	FFr4,254.0	718.7	9.7	FFr586.0	97.3	NMF

Source: PaineWebber.

Notes: Exchange rates are as of December 31, 1993. Percentage changes are based on local currencies (DM = German mark; DFL = Dutch florin; and FFr = French franc). NMF = not a meaningful figure.

Table 4. Major Tire Companies' Debt and Capital Structures
(dollars in millions)

Company	Debt 1991	Debt 1992	Percent Change	Debt to Equity 1991	Debt to Equity 1992
Goodyear	$2,641	$2,038	−22.8%	96.7%	105.6%
Bridgestone	6,208	6,531	5.2	158.1	160.3
Continental	1,131	1,292	14.2	142.8	153.0
Pirelli	2,646	2,068	−21.8	244.9	140.2
Michelin	6,474	6,449	−0.4	340.9	344.3

Source: PaineWebber.

Note: FAS No. 106 reduced Goodyear's equity in 1992. Exchange rates are as of December 31, 1993, for 1991 and 1992 numbers.

ity, for instance. A company that "cooperates" the first time soon gets burned and learns not to cooperate again. Inevitably, then, all defect and lose money. Every few years, the tire companies beat themselves up, fall into the bottom right corner, and stay there until the pattern starts over again.

Less Developed Markets

Many areas of the world do not have the severe structural problems that lead to the Prisoner's Dilemma of tire manufacturers in developed countries. Therefore, returns on investment are a lot higher outside North America than inside.

Figure 3. The Tire Industry's Dilemma

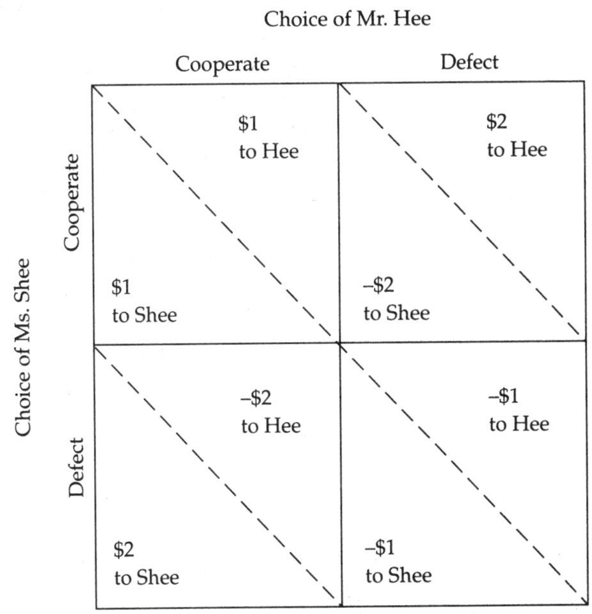

Source: PaineWebber.

Moreover, as noted, growth rates in some of the underdeveloped tire markets are much higher than in the developed markets. As an illustration, **Table 5** shows cars per 1,000 people in Eastern Europe,

Mexico, and the Pacific (non-Japanese) markets. Recall that the figure for the United States was more than 750. If two companies want to compete in these less developed markets, they can both win; they can both improve returns without cutting each other to pieces.

The emerging markets are also much more fragmented than the developed markets. Consider these figures for the number of tire and rubber companies in developing regions:

Asia	81
South and Central America	15
Eastern Europe	33

Nine of the Asian companies are state owned, as are a dozen of the East European companies. Asia includes China, and no one knows exactly how many tire companies are in China; so, Asia has *at least* 81 tire companies.

These companies are not well capitalized. Rivalry is not as intense in these markets as in developed markets, and consumers are not sophisticated. A well-capitalized player from the developed world, one of the major six firms, could easily improve its

Table 5. Characteristics of the Non-U.S. Tire Industry

Country	Cars per 1,000 People
Eastern Europe	
Bulgaria	142
Czechoslovakia	222
Hungary	206
Poland	157
Romania	51
Russia	122
East Germany	300
Mexico	118
Pacific	
India	2.3
Malaysia	91.2
Singapore	93.5
Indonesia	8.7
Taiwan	60.6
South Korea	32.1
China	1.7

Source: PaineWebber.

returns by entering one or more of these markets.

Solutions to the Problems

The solutions to the problems created for the tire manufacturers by the characteristics of the modern tire and rubber industry were introduced by the CEOs of the two companies discussed in this section.

The Goodyear Approach

Goodyear brought in Gault to head the company in 1991. Gault had spent 30 years at General Electric; in fact, he was a candidate along with Jack Welch to run GE. When GE gave the job to Welch, Gault went to Rubbermaid. He turned Rubbermaid around and then retired. When Goodyear was in trouble, and was almost bankrupt, Gault was on the board of directors, and they talked him into rescuing the company.

Gault's philosophical approach is intended to change the way the tire industry works. Gault argues that no marketing has ever been done in the tire business, but because a tire is largely a consumer product (rather than a commodity product), a company that markets well should be poised to benefit in the industry. Gault also believes that the theory that consumers will replace their tires with the same brand that was original equipment is a myth, particularly at the low end. Tires on a low-end Chevrolet, for example, generate no brand loyalty. Brand loyalty is evidenced at the high end, such as on a Mercedes or BMW, and on high-end models such as the Mustang GT (but not the regular Mustang) or the Cadillac Seville STS (but not the Seville).

The corollary to the brand-loyalty myth is the adage that tire manufacturers should go to any extreme to obtain OE business. Gault believes that following this advice is also bad business. He favors letting the other companies give GM tires for nothing; Goodyear has other fish to fry, particularly in the replacement market.

Gault believes tires should be sold where consumers want to buy them. He wants to show the tires to as many consumers as possible. Therefore, if consumer buying patterns are changing, the company should adjust accordingly.

Goodyear and Kelly-Springfield worked as independent companies at opposite ends of the spectrum with no cooperation. Today, Gault has them working together to segment and attack the replacement market strategically. Goodyear is applying Gault's philosophy through several strategies.

■ *The product.* Gault believes Goodyear needs to differentiate its products. So the company launched the Aquatred—the tire with a big groove down the middle that improves performance on wet

roads. Goodyear has also launched a Wrangler directional-tread truck tire; a new touring tire, the Regatta; and some medium-duty truck tires. Goodyear has had more new-product launches during the past two years than during any previous two-year period in the company. The products had all been on the shelf, but the company had simply not been aggressive in launching its new products.

Another solution Goodyear has for the commodity-product problem is marketing. When Goodyear launched the Aquatred, Michelin already had a wet-road tire, which it sold but did not *market*. Nine months later, the Michelin CEO reported that Michelin had test-driven the Aquatred against its own wet-road tire and the Michelin outperformed its competitor. Meanwhile, Goodyear had sold a million Aquatreds and still nobody knew Michelin had a competitive tire. What good is a superior product if nobody knows about it? That lack of focus on marketing is a fundamental problem in the industry.

Gault does not want to launch a new product and let it go unnoticed. Advertising expenditures for Goodyear, Michelin, and Bridgestone-Firestone, shown in **Table 6**, indicate that since Gault took office, Goodyear has been spending far more money on advertising than any of the other tire companies. Cooper does not spend much at all. Michelin actually showed a decline in spending between 1991 and 1992. **Table 7** breaks down advertising expenses by brand. Spending by all but BF Goodrich and Uniroyal was up in 1992, but Goodyear and Kelly-Springfield advertising expenditures increased significantly.

■ *Excess capacity.* Gault has attacked the capacity problem by expanding distribution. The days of the single-line, independent franchise tire company may be numbered; tires must be offered in the outlets where consumers want to shop. Gault added Wal-Mart, Kmart, Sears, Big O Tire, and Canadian Tire. In fact, the number of outlets selling Goodyear or Kelly-Springfield tires has increased by about 30

Table 6. Advertising Expenditures
(thousands)

Company/Dealer	1991	1992
Bridgestone/Firestone	$ 5,184.9	$ 7,060.3
Cooper	287.7	331.1
Cooper dealers	102.0	257.6
Total Cooper	$ 389.7	$ 588.7
Goodyear	54,862.5	74,600.5
Goodyear dealers	10,092.6	20,213.5
Total Goodyear	$64,955.1	$94,814.0
Michelin	27,108.2	22,745.3
Michelin dealers	2,082.7	3,252.2
Total Michelin	$29,190.9	$25,997.5

Source: PaineWebber.

Table 7. Advertising Expenditure by Brand
(dollars in thousands)

Tire Brand	1991	1992	Percent Change
Bridgestone	$ 2,350.0	$ 3,364.8	43.2%
Firestone	2,834.9	3,695.6	30.4
Cooper	389.7	588.7	51.1
Goodyear	62,133.6	89,850.8	44.6
Kelly-Springfield	2,821.5	4,963.2	75.9
Michelin	18,446.8	21,346.6	15.7
BF Goodrich	9,642.9	4,004.2	−58.5
Uniroyal	1,101.2	646.7	−41.3

Source: PaineWebber.

percent since 1991.

The expanded distribution was a calculated risk. Taking the Goodyear brand to Sears posed the risk that the independent tire dealers and franchisees would defect from Goodyear. To lessen that risk, Gault gave Sears the old tires and continued to launch the new products at the dealers. The dealers got both the Aquatred and the Regatta first, for example. In addition, Gault supported them with increased advertising dollars.

The result was that the dealers did not lose any share. Cooper, Michelin, and Bridgestone may think that any day now the dealers will be running over to them, but two years have passed and Goodyear dealers have not underperformed the market.

Tire dealerships still dominate the tire market, as shown in **Table 8**, but the Wal-Marts, Kmarts, and Sears are doing extremely well in the business. Goodyear does not supply the warehouse clubs *yet*; if consumers want to buy their tires at warehouse clubs, however, Goodyear will eventually have to be there.

When Gault went to Goodyear, it was running at about 75 percent capacity utilization. Increasing the outlets took utilization to 95 percent.

▧ *Well-matched rivals.* Goodyear's solution to the rivalry problem is to attack the fixed costs in order to surpass the field of equally matched competitors. Changes in Goodyear's selling, general, and administrative expenses (SG&A) and debt are shown in **Table 9**. The company's SG&A as a percentage of sales is expected to have dropped 100 basis points, to 16.7 percent, between 1990 and 1993. SG&A has not grown at all, despite a significant increase in advertising money, since Gault joined Goodyear. The company paid for the advertising increase by cutting costs in other places.

Goodyear's debt levels peaked at $3.4 billion in 1990; today, it is down to $1.5 billion and is moving lower. Goodyear has thus quickly built a competitive advantage by reducing debt. One issue for the future is how the company will use this advantage.

▧ *Customer purchasing power.* Goodyear's solution to this problem is to reduce its dependence on the OE market: Why give those who pay the least (the OE manufacturers [OEMs]) first dibs on capacity and end up back-ordering the people who pay the most (the private-label customers)? Inevitably, the private-label customers will buy from somebody else. Although demand is currently tight, to build a new tire plant just so the company can sell GM tires for next to nothing is pointless. Rather, over the long term, Goodyear will cut back on OE business—not eliminate it, because it is important to the company—

Table 8. Distribution Outlets' Industry Shares

Outlet	1988	1989	1990	1991	1992
Tire dealerships	56%	54%	54%	54%	54%
Service stations	7	7	7	6	5
Tire company stores	12	13	13	12	12
Miscellaneous outlets	2	2	1	1	1
Auto dealerships	2	2	1	1	1
Chain stores, department stores	17	17	18	19	19
Warehouse and discount clubs	4	5	6	7	8

Source: Modern Tire Dealer.

Table 9. Goodyear's SG&A Expenses and Debt
(dollars in millions)

Item	1988	1989	1990	1991	1992	1993[a]	1994[a]
SG&A	$1,745.1	$1,863.7	$1,999.6	$1,911.7	$1,997.3	$1,958.7	$2,061.6
SG&A/sales	16.1%	17.1%	17.7%	17.5%	16.9%	16.7%	16.7%
Debt[b]	$3,217.0	$3,030.0	$3,372.0	$2,130.0	$1,564.0	$1,471.0	$1,277.0
Debt/equity	158.7%	141.3%	160.7%	78.0%	81.0%	63.6%	46.9%

Source: PaineWebber.
[a]Estimates.

[b]Debt is long-term debt.

by getting out of the low-margin business, such as supplying Chevy Cavaliers, Saturns, or Ford Escorts. This strategy, reducing dependence on the OEM business, is designed to increase profits and decrease volatility.

The launch of new products in the replacement market is another aspect of reducing OEM power. The intention is to make money right away, without waiting for repurchase of an OE brand, and allow the competition little time to react. The Aquatred, for example, was launched directly to the replacement market. Some managers of other companies were skeptical about this Goodyear strategy. They doubted that a product launched in the replacement market would make a big enough splash to attract attention. Today, after $90 million and Super Bowl advertising, the Aquatred has made a pretty big splash. Goodyear has launched a private-label Aquatred with TBC, and it has launched a Kelly Aquaflow and an Eagle Aquatred. Gault has created an "aqua" segment in the tire industry and plans to dominate it.

One benefit of reducing dependence on the OEMs is that a tire company's product-development and marketing decisions can be based on consumer tire preference rather than OEM tire preferences. OEMs want a cheap tire, and they want a fuel-efficient tire. Drivers want a safe tire. That is a fundamental difference. Why should a company spend a lot of money developing a cheap, fuel-efficient tire when replacement-tire buyers will pay much more for a safe tire? Because of the Aquatred, Goodyear is now the safety company. The product is enjoying a halo effect.

The Cooper Tire Approach

Cooper Tire is one of the most successful tire companies in the world. Cooper's operating margins run about 13 percent, in comparison with Goodyear's 6–7 percent.

Cooper Tire is primarily a private-label tire company that sells almost exclusively in the U.S. market under the Cooper brand but also under other manufacturer's brands, such as Western Auto, TBC, and Winston Tires. It does not generally sell consumers their first replacement tire, but it will sell them their second or third replacement tire, when brand loyalty has diminished.

In the 1970s and 1980s, numerous gasoline stations shifted from selling automobile service along with the fuel they sold to selling snack foods along with self-service fuel. Consumers who in the 1970s could go to their local service stations to have tires installed on their cars had to turn primarily to the independent tire dealers. This shift played directly to Cooper's advantage, because the independent

dealer is Cooper's primary customer.

Another trend that has been helpful to Cooper is the big increase in the number of ten-year-old (and older) cars on the road in the United States. These cars are typically bought by low-income individuals in the used-car market for relatively little money, and if the car is worth $500, the owner is not likely to put a $500 set of tires on it. Instead, he or she will put a $200 set of tires on it. This trend in older cars played into Kelly-Springfield's market also.

■ *Product, excess capacity, and competition.* Cooper takes advantage of the commodity nature of the product. Its approach is based on the theory that, in a commodity business, the low-cost producer will be the one best able to survive any price war. Cooper is a low-cost producer in what is essentially a commodity business; it has no advertising and no R&D. Cooper is happy to sit back, relax, look at what is big in OE, and then reverse-engineer it. It differentiates itself from the competition by maintaining low-cost production. In addition, it keeps its balance sheet in great condition.

■ *Customer purchasing power.* Cooper has nothing to do with the OE tire market. It supplies the OE market with rubber products on which the returns are somewhat better than on tires, but it simply does not want to be an OE tire supplier.

■ *Strategic limitations.* The drawbacks to Cooper's strategy are as follows: First, Cooper may be technologically disadvantaged; it will not have the first and the newest product to market.

Second, it has little market diversity. Because it is 80 percent a U.S. replacement-tire company, if the North American replacement market declines, as it did in the summer of 1993, Cooper will suffer. Goodyear, in contrast, has only 20–25 percent of its business in the U.S. replacement-tire market. Goodyear also sells general rubber products, sells in the U.S. OE market, and sells in Europe and Latin America.

In addition, Cooper has limited resources relative to larger companies. As Bridgestone and Michelin recover, they may recognize the substantial amounts of money being made in the private-label business, and they may want a piece of that for themselves.

The competitive threat of Goodyear and Kelly-Springfield working together closely, as with the Aquatred, illustrates Cooper's vulnerability. After it became apparent that Aquatred and the strategy of introducing such products directly in the replacement market were going to make a big impact in Cooper's market, Cooper decided that it would have an aqua tire of its own by 1993 and that it would be 40 percent cheaper than Goodyear's. At this juncture, Goodyear's new strategy of working with

Kelly-Springfield became increasingly important. Gault knew that low-price knock-offs of the Aquatred would appear in the replacement-tire market, but he could simply give the technology to Kelly, and Kelly could offer a low-cost product in front of, or at the same time as, the knock-offs.

Cooper was indeed late to the market. General was actually the first low-price knock-off. TBC, the largest tire distributor in the United States, went to Kelly for its aqua tire. Big O Tire is sharing an aqua-tire mold with ten private-label customers.

Three months after Cooper decided to build an aqua tire, the company decided its customers do not want one, so it canceled (or postponed) its plans for an aqua tire. TBC, in contrast, has stated that its customers love the aqua product and that it did not order enough of them, and Goodyear's Aquatred was quite successful. Apparently, customers did want an aqua but they were already getting it from Cooper's competitors.

In the end, Cooper decided that it needed an aqua tire after all. CEO Ivan Gorr said, "Our customers want one. It is not a large market, but we need it as a merchandising tool." He noted that the company probably would not make any money on the product.

If the Aquatred story is an isolated instance, it will not change the industry; if it is a sign of the way the industry is going in the future, it means a fundamental change in the rules of competition and risks for a company like Cooper. The change in new-product launches creates a change in the decision tree that replacement-tire and private-label companies follow. The old approach was to look at the OE market when a new product was introduced to determine whether the after-market for it would be large. If the product was on a high-selling new car, then the decision was: yes, develop the product and make a lot of money. If the OE market indicated the number of sales would be small, then the old approach dictated not spending resources to enter that market.

Decisions in the new environment must be made without the OE-market input. Now the tire company has to build the product first. If the market is big, the company will make money. If the company spends a lot of money to build a product and the market turns out to be small, it loses a lot of money. If it does not build the product and the market turns out to be big, it leaves money on the table. Inherently, therefore, the risk for a replacement-tire product is greater today than it has been. Companies make decisions based on estimates and probabilities.

Tracking the Industry

In tracking the industry on a day-to-day basis, the

first thing to examine is the price environment. Figuring out what is going on with prices per se, however, is very difficult. Dealers will reveal a little bit, and tons of tire ads can be found almost daily in the newspapers. Also, the government publishes data. This information may not be totally reliable, but it is consistent; so if it is unreliable, it is consistently unreliable. **Figure 4** shows year-to-year changes in the producer price index, which comes out every month, for the past three years. As shown, 1991 was a great year, prices slipped in 1992 and then improved, and 1993 started off well but is now faltering.

Figure 4. Producer Price Index: All Tires
(year-to-year percentage change)

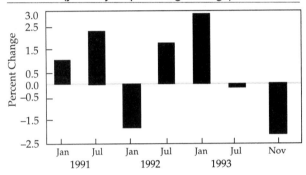

Source: PaineWebber.

Another important factor to examine is materials; about 50 percent of the materials costs of a tire company is rubber, synthetic and natural. Synthetic rubber is typically, depending on the tire, used more than natural rubber but they are somewhat substitutable. Synthetic rubbers are composed of various commodity chemicals—petrochemicals, to be precise—which means their prices are driven by the price of oil. The cost of oil, for chemicals and for energy, is an important element in tire making. In fact, every dollar increase in the price of oil leads to about a 17-cent increase in costs per tire.

That increase assumes, however, that the commodity chemical companies can pass along the oil-related price increases. Luckily for the tire industry—and unluckily for the chemical industry—overcapacity in some commodity chemicals constrains that pass-through. As **Figure 5** shows, from 1988 through 1990, prices for the chemical ingredients of synthetic rubber were high; then in 1991, prices started to fall. They remain sluggish in early 1994.

Natural rubber prices appear daily in the *Wall Street Journal*. Because the rubbers are somewhat substitutable, prices of natural rubber have somewhat mirrored the pattern of synthetic rubber, as shown in **Figure 6**.

To determine what is happening to margins, an

Figure 5. Prices of Ingredients of Synthetic Rubber
(cents per pound)

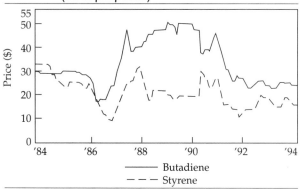

Source: PaineWebber.

Figure 7. Tire Manufacturers' Margins

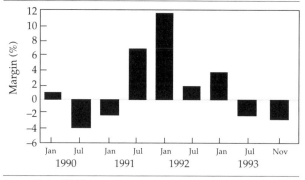

Source: PaineWebber.

analyst can compare the percentage change in tire prices with the percentage change in materials costs. This comparison does not indicate exactly how things are going, because the business involves large fixed costs and because demand and mix issues enter the picture; large tires provide a much higher profit than small tires, for example. In general, however, if prices are increasing faster than materials costs, tire company margins are likely to widen, which is essentially what has happened. As **Figure 7** shows, 1991 through early 1992 was a time of the best of all worlds in this industry—rising prices, falling materials costs, and rising demand. Some analysts were fooled, in fact, into thinking 1991 and 1992 could be setting a trend and volumes would grow from that trendline. Now, however, the industry is in almost the worst of all worlds—weak prices, weak demand, and materials costs that are not declining.

Analysts can also track the demand side. One approach is to use data on tire demand published by the Rubber Manufacturers Association. The data are lagged by about three months, however, so they tell only what has been. To predict what will be, analysts can examine such data as the all-systems vehicle mileage, which is total miles traveled and only slightly lagged, collected by the U.S. Department of

Transportation. As shown in **Table 10**, those data indicate demand is reasonably strong.

Another set of demand data to track is truck tonnage. The American Truck Association publishes the data shown in **Table 11** on how much tonnage is being hauled by trucks. Heavy-truck demand is strong domestically at the moment.

Truck tonnage and miles driven are leading indicators of retread demand and heavy-truck tire demand. Thus, such statistics are more important for retreaders, such as Bandag, Treadco, Brad Ragan, or Oliver (a division of Standard Products), than for new-tire manufacturers. Bandag's domestic unit sales have been up about 9 percent.

For valuing the company stocks, comparing the tire industry with general industrial production and capacity utilization is useful. The point is to determine whether the industry is growing faster or slower than the general economy. If it is growing faster, the companies' stock prices are likely to grow faster than the general market. **Table 12** allows a comparison of 1991–93 figures for the general economy with those for the rubber and plastics industry. The table does not break out tire data, but it does give a general idea of what is going on in the industry.

Tracking the Stocks

The relative P/Es reveal that a lot of the valuation risk is external to the industry. **Table 13** shows four companies' P/Es relative to the S&P 500 and historical levels, and the companies' total value (total capitalization; market value of equity plus debt) to EBITD (earnings before interest, taxes, and depreciation). Valuation risk was a problem in 1993, but it decreased as 1994 began.

Goodyear can be used to illustrate building a valuation case for one of the tire companies: First, consider Goodyear's P/E relative to the S&P 500. As shown in **Figure 8**, prior to 1986, the market would pay somewhere between a 90 percent and a 120 percent multiple for Goodyear stock; after 1987, it

Figure 6. Rubber Spot Prices
(cents per sheet pound)

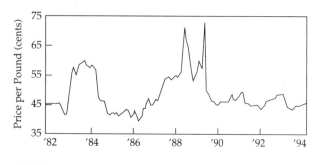

Source: PaineWebber.

Table 10. All-Systems Mileage

Month	1989	Year-to-Year Percent Change	1990	Year-to-Year Percent Change	1991	Year-to-Year Percent Change	1992	Year-to-Year Percent Change	1993	Year-to-Year Percent Change
January	159.8	7.3%	163.2	2.1%	157.9	−3.2%	165.6	4.9%	168.5	1.8%
February	146.7	3.5	153.7	4.8	153.4	−0.2	159.7	4.1	160.2	0.4
March	175.0	4.2	180.1	2.9	179.1	−0.6	183.8	2.6	184.7	0.5
April	174.3	4.5	180.0	3.3	179.5	−0.3	184.6	2.8	189.6	2.7
May	184.8	3.8	189.1	2.3	191.9	1.5	195.7	2.0	201.0	2.7
June	184.1	3.0	189.7	3.0	193.5	2.0	196.6	1.6	201.8	2.6
July	191.0	3.4	195.8	2.5	198.4	1.3	204.5	3.1	210.7	3.1
August	194.2	5.3	198.1	2.0	204.1	3.0	206.2	1.0	212.3	3.0
September	177.3	3.6	179.4	1.2	183.6	2.3	190.5	3.8	195.8	2.8
October	182.6	4.3	182.6	0.0	188.5	3.2	194.8	3.3		
November	169.7	4.1	171.6	1.1	169.7	−1.1	178.0	4.9		
December	167.5	1.6	168.6	0.7	172.8	2.5	179.9	4.1		
Total	2,107.0	4.0%	2,151.9	2.1%	2,172.4	1.0%	2,239.8	3.1%	1,724.6	2.2%

Source: U.S. Department of Transportation.

was paying 50–70 percent of the market. In 1986, Goodyear had taken on $2 billion in debt to increase capital spending and build two new, state-of-the-art tire plants to supply OE tires. In effect, it spent a lot of money to build plants to supply GM with low-profit tires. It also took on more debt to fight off a takeover attempt. Goodyear's oil pipeline, which was a money loser, started to depreciate, and then the OE tire market fell apart. Prior to Gault's entrance, Goodyear's situation was terrible.

Figure 8. Goodyear P/E Relative to S&P Composite Index

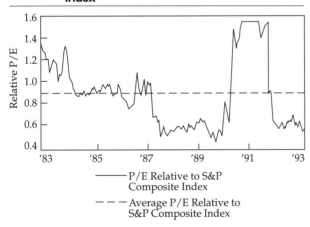

P/E Relative to S&P Composite Index

— — — Average P/E Relative to S&P Composite Index

Source: PaineWebber.

Currently, even in this difficult environment, the company continues to show earnings gains of 20–30 percent. The stock market, however, is still treating it like some big, bad cyclical stock. Goodyear's markets are mixed; European sales and North American replacement sales are lousy. What is going well for Goodyear at the moment are general products in North America and OE in Latin America—plus ag-

gressive cost cutting. As Goodyear posts earnings gains, the stock market will probably resume treating the company as it did in the early 1980s.

Cooper is a quality company that has reported a lot of quality earnings, and as **Figure 9** shows, its valuation sometimes gets out of hand. Cooper was trading at 120 percent of the market in early 1993. It had a huge P/E because it had a stellar 1992—volume up, prices up, materials costs down—and investors built a trend out of that improvement. In early 1993, inventory started to increase and revenues started to decline. The margins held at first because Cooper was producing more than it was selling; it kept the plants running. Suddenly, demand dropped and margins plunged. Cooper's valuation has since improved, and its quality of earnings should recover.

Whereas Goodyear entailed earnings risk for investors, it posed little valuation risk because of its low P/E. Cooper entailed not only an earnings risk

Figure 9. Cooper P/E Relative to S&P Composite Index

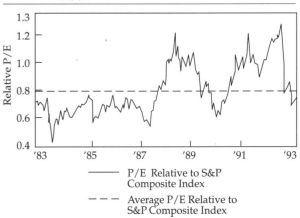

P/E Relative to S&P Composite Index

— — — Average P/E Relative to S&P Composite Index

Source: PaineWebber.

Table 11. Truck Tonnage Index
(1967 = 100)

Month	1988	Year-to-Year Percent Change	1989	Year-to-Year Percent Change	1990	Year-to-Year Percent Change	1991	Year to Year Percent Change	1992	Year-to-Year Percent Change	1993	Year-to-Year Percent Change
January	175.6	13.5%	177.1	0.9%	169.5	-4.3%	178.7	5.4%	196.0	9.7%	217.0	10.7%
February	173.6	8.4	171.0	-1.5	170.6	-0.2	174.8	2.5	194.1	11.0	213.1	9.8
March	175.9	9.5	167.7	-4.7	175.0	4.4	169.2	-3.3	198.3	17.2	209.4	5.6
April	177.1	12.2	173.2	-2.2	175.5	1.3	180.2	2.7	202.8	12.5	209.1	3.1
May	178.9	12.1	172.6	-3.5	176.4	2.2	176.8	0.2	202.6	14.6	215.4	6.3
June	181.6	13.0	169.5	-6.7	175.1	3.3	176.2	0.6	201.5	14.4	216.7	7.5
July	174.5	7.1	160.1	-8.3	176.9	10.5	188.0	6.3	209.9	11.6	214.1	2.0
August	178.3	8.8	168.5	-5.5	180.9	7.4	189.5	4.8	203.2	7.2	213.0	4.8
September	178.7	6.4	165.4	-7.4	176.5	6.7	188.2	6.6	200.6	6.6	212.1	5.7
October	177.4	4.4	166.9	-5.9	179.0	7.2	189.6	5.9	200.9	6.0	214.9	7.0
November	177.3	2.7	165.9	-6.4	176.1	6.1	189.4	7.6	199.8	5.5		
December	177.9	2.5	165.5	-7.0	166.2	0.4	185.2	11.4	205.1	10.7		
Average	177.2	8.3%	168.6	-4.9%	174.8	3.7%	182.2	4.2%	201.2	12.3%	213.5	6.2%

Sources: American Trucking Association and PaineWebber.

Table 12. Industrial Production and Capacity Utilization

	Industrial Production				Capacity Utilization			
Year	Rubber and Plastics	Year-to-Year Percent Change	All Industries	Year-to-Year Percent Change	Rubber and Plastics	Year-to-Year Percent Change	All Industries	Year-to-Year Percent Change
1991	104.5	–2.5%	104.1	–1.8%	80.4	–5.8%	79.2	–3.5%
1992	109.7	5.0	106.6	2.4	82.2	2.2	79.8	0.8
1993								
January	113.6	5.6	109.3	4.6	83.9	3.0	81.2	3.0
February	112.7	4.0	109.9	4.4	83.1	1.5	81.5	2.8
March	112.9	3.2	110.1	4.2	83.0	0.6	81.6	2.7
April	113.6	4.1	110.4	3.8	83.4	1.5	81.7	2.2
May	113.8	4.3	110.2	3.3	83.3	0.6	81.5	1.8
June	112.4	2.5	110.4	4.1	82.1	–0.2	81.5	2.5
July	113.0	2.1	110.9	3.8	82.3	–0.6	81.8	2.3
August	113.0	2.1	111.1	4.2	82.2	–0.5	81.8	2.6
September	114.5	5.6	111.0	4.5	83.0	2.7	81.6	2.9
October	114.8	4.5	112.2	4.4	83.0	1.6	82.4	2.8
November	114.9	3.2	113.2	4.4	82.9	0.4	83.0	2.8

Source: Federal Reserve Board.

but also valuation risk. With a P/E multiple of 25, the sudden fall in the earnings also brought down the P/E. A point was reached in early 1993, when Goodyear's market value of equity plus debt was just over two times Cooper's but Goodyear's revenues were eight times Cooper's. Something was not right, and that suspicion was confirmed by Cooper's earnings statement in the second quarter of 1993. Goodyear remains about 20 percent cheaper than Cooper, as seen in **Figure 10**.

Bandag is a U.S. retreader of truck tires. It supplies the tread rubber and has the largest share of that market. Many trucking associations use retreads because the economics favor them over new tires. The big slabs of rubber often seen on highways are retreads that have come off truck tires.

TBC is the largest tire distributor in the country. It is being affected by a weak replacement market, and the stock market has been spooked by its poor earnings, but valuations are improving.

Conclusion

The rubber and tire industry has many structural

Figure 10. Goodyear P/E Relative to Cooper P/E

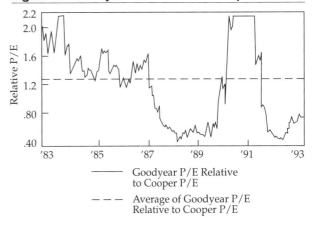

——— Goodyear P/E Relative to Cooper P/E

– – – Average of Goodyear P/E Relative to Cooper P/E

Source: PaineWebber.

problems, which are exacerbated by weak current demand and poor pricing. Some companies are following approaches to cope with those problems, however, and valuations are improving. In the near term, analysts should monitor demand and, more importantly, the quality of earnings.

Table 13. P/Es of Tire and Rubber Companies

	P/E		P/E Relative to S&P 500			Total Capitalization/ EBDIT	
Company	1993	1994	1993	1994	Historical	Current	Historical
Bandag	18.6	16.6	94%	95%	75–140%	10.4	5.0–12.6
Cooper	19.6	17.3	99	99	90–150	9.3	6.0–14.3
Goodyear	14.5	12.9	73	74	45–150	5.5	4.5– 9.0
TBC	16.2	14.3	82	82	50–105	10.9	5.0–15.8

Source: PaineWebber.

Note: As of January each year.

Question and Answer Session

Stephen J. Girsky

Question: Given the poor industry fundamentals, has any wealth been created in this industry during the past 10–20 years?

Girsky: No wealth has been created, but Goodyear is finally creating shareholder value. Michelin has made money in two of the past ten years. Cooper has created value for its shareholders, although value has been lost in the near term, which may or may not be a temporary setback. Aside from those two companies and some smaller players, the total value of this industry reflects little wealth creation or shareholder value.

Question: How does recycling affect the economics of the industry?

Girsky: Recycling will definitely be a growth business in the future. Tires do not degrade, so the problem is that big piles of tires are accumulating all over the place. Some recycling companies crumble them to use in cement or asphalt; they can pull the energy back out of the tires. That sort of recycling is still in its infancy, however.

Question: Do the manufacturers face litigation over the disposal of old tires?

Girsky: No litigation has occurred so far. The liability is unclear because the manufacturers sell the tires to the dealers. Some states are imposing a tax—for example, a dollar per tire on a new-tire sale—to pay for the disposal.

Moderator: In some case, states or municipalities have tried to col-

lect damages when a big tire dump started burning because that situation is a mess.

Question: What is the differential in cost between synthetic and natural rubber?

Girsky: Because the rubbers are somewhat substitutable in a tire, the cost differential is small. If one does get out of line with the other, companies correct the disparity right away.

Question: How are the tire companies performing in Europe, where the recession lingers, and what about consolidation in that industry?

Girsky: The companies got a little lucky in Europe. The snows came early in the winter of 1994, and in contrast to the United States, winter tires are a big business in Europe. The winter of 1993 was a lousy year for winter tires; tons of inventory were sitting around. When the snow came this year however, the companies were able to move that inventory out; so, the replacement-tire side has not been bad.

The OE side in Europe is still miserable, and the companies have many problems. Pirelli is highly leveraged and in a lot of trouble. The majority of its sales are in Italy, which is one of the weakest auto markets on the continent. Continental is heavily in Germany, which is stuck with high labor costs and a strong deutsche mark. In addition, these companies may not be large enough to compete in the 1990s.

Consolidation, however, does not seem to be likely. Pirelli and

Continental tried to get together, but it did not work out. Michelin cannot buy them. Goodyear has little appetite for buying a European tire company because it believes the West European market is and will remain unhealthy, in contrast to Latin America and Asia. Severe distress, more than at present, would be needed to force consolidation on the European companies.

Question: Have Bridgestone and Michelin pulled in their horns on geographical expansion, and if so, does Goodyear have a window of opportunity?

Girsky: Yes to both questions. Although Michelin and Bridgestone have recovered or are in the process of recovering from a profitability standpoint, they still have leverage that they need to work down in order to be competitive in the future.

Gault has accomplished his first two priorities at Goodyear—reducing debt and improving earnings per share. Now that he has built a competitive advantage, I expect to see a strategic plan announced. It will include heavy emphasis on Asia and Latin America, where the returns are much better than in North America, and some on Eastern Europe. Gault is retiring, so he will no doubt put the people in place to carry out geographical expansion. Gault has little desire to add capacity in, for example, Western Europe, but capacity has doubled in Thailand, Malaysia, and Indonesia. The company has announced a joint venture in India. Goodyear could use that capacity to export to North America.

Question: Can the high-end manufacturers, such as Goodyear or Michelin, do anything to make reverse engineering of their new products more difficult than it is?

Girsky: They claim they can, but history says otherwise. Michelin introduced the radial. Now everybody has radials. Goodyear sued General for patent infringement because General launched the Hydro 2000, but patent-infringement suits have generally been unsuccessful in this industry. So impeding reverse engineering is difficult. Goodyear has reduced the time competitors have for successful reverse engineering, which is a logical first step.

Question: Who are the suppliers of rubber for new automotive models such as Chrysler's JA or Ford's Windstar? Would such contracts mean significant business for them?

Girsky: I do not know which companies are supplying the Windstar; I would be shocked if Goodyear was not on the JA in some way. It is already on Chrysler's LH model and on all the Jeep Grand Cherokees.

Such business is meaningful only at the margin. Goodyear has about 80 percent of Chrysler's business, and Michelin the rest. Goodyear has about 40 percent of Ford; General, Bridgestone, and Michelin the rest. GM is about 50 percent Michelin, 30–40 percent Goodyear, and 5–10 percent General.

Question: *Consumer Reports* magazine has some influence with respect to the purchase of automobiles; do any of your contacts indicate that its ratings of tires are meaningful?

Girsky: *Consumer Reports* raved about the Aquatred when it first came out, saying it did better on wet roads than a General tire tested on dry roads. Having the Aquatred come out on top was one of the lucky breaks Goodyear got last year. Such ratings are part of the halo effect. So, at the margin, it probably helped sales.

Goodyear lost to Michelin in the J.D. Power and Associates Customer Satisfaction Index on OE tires, but Goodyear could never have won because of the way J.D. Power did the study; Michelin has launched many more OE tires than Goodyear.

Michelin does not think such rankings help. The companies differ in strategy and approach, however. Goodyear is going for safety; Michelin is going with high-quality, 80,000-mile, fuel-efficient tires. Michelin thinks the consumer wants long-lasting tires. Seeing how these differences play out in the future will be interesting.

Question: Do you foresee a large-scale introduction of "run-flat" tire technology any time soon?

Girsky: That technology is the next generation. Goodyear has a tire on the current Chevy Corvette that will run without air at 50 miles an hour for 200 miles. Bridgestone has a similar one, but it is a replacement tire and not sold as OE. Goodyear has had a run-flat tire for some time but the problem was to know when it was flat. Now cars have electronic displays that light up to indicate the tire is low on air.

Consumers will probably pay for this kind of tire; no one wants to be stuck, or have a family member stuck, out on the road late at night with a flat tire. The tire companies and OEs can work together on marketing run-flat tires. The product will also encourage brand loyalty, because if the tire is built for a special wheel that will run when the tire is flat, the consumer must go back and buy that brand of tire. That creates a bang for the buck in the replacement market.

Moderator: In addition to consumer demand for such a tire, OEs will be big proponents of this product because of the space and the weight the spare tire, jack, and all that gear involve. Auto companies are always looking for a way to take even as few as 10 pounds out of a vehicle structure. If the spare is eliminated, automakers can probably take out maybe 30 pounds in total and improve their packaging.

Question: Do you expect any reduction in tire overcapacity in the next few years?

Girsky: Overcapacity happens in waves. North American manufacturers were in a lot of trouble—plant closures, for example—during the late 1980s and early 1990s. Now the problem has shifted to Europe. Meanwhile, Bridgestone is adding capacity in the United States because importing from Japan has become completely uneconomical. In fact, with the yen: dollar exchange rate at 110, Goodyear says it can make money sending tires to Japan to put on cars that are then shipped back here.

The exit costs in this business are very high, which inhibits taking capacity out of the business. Industry analysts hope for a balanced level eventually, but I do not see it in the near term. The excess capacity simply moves around.

Question: Where will tires be sold in the future? Through what distribution outlets?

Girsky: People who buy tires based on price will go to one place; those with brand loyalty will go to another—a Goodyear dealer, for example. Some people are channel loyal. When Goodyear added Sears, it was recognizing that people buy tires at Sears because it is Sears, not necessarily because they can get what they want there; they do lots of other things there.

For the price conscious, the warehouse clubs have grown and grown. Every year they grow and increase their market share, and every year the tire companies say the clubs will never be big players or long-term players. In reality, the warehouse clubs will continue their penetration in the United States. I am not sure that they will be huge players, however.

I do foresee consolidation on the retail side. The mom-and-pop stores are going to have trouble competing against the big retail outlets—the Wal-Marts and the Kmarts of the world. Also, the replacement market will have increased power. It will never match that of the OE market, but it will be more diverse.

Question: Where do you see the replacement tire business in 1994 versus 1991? And if 1993 is down, do you view it as flat relative to 1991?

Girsky: The replacement tire market could be up 2 percent in 1994. This market does not change much; for it to grow more than 5 percent or shrink more than 5 percent in any given year would be unusual. When the full data for 1993 are available, they could show the replacement market as flat or down a few percent. I think 1994 will be up a little from 1993, so in general, it will be better than 1991.

Question: Do you think recently announced price increases will stick?

Girsky: Historically, about 40 percent of announced price increases stick. I find it odd that companies start announcing these price increases in January to take effect March l. A company could be sending a message to all its competitors that March l is the day; the competitors have six to eight weeks to think about it, and sure enough, everyone gets the message and raises prices. Another thing the companies may be trying to do is to pump up first-quarter demand; a lot of wholesalers will buy tires in front of a potential price increase. If true demand is not there, the price rise is not going to stick. I doubt they will get 3 percent; 1 percent or 1.5 percent will be a victory.

Question: What is the price differential between a Goodyear OE tire—that is, what GM, say, pays for a tire—and that same tire at a Goodyear store?

Girsky: I would guess GM probably pays $25–$30 for a tire for which the consumer pays about $75 at the store.

Question: Do prices in the OE market and prices in the replacement market influence each other?

Girsky: No, there is no direct correlation.

Question: Can Cooper spend like the big guys on marketing, and if it does, what are the implications for its cost structure?

Girsky: Spending on marketing would not be in Cooper's nature or history. Building a brand from nothing is very tough; Bridgestone has experienced this problem; in fact, it bought Firestone because it wanted a brand. To market like the big companies do, therefore, would cost Cooper a lot of money, and the company is not interested in that.

A big issue concerning Cooper is the company's attitude that nothing changes very fast in this business so it does not have to worry about change. That attitude may or may not be true.

Question: How does discretionary advertising expense on Goodyear's part—blimps and racing, for example—affect its cost structure? Does such spending reduce Goodyear's competitiveness?

Girsky: It is hard to measure the bang for the buck in these areas. When Gault arrived at Goodyear, management was debating internally why the company was in the racing business. It spends $30–$50 million on racing tires. In the end, Goodyear stayed in the racing business because of the high visibility. In the past, the company gave the tires away; today, the company gives tires to, say, the top three drivers, and other people pay for their tires. The company also previously paid for its grandstand at the Indy 500; it now gets the grandstand for free.

I don't know whether racing provides a good return on investment. Perhaps the money could be better spent somewhere else. Some half a million people go to the Indy 500, however, so Goodyear gets a lot of exposure. Firestone is getting back into furnishing Indy tires, which will create some healthy competition.

The blimp is another interesting issue. When it was the only blimp in town, one could make a case for it. Now that it is not the only blimp in town, its effectiveness is questionable.

Moderator: The stories about Gault are endless, but a particularly good one relates to racing tires. In the auto magazines, when the Indy winner and car are pictured, the big tires have

"Goodyear" on them in white letters. At the racetrack, however, the tires do not have that printing. When Gault asked why, he was told that the tires do not come from Goodyear with the printing, so after each race, "Goodyear" is inked onto the tires for the photo sessions. Gault wanted everybody to see "Goodyear" on every tire, however, not just in the magazine, so he had the company find a way to mold the name into the tire.

Girsky: Gault is also leveraging the racing-tire publicity more now than in the past. He makes some people pay for it, for example, and he has some of the drivers attend the annual meetings. They are also showing up at other events for him now. In addition, because Goodyear has been the only tire supplier at Indy, the company was able to run an ad reading, "These are the only tires that can take Turn One at Indy."

Question: The Aquatred, Wrangler, and some of the other new products were in the Goodyear pipeline before Gault arrived. Can subsequent new products be as dramatic?

Girsky: They were in the pipeline, but Goodyear was doing nothing with them. At an analysts' meeting, Goodyear allowed us a peek at the Aquatred, but when we asked the CEO at the time, "When are you introducing this? How much is it going to cost? What are the benefits?," he would not answer.

That attitude was one of the fundamental problems Gault confronted. Goodyear had great products on the shelf and should have been using them to push an advantage. The Aquatred was a consumer product that could be used to differentiate the company.

Goodyear is now expanding the Aquatred line with the Eagle Aquatred. It is a little different, in that it is speed rated and designed for the Lexus, Corvette, or other high-end models. The Regatta is a new touring tire. The company had asked dealers what it could do to make their jobs easier, and the dealers responded that the tires were ugly, that the company needed something different, something that looked fresh. The result was the Regatta.

Goodyear has been doing much more market research—finding out what the customer wants—than ever before in this industry, which will probably give it an advantage.

Question: Goodyear is really the only American tire company left. How long does Gault stay at Goodyear, and is there a clear successor? How strong is management at Goodyear if you set aside Gault, and has the Gault effect on the stock played out fully yet?

Girsky: These questions are common; investors want to know if they should sell their Goodyear six months before Stan Gault leaves or six months after. Gault is supposed to retire at the end of 1994. He owns at least one million shares of stock, and I believe he wants to see that stock go up between now and then. He will not be judged on the stock price at the end of 1994, however, he will be judged on the stock price at the end of 1996.

Therefore, today is the time for Gault to build the future strategy. It is time to communicate a strategy and put people in place to execute it. Only Gault can communicate that strategy to the investment community because he has such a rapport with the community. The next generation of managers at Goodyear, no matter who they are, will not be able to have the same effect on the market as Gault has.

Rumor has it that Gault wants an outsider to head the company and that he wants a marketing type. Whatever choice Gault makes, Goodyear has plenty of high-quality people who have survived the political wars, and have avoided the political wars altogether, who could lead the company. I am not worried in the least about management succession at this company.

The Future of the Global Automotive Industry

Martin L. Anderson
Associate Director, International Motor Vehicle Program
Massachusetts Institute of Technology

Change in the global auto industry is causing shifts of power, particularly from assembly to distribution, restructuring, and altered determinants of success. Future growth will come to the companies that are made hungry and creative by a lack of resources, that focus on systems and on gaining and applying knowledge, that develop close relationships with customers, that have vision, and that, above all, have energetic managers adept at networking.

Although investors can make a ton of money on the cyclical movement of the automotive equities for various market-related reasons, some strong fundamental, long-term, underlying trends are at work in the global industry. These trends are easy to identify but also easy to forget. This presentation reviews basic trends and the forces behind them.

The global perspective is not that of the 15-million-unit North American market but of a 50-million-unit market. This market is continuing to grow. From the standpoint of vehicle output, at the assembler/producer level, the global industry will likely grow at a 2–4 percent rate for the long term.

The high social utility of vehicular travel tends to reinforce long-term industry growth. Any country that gets any form of income will spend it on automobiles. In Central Europe after the Berlin Wall collapsed, one of the first things people did was to pull their money out of their mattress and buy Mercedes, Volvos, high-end Saabs, and BMWs. The global demand, latent or otherwise, is strong. Therefore, at the global level, barring wars or major political upheavals, the industry will continue to grow.

The developed vehicle markets, which have decomposed into many segments since the 1970s, will remain fragmented. The multiplicity of global producers has reinforced this fragmentation: Even if all the companies try to slow their product development cycles, the total rate of new models in the market will not slow significantly.

Competitive Forces

Some fundamental competitive forces are influencing markets and industry leadership around the world. The first major factor is the competition between the U.S. and Japanese industries. The U.S.–Japan balance of power has not yet been worked out. Since about 1980, Japan has been winning. Today, for a variety of reasons, Japan has slowed down, but it has not stalled. The Japanese auto industry has slowed down previously (in the late 1950s, 1973, and briefly in the 1980s), and each time the Japanese have restructured and come back strong. If the U.S. industry makes use of the strength it has gathered, particularly during the past five-to-seven years, the battle will be relatively even. If not, some of the Japanese competitors will come on strong again. This particular power struggle will determine much of what will happen in the global industry during the next 10–12 years.

Competition for the markets ringing the Indian Ocean is extremely complicated because the markets are highly segmented and culturally distinct. Growth in the Asian markets is expected, but whether these markets will spawn Western-style vehicle fleet sizes is questionable. Cars are a cultural, emotional commodity. Thus, the competition will be complex, and what develops will be a major factor determining Asian demand 8–15 years from today. Everybody is waiting for the mainland Chinese market to open, but the timing is uncertain. As with the Russian market, Chinese demand, when it truly begins to accelerate, is likely to be "infinite and growing" for a long time.

The auto companies in the developed countries of Europe are at the stage the Americans were at in the mid-1970s. They are just beginning to wake up to the full intensity of global competition. Thus, the European auto companies will be under extreme pressure for the next five-to-seven years. European emissions regulations will put Europeans under cash flow pressure similar to what American automakers faced in the early 1980s. The auto companies' challenges have little to do with the political situation involving the European Union, but that wrangling is not helping their competitiveness. How Europeans come out of the current structural market shift will determine to a great extent who the world players are in 2005.

The industry in Central Europe, including Russia, is an enigma at the moment. It may, however, become a high-quality, high-skilled, low-cost place to produce components that gives assemblers in the developed European countries more options than they have at present. The area contains some really good auto people and some extremely good crafts people, who have been held back for about 50 years. They can probably become a force similar to what Spain has represented since about 1985 in Europe and what Mexico may represent to the United States.

The situation in Mexico and South America has in the past been similar to the Asian situation: The auto industries have risen and fallen; they have been profitable and they have been unprofitable. Something fundamentally different is now occurring in Mexico, however. It has built an industry at the component level and later will build up a motorized infrastructure. Mexico has probably preempted Brazil as the place where the industry in South America is going to grow up.

Strategic Growth Factors

During the past 15 or so years, the global automotive industry has become more stable than in its earlier history; the war zones have shrunk somewhat, and companies are not thrashing each other as hard. Japan's strength has dropped off during the past three-to-four years, the U.S. automakers' strength has picked up, and the industry is in a pause. The stability is temporary, however. The issue for the next 20 years will be decided by what happens during the current relative stability. That issue is: Where will the new growth be?

To identify and understand the likely growth companies in the global industry, analysts need to review how growth occurs within a somewhat mature industry. One fact often unnoticed by analysts concentrating on regional markets is that, viewed on a global scale, the top leaders in any industry change every ten years. If the scope of analysis is only the North American producers, the top competitors appear to have been relatively stable for the past 50 years. If the scope is global, however, new companies will be seen to have emerged to dominate the

leadership. In any ten-year slice of a global industry, the list of the top five or ten players always changes; a new competitor always comes out of nowhere and generates value. What drives this growth?

▪ *Scarce resources.* The companies that have grown have almost always had some form of scarce resources. Scarce resources are key to growth because they create hungry organizations. Toyota and General Motors will illustrate.

Until four years ago, Toyota had always managed to create growth, but not because of its wealth. Analysts sometimes refer to Toyota as "Toyota Bank" because of its vast financial resources. Although Toyota was a rich organization, however, it consciously—as a management strategy—forced people to live as if their resources were scarce. The company had lots of cash, but it never provided the cash to the product development teams and the manufacturing organizations. For example, the GM–Toyota joint venture, NUMMI (New United Motor Manufacturing, Inc.), had two floors in 1984 and petitioned Toyota to redo the escalator between the floors for $250,000. Toyota management said it would give $250 for a sign reading, "Walk up the escalator; it is good for your heart."

General Motors, on the other hand, before its problems began, had experienced a long period with lots of resources. Moreover, it was operating primarily in a North American market that was protected from the rest of the world market until about 1973. Therefore, its resources were never challenged. Such a company has a hard time thinking its way and acting its way into a growth curve.

To find growth in the future, look for the hungry people and the hungry companies.

▪ *Focus on knowledge.* Also look for the companies built on knowledge and learning, not personal power. Although most people think the cost of a vehicle is mainly materials and assembly labor, deeper analysis indicates that most of the cost is the know-how and labor of all kinds of workers—from managers to designers to technicians and so on—and of outside equipment makers, and of capital suppliers. In addition, the automobile is a set of engineering systems (fuel, braking, transmission, sound, etc.) organized to come from systems of companies. Therefore, the dominant cost dimensions of a vehicle are determined by knowledge and systems.

The growth companies of the future will be organizations that know how to manage fragile investment in intellectual capital and that are designed to take in information, use it quickly, and not worry about who remains in power or who owns the information.

When analysts talk to companies, they can immediately sense whether they are knowledge-based or power-based, bureaucratic organizations. Look for those based on the search and use of knowledge.

■ *Close relationship with customers.* The growth company will have active involvement in customers' lives. Involvement does not mean merely studying the customer. GM has a new campaign in which it must "analyze" its customers to develop its vehicles. That approach is not as useful as what Honda used to do, which is live with customers and watch in depth how customers use their vehicles. Many companies other than Honda now live with their customers. GM's Cadillac Division did, and the result was a dramatically different car.

■ *Vision.* The growth companies will have vision, and the vision will be shared by all employees. That sounds like "motherhood," but it is really true: A company must know where it is going, and it must share this destination with its employees.

■ *Networking.* The final major characteristic of the future global growth companies will be energetic managers who network and build trust among the systems of companies that create a vehicle. In Europe and North America, the auto industry has typically been vertically organized around manufacturing processes. (Japan's cultural history led to a more weblike structure.) Market fragmentation, globalization, and rapid product cycles are forcing a change, however, in the typical Western structure. The old style of vertical integration has become a liability, and new forms of networked organizations are proving to be the most flexible and profitable. This pattern is similar to the dominant pattern in the electronics industry, with its prevalence of complex alliances and contracting. To oversimplify, what has happened in the auto industry is that the product development cycles have become so short that the stability that used to be possible in product development is disappearing. Therefore, companies cannot build a GM-type, vertically integrated industry; they must do what has been normal behavior in the electronics industry for 10–15 years—networking, constantly searching for people who will help, gaining their trust, and figuring out together how to make money in a short time. Chrysler, for example, is doing it today. BMW is doing it. Networking will be the dominant force in creating growth in the worldwide auto industry during the next decade, and it presents a unique challenge for the companies: how to create value with partners one does not own.

Honda's growth illustrates well the benefits of a networking strategy. Honda had few resources, a small knowledge base, no *keiretsu*, and no government support. The government refused to support the company's efforts. The company had great vision, however, and a lot of creative technology. It went out and networked. The result of the network-ing is a strong supplier relationship. For example, Asahi Glass Company networked with Honda and shaped Honda's growth curve. Today, if a supplier wants to sell glass to Honda, that company has a low probability of making a sale.

Assessing the Auto Producers

Can another company duplicate Honda's experience? Will it be the Koreans? Three Korean companies together form the total Korean auto industry. About every three years, someone declares that the Koreans will take over the auto industry. Unlike Honda, however, the Korean companies do not have a vision, so it will be difficult for them to duplicate the success of Honda. They do not have the same growth elements that Honda had. Most of the Korean auto companies are extensions of large bureaucracies that have provided funding and given orders to produce cars. The Koreans need both technology and an offshore base, and they are using a build-and-export model that the Japanese have worn out.

Thus, the question remains: Which producer will have the growth? Will it be Chrysler? Everybody loves Chrysler; some lived through the Chrysler bankruptcy, watched it hit the wall twice, and cheered as, with scarce resources but with vision and energy, the company came back. It has enhanced product development by networking with dealers and with suppliers. Chrysler must keep the product hits coming, however; otherwise, its credibility will begin to drop off.

The situation is similar for Saturn, which was a wonderful operation when it had a 28-day supply of inventory. Today, it has 98 days of inventory. The test of that organization, therefore, is right now: Can it keep that trust and networking going in the face of slow sales? It probably can, but the test will be tough.

Growth will be coming from the Japanese producers. They have been through slowdowns before, and every time they get hit, they think up something new. The key will be their ability to digest an international production base.

GM is resurrecting itself, but it still has too many resources. The big problem for GM from an operating standpoint is that many people in the company have not recognized the challenge because they are still having meetings about having meetings. In a large organization that has lots of resources, people do not feel problems in their guts; the need for change does not hit them. GM has a lot of wonderful, extremely skilled people, but it is difficult to pull the old organization apart and give them direction, get them cranked up, and get them going in new directions. Nevertheless, GM will probably come back strong after it recognizes the situation—after, say, two more market cycles.

BMW is a classic example of a company that was pushed back by the Japanese in many of its markets and then relearned many lessons. BMW is beginning to hit stride again, just as it did in the early 1970s.

Many people, especially in Washington, D.C., and in southern California, are expecting new industries to crop up in connection with electric vehicles, but do not bet the ranch on this prospect yet. A number of basic problems are working against the growth of electric automobiles; for example, 3 British thermal units of fossil energy are needed to create 1 Btu of electricity in a car. New electric vehicles will come into the market, but this segment is not going to dominate the market.

Changes in the Industry System

The auto industry is a massive system of links between dealers, assemblers, and suppliers, and the global industry is worth at least $1.5 trillion. That figure includes assembly, distribution, service (which includes dealers, after-market service, and used cars), and suppliers. This structure can create new growth businesses outside the assembler segment. The companies may not be $30 billion businesses, but they will certainly be $1 billion and $2 billion businesses.

Everybody pays attention to assembly, but most of the value in the industry is created outside the assemblers. People talk a lot about companies reducing labor from 34 hours a car to 15 hours a car, but those figures pertain only to assemblers. The industrywide system that puts a car together takes something on the order of 125–175 labor-hours and often an additional 25–50 hours of management time. More hours are added by the distribution system through dealers, maintenance, and repair.

Thus, some 50,000 people in the industry system may be trying to get good cars out the door for a given brand of vehicle. These people must interact as a system: If a salesperson says something stupid to a customer who walks into a dealership, that salesperson has destroyed the system; 50,000 people contributed 125–175 hours of work to a car, and now the consumer does not want the car. Coordination is what counts in this system.

System coordination, not the labor at assembly plants, is the strong point of the Japanese system. The Japanese would love for auto analysts and competitors to continue paying attention to reducing labor content in assembly plants, because the real key is in the suppliers and the distribution infrastructure.

Systematic changes occurring in the industry hold significance for analysts who are intent on following the shifts in value. During the 1970s and 1980s, most structural change was taking place at the assembler level. Now, the most significant structural changes are taking place among the supply base, the distribution system, and in the postassembly processes (service, repair, used vehicles, recycling, financing). Value creation—product and equity—is moving beyond the province of assemblers to a wide variety of hardware and service providers.

Concentration has been growing among suppliers and dealers. The top ten North American original-equipment (OE) suppliers are billion-dollar companies. The top ten dealers in North America are also billion-dollar businesses, or approaching this size.

A rough estimate of the annual global sales in distribution and services is $300–$400 billion a year. Not much of this part of the value chain is available in public equity today, however; these segments contain many very rich, privately held companies. The trick is to get them to go public, which they may do.

Since about 1974, the automotive industry has been experiencing a "cost-push" problem as variable costs have become fixed. In North America, cost-push pricing has slowed per capita vehicle demand for years. Producers have won some hard battles for quality and vehicle design, and they have achieved breathing room through trade actions, European product mistakes, medium-term currency conditions, and Japanese economic conditions, but they have not been able to reduce real costs. Therefore, the market is open for price competition as in no market since the 1970s.

As the cost of producing a car rose for the assemblers, those pressures spilled over into two places. The first thing the assemblers did was lean on their suppliers; they cut prices and, therefore, the suppliers' margins. Now, the assemblers are beginning to cut margins in distribution and at the dealerships. Thus, 20 years of accumulated cost pressure, primarily in North America and Europe but some in Japan, have moved to the end of the system.

Because the whole system has now been affected, the whole system may change. Making money in the dealer business is becoming more and more difficult. Dealers worldwide are lucky if they can net 1 percent of sales. Dealers need to earn more, so they have begun to use their unique power to change the structure of the industry.

Demanding customers give dealers their power. Thirty years ago or so, customers could choose among few types of cars. Today, buyers can choose among many different types of cars, and they can find something tailored specially for them. Moreover, if they do not like it, they can complain. This market demand is what fragments the vehicle market; it takes power away from the large, integrated companies like GM and gives it to niche players. More importantly, customer demands give dealers a form of control. The importance of dual dealers or multibrand stores is that, through them, dealers create a portfolio business that can satisfy demanding customers. They have created a power base.

A different type of distribution business is under way in North America and will develop later in Europe. Smart, sophisticated dealers recognize the potential for creating financial value through portfolios of businesses. A car is sold three-to-seven times during its lifetime, and the essential question for any dealer is how many times it can make money selling the same car.

The portfolio business was designed to enable a dealer to "sell" a car multiple times. The business works as follows: If a customer is really willing to buy a new car, the dealer will sell him or her one. (The customer has to keep the car for up to 12 years, however, in order to win after paying the large depreciation hit, and most people do not keep their cars that long.) The portfolio dealer will also sell the customer a used or program car.

Program cars are a really hot business, primarily because consumers have realized that if they wait six months after a new model comes out, they can buy one at a 20–30 percent discount. Even though the Hertz Rent A Car and Avis Rent A Car program cars have moved toward auction markets, which will absorb the best used cars, smart dealers have identified other sources of program cars. This strategy indicates that dealers are thinking more like manufacturing and service conglomerates and less like dealers. The strategy will be to sell a portfolio of services, new cars, and used cars. If they need a "supplier base," a source for used cars, they will create networks to provide it.

Another dealer strategy is leasing cars. In this strategy, the dealer is selling the depreciation only; the customer does not have to buy the car for life, he or she just pays for constantly driving a new car. From the perspective of the new portfolio-building dealer, leasing is a systematic way to sell consumers depreciation. The customer's income level allows the customer to continue to afford the lease even if interest rates increase. Then, depending on how the lease is structured, dealers may have the opportunity to resell that car to the person waiting for a "new" used car (like a program car).

European and Japanese companies have long recognized the profitability of multiple sales of the same car. Toyota, Nissan, Mercedes, and others have used-car companies that repackage used cars and sell them in Asia, Turkey, and elsewhere. Some U.S. dealers are following a scaled-down version of this strategy. The dealers think of the strategy as not

selling cars, however, but selling paper. From the dealer's point of view, all kinds of customers are coming in looking for different types of transportation products—used, new, or leased—and the dealer is trying to generate various contracts in the form of notes or leases.

The result is the creation of financial factories. Today those factories are the captive finance companies of the assemblers, who understand the paper business best and are today providing the best financial product for the customers. That situation could change, however. The dealers who are building portfolio businesses could arrange financing independently of the assemblers' finance factories. Such dealers would have negotiating power and could pull from the factory of their choice. This kind of change would fit with the factors that are pushing the assemblers away from distribution—lack of skill in distribution and the rising costs to car companies of maintaining expensive distribution systems.

Some people at the vehicle producers would like to eliminate their captive dealer networks because, then, the dealers who are really good at distribution could take over, and the producers could do something else with the money presently spent on dealerships and servicing distributors. The people at the car companies who think this way are often the manufacturing people. They used to be the conservatives who would not change; but today, many marketing people are the ones who are still thinking about life as it was ten years ago.

Enough of the new kind of thinking about distribution is under way that it may produce a completely different way of doing business internationally. Distribution structures that follow the new model already exist in the Third World. As European dealer structures become less factory dominated, European and North American dealer groups may quickly occur.

One last area to note in connection with dealers is digital technology. Digital communication technology makes possible all kinds of changes in an industry structure. Although this factor has been somewhat like the Chinese market—always just around the corner—the dealership segment of the automotive industry is truly beginning to experience the benefits of digital communications. Imagine, for example, an "automated teller machine" that has in it a two-way multimedia, video-driven data base. Such a device is not pie in the sky; it exists, and it contains a realm of information that can be passed from the company to the customer. When auto customers walk up to such a device, they can touch the screen and ask it to tell them about vehicles. They can access branched data bases about the vehicles' options, and they can also ask about such matters as lease costs.

Another characteristic of such a machine is that it can clock the milliseconds a person stays at each level in the data base, so it can reveal which options packages are of most interest to the customer. Such information is not very useful in a single interaction, but the 2–4 million such transactions that take place each month can provide product development people a rich data base. The assemblers can also use such information to coordinate scheduling, factory loading, and so forth. Companies like Toyota and Honda have the sort of global forecasting and delivery systems that can take great advantage of this kind of technology.

Use of digital communications technology will not suddenly explode in the automotive industry, but during the next five-to-seven years, analysts should follow companies that are likely to provide this service to automobile producers.

In summary, because of the current high price umbrella, the global industry system can expect some form of new entrant that can reduce the effective cost of buying new vehicles. The new entrant is unlikely to be a new auto company, despite Honda's example, but it might be a focused division, a powerful platform team, or a new venture among existing players. An alternative is that a building accumulation of financial power in distribution may restructure this part of the industry system and may force the assemblers to do business in a different way.

Conclusion

In the next 20–30 years, the automobile industry will experience growth on a unit basis. Moreover, the traditional 25 or so auto producers familiar today will still be around, and they will create value and destroy value as they have done in the past. In the developed countries, however, the system has become so overloaded with cost that assemblers, suppliers, and distribution groups are developing a new form of business relationship, networking. Managers at all levels of a company will need to figure out how to work with people they do not own or control. Therefore, as analysts perform their technical analyses of the industries, they should also probe whether the managers are able to network. The future of the global auto industry depends on it.

Complex fragmentation in the global automotive industry will force a constant shifting of positions among assemblers, suppliers, and new entrants. Companies that cannot hold the position of full-line producer may become contract assemblers; consortia may form around emerging technologies or product segments—sport/utility vehicles, for example, or urban cars. The assemblers will battle to hold on to their core competencies, but changes in the determinants of success will be more rapid in the future than in the past 40 years. Some will win with car designs, some with financial positioning, some with networking skills, and some with distribution position.

Question and Answer Session

Martin L. Anderson

Question: Have the determinants of profitability in the automobile industry shifted from machinery to systems?

Anderson: That is exactly right. In the computer and auto industries, the cost structure and the profitability determinants have shifted from hardware to software. Behind the health care costs and other large costs in the automotive industry, the dominant costs are the management of knowledge and types of software. Hardware has almost become a commodity, and profitability is determined by the software and by reconfiguring software services to allow knowledge management.

Question: What will the European market look like in, say, ten years?

Anderson: Demand will remain relatively strong, and the major players—such as Ford, GM, Mercedes-Benz, and BMW—will remain major in the next ten years, largely because of their global resources. I do not know where companies such as Renault will be. Volkswagen needs to be reconfigured, and options for using East European or Central European suppliers of components may give it some flexibility.

A major question is: When will the Japanese resume making their moves in Europe? Despite their current financial problems, the Japanese intend to be in Europe. They clearly have Europe on their screens for the long term, and they have been successful in using the United Kingdom as an island platform. One combination could well be Japanese companies and French companies, despite the current French protectionism. The French tend to be protectionists in most of their industries until an industry caves in; then, they immediately partner with the company they were trying to keep out.

Question: How is the concept of dealership that you described different from the way GM set up Saturn dealerships?

Anderson: Saturn is part of a producer's system. In fact, one reason Saturn has made its no-haggle pricing stick is that the entire Saturn operation is geared to having that approach work. The dealers know they are not going to lose money by participating in the process. This approach is fundamentally different from independent dealers creating portfolios and negotiating with producers.

The poor characteristics of the Saturn operation, such as its high capital costs and its slow launch timing, were inherited from the old GM culture. In order to minimize such problems, GM had to let the Saturn operation loose. Cutting them loose may be the way to fix other operations, such as Oldsmobile. The Cadillac operation is ready to be cut loose. GM is likely to initiate a series of forays like Saturn, create independent entities that then help GM out.

Saturn may well be one of those franchises that the new dealers will want in their portfolios, and GM will realize that it does not have to control every dealer, that the command-and-control approach is, in reality, counterproductive.

Order Form₀₃₃

Additional copies of *The Automotive Industry* (and other AIMR publications listed on page 118) are available for purchase. The price is **$30 each in U.S. dollars**. Simply complete this form and return it via mail or fax to:

AIMR Publications
P.O. Box 3668
Charlottesville, Va. 22903
U.S.A.
Telephone: 804/980-9712
Fax: 804/980-9710

Name _____

Company _____

Address _____

_____ Suite/Floor _____

City _____

State _____ ZIP _____ Country _____

Daytime Telephone _____

Title of Publication	**Price**	**Qty.**	**Total**
_____	_____	_____	_____
_____	_____	_____	_____
_____	_____	_____	_____

Shipping/Handling
- ❑ All U.S. orders: Included in price of book
- ❑ Airmail, Canada and Mexico: $5 per book
- ❑ Surface mail, Canada and Mexico: $3 per book
- ❑ Airmail, all other countries: $8 per book
- ❑ Surface mail, all other countries: $6 per book

Discounts
- ❑ Students, professors, university libraries: 25%
- ❑ CFA candidates (ID #_____): 25%
- ❑ Retired members (ID #_____): 25%
- ❑ Volume orders (50+ books of same title): 40%

Discount $—_____

4.5% sales tax
(Virginia residents) $_____

8.25% sales tax
(New York residents) $_____

7% GST
(Canada residents,
#124134602) $_____

Shipping/handling $_____

Total cost of order $_____

❑ Check or money order enclosed payable to **AIMR**   ❑ Bill me
Charge to: ❑ VISA   ❑ MASTERCARD   ❑ AMERICAN EXPRESS

Card Number:_____   ❑ Corporate ❑ Personal

Signature:_____   Expiration date: _____

Selected AIMR Publications*

The Telecommunications Industry, 1994 . . . . $20
  Randall S. Billingsley, CFA, *Editor*

Managed Futures and Their Role in Investment Portfolios, 1994 . . . . $20
  Don M. Chance, CFA

Fundamentals of Cross-Border Investment: The European View, 1994 . . . . $20
  Bruno Solnik

Good Ethics: The Essential Element of a Firm's Success, 1994 . . . . $20
  H. Kent Baker, CFA, *Editor*

A Practitioner's Guide to Factor Models, 1994 . . . . $20

Quality Management and Institutional Investing, 1994 . . . . $20
  Keith P. Ambachtsheer, *Editor*

Managing Emerging Market Portfolios, 1994 . . . . $20
  John W. Peavy III, CFA, *Editor*

Global Asset Management and Performance Attribution, 1994 . . . . $20
  Denis S. Karnosky, Ph.D., and Brian D. Singer, CFA

Franchise Value and the Price/Earnings Ratio, 1994 . . . . $20
  Martin L. Leibowitz and Stanley Kogelman

Investing Worldwide, 1993, 1992, 1991, 1990 . . . . $20 each

The Modern Role of Bond Covenants, 1994 . . . . $20
  Ileen B. Malitz

Derivative Strategies for Managing Portfolio Risk, 1993 . . . . $20
  Keith C. Brown, CFA, *Editor*

Equity Securities Analysis and Evaluation, 1993 . . . . $20

**The CAPM Controversy: Policy and Strategy Implications for
Investment Management**, 1993 . . . . $20
  Diana R. Harrington and Robert A. Korajczyk, *Editors*

The Health Care Industry, 1993 . . . . $20
  James Balog, *Editor*

Predictable Time-Varying Components of International Asset Returns, 1993 . . . . $20
  Bruno Solnik

The Oil and Gas Industries, 1993 . . . . $20
  Thomas A. Petrie, CFA, *Editor*

**Execution Techniques, True Trading Costs, and the Microstructure
of Markets,** 1993 . . . . $20
  Katrina F. Sherrerd, CFA, *Editor*

Investment Counsel for Private Clients, 1993 . . . . $20
  John W. Peavy III, CFA, *Editor*

---

*A full catalog of publications is available from AIMR, P.O. Box 3668, Charlottesville, Va. 22903; 804/980-9712; fax 804/980-9710.